STUDIES IN IRISH HISTORY

edited by

T. W. MOODY
Professor of Modern History
University of Dublin

R. DUDLEY EDWARDS
Professor of Modern Irish History
National University of Ireland

J. C. BECKETT
Reader in Modern History
Queen's University, Belfast

VOLUME VII

THE WILLIAMITE CONFISCATION
IN IRELAND
1690—1703

THE
WILLIAMITE CONFISCATION
IN IRELAND
1690–1703

by

J. G. SIMMS

FABER AND FABER LTD
24 Russell Square
London

First published in mcmlvi
by Faber and Faber Limited
24 Russell Square London W.C.1
Printed in Great Britain by
Latimer Trend & Co Ltd Plymouth

CONTENTS

7

PREFACE

There has hitherto been no detailed account of the confiscation of Irish land which resulted from the defeat of the Jacobites. General historians have expressed very different views about its consequences for Catholic landowners, and the subject is one of the puzzles of Irish history. W. F. T. Butler, in his pioneer work, *Confiscation in Irish History*, pointed out the difficulties presented by the statistics in the report of the parliamentary commissioners of 1699, which form the basis of most references to the subject.

In this book the attempt has been made to solve the problems raised by Butler about the ownership of Irish land before and after the war of 1689–91. The book is largely based on manuscript sources not hitherto used by those who have written about the Williamite confiscation. The most important of these are the books which accompanied the parliamentary commissioners' report and contain the full record of their investigations; the Annesley manuscripts, which contain the proceedings of the trustees for the forfeited estates; and the Books of Survey and Distribution, which record in detail the ownership of Irish land during the seventeenth century. These sources have been used to establish a framework, which indicates that Catholics owned considerably more land both before and after the Jacobite war than Butler estimated. In particular, the full record of the parliamentary commissioners shows that their published report was misleading, and that the treaty of Limerick (together with the analogous articles of Galway) was of much greater importance in preserving the estates of Catholics than appears from that report. The comparative effects of the Cromwellian and Williamite confiscations have been shown by maps indicating the proportions of Irish land held by Catholics in 1641, 1688 and 1703.

The Williamite confiscation was one of the major questions of both English and Irish politics for a number of years after the war and was

9

PREFACE

not finally concluded until 1703. During this period much of the land of Ireland was subject to a bewildering series of changes of ownership. Some of the confiscated estates were restored under the treaty of Limerick or by special agreement; the disposal of the remainder was the subject of contention between William and the English house of commons. William's lavish grants were the cause of strong protest; eventually the commons compelled him to agree to an Act of Resumption which cancelled nearly all his grants and vested the property in trustees, who auctioned it in Dublin. In the Irish parliament controversy centred on the interpretation of the treaty of Limerick. A full examination of the political and constitutional problems presented by these conflicts is beyond the scope of this book, in which the subject is treated only in so far as it affected the history of the confiscation.

The fortunes of a number of families were affected—adversely or otherwise—by the confiscation, the records of which contain much material of personal and social interest. The book does not set out to give family histories in detail, but the various processes—forfeitures, pardons, Limerick claims, auction-purchases, etc.—have been illustrated from the records by examples relating to individual families, many of which have preserved their continuity into modern times.

The general conclusion drawn is that the treaty of Limerick and the dispute between William and his English commons made the confiscation much less comprehensive than it would otherwise have been; but that many of the Catholics who thus succeeded in retaining their estates were induced to change their faith in the course of the eighteenth century by the pressure of the penal laws.

It remains for me to express my gratitude to those who have helped me: to the officials of the various libraries and repositories in which I have worked, especially to those of the National Library of Ireland, the Public Record Office of Ireland, the Royal Irish Academy and the library of Trinity College, Dublin; to Sir Gyles Isham, Bart., for his kind permission to refer to the correspondence of John Isham; to Professor T. W. Moody and Professor R. Dudley Edwards, to whose advice and guidance I am deeply indebted; to Dr R. C. Simington, whose knowledge of seventeenth century Irish land records is unrivalled; and to the Board of Trinity College, Dublin, for a generous grant in aid of publication.

J. G. SIMMS

Trinity College
Dublin

10

ABBREVIATIONS

The abbreviations used in the footnotes are for the most part taken from the list in *Irish Historical Studies*, iv. 6–35. Apart from those which are self-evident, they are as follows (for fuller particulars see the bibliography):

Anal. Hib.	*Analecta Hibernica.*
Annesley MSS	Manuscripts of the Annesley collection, Castlewellan, co. Down (microfilms in N.L.I.). References relate to the volumes listed in the descriptive catalogue (*Anal. Hib.*, xvi. 359–64).
B.M.	British Museum.
Cal. S.P. dom.	*Calendar of state papers, domestic series.*
Clarke corr.	Correspondence of George Clarke (T.C.D., MSS K.5. 1–13). References relate to volume and letter numbers.
Commrs' report	*The report of the commissioners appointed by parliament to inquire into the Irish forfeitures.*
H.L. MSS, n.s.	*House of lords manuscripts*, new series.
H.M.C.	Historical Manuscripts Commission.
I.H.S.	*Irish Historical Studies.*
N.L.I.	National Library of Ireland.
P.R.I. rep. D.K.	*Report of the deputy keeper of the public records in Ireland.*
P.R.O.I.	Public Record Office of Ireland.
R.I.A.	Royal Irish Academy.
T.C.D.	Trinity College, Dublin.

Dates are given in the old style, except that the year has been treated as beginning on January 1.

1

INTRODUCTORY

The Williamite confiscation was the last of a series which in the course of a century and a half changed the ownership of the greater part of Ireland. Its history covers the thirteen years between the battle of the Boyne and the final disposal of the forfeited estates. It consists of a complex of forfeitures and restorations, grants and resumptions. In the course of these proceedings most of the Catholics who still owned land ran the gauntlet in some form or other. Some succeeded in recovering or preserving their estates, whether under the treaty of Limerick or otherwise. Some lost their lands irrevocably. After 1703 there were no more confiscations on the wholesale scale of the sixteenth and seventeenth centuries. Stability had at last been reached, and the stage was set for the period of the penal laws and the supremacy of the 'Protestant nation'.

In the history of these confiscations 1641 makes a natural dividing line. Before 1641 they were directed against those who adhered to the old Gaelic civilization; after that date religion formed the primary line of cleavage. The earlier confiscations, from the seizure of Leix and Offaly to the Ulster plantation, marked the successive reduction of more or less independent territories, and their settlement with English or Scottish grantees. The lesser expropriations carried out by James I in Leitrim, Longford, Wexford and elsewhere were not technically forfeitures. They were based, not on any charge of rebellion, but on the legalistic revival of old crown titles. They resulted in a number of landowners being deprived of a great part of their property. In these confiscations almost all the victims were the Gaelic Irish. Catholics of Norman or English origin, (with some exceptions, notably the Desmonds who had 'gone Irish') continued to hold their lands. In spite of religious differences they allied themselves with the Protestant government of England rather than with the Catholic chieftains of Ireland.

13

INTRODUCTORY

From 1641 the situation changed. Parliamentarians made no distinction between the 'old English' of the pale and the Gaels of the south and west. Fingall and Gormanston, no less than MacCarthy and O'Dempsey were Irish Papists. The same description served for Catholic descendants of Elizabethan settlers, Bagenals, Brownes or Colcloughs. The Cromwellian settlement was frankly on a religious basis. All Catholics, except the very few who proved their 'constant good affection' to the parliament of England, forfeited their lands. Although Ormond and a limited number of other Protestants also forfeited, the general rule was that 'Protestant land' was excluded from the settlement.

From 1641 to 1703 two wars and three settlements formed different phases of one continuous process, the struggle between Catholic and Protestant for the land of Ireland. Of the three settlements the Cromwellian was the most drastic and the least complicated.[1] It involved the expropriation of virtually all the Catholic landowners east and south of the Shannon, and the division of most of Connacht and Clare between the transplanted Catholics and the original proprietors. The restoration and Williamite settlements were considerably more complicated. They involved the resolution of conflicting interests and the individual decision of a great number of claims. Neither settlement has been the subject of a full-scale independent study. Very diverse views have been expressed about the general results of both settlements and the subject has remained one of the vexed questions of Irish history.

All accounts of these settlements have suffered from the want of a firm statistical basis. Estimates of the area held by Catholics and Protestants in 1641 and 1688 have varied so widely that it has been impossible to assess with any degree of certainty the combined effect of the Cromwellian and restoration settlements, or to understand the strength and attitude of the rival groups during the different phases of the struggle. An assessment of the 1688 position is an essential part of the background against which the extent and effect of the Williamite confiscation must be judged.

The first attempt to analyze the territorial statistics of the Cromwellian and restoration settlements was made by Petty. In his *Political anatomy of Ireland*, written in 1672, he calculated that in 1641 Catholics held about two-thirds of the profitable land (which he estimated at seven and a half million Irish acres), and that as a result of the restoration settlement they held rather less than one-third.[2] Later on, in his *Treatise of Ireland*, he observed that in 1683 Catholics had about half the area

---

[1] Prendergast, *The Cromwellian settlement of Ireland*.
[2] Petty, *Economic writings*, i. 135–7.

INTRODUCTORY

which they had held in 1641.[1] There were various other contemporary estimates for the proportion of Ireland held by Catholics at the conclusion of the restoration settlement. Richard Cox put the Catholic share at a fourth of the whole,[2] and Richard Lawrence put it at about a fifth.[3]

W. F. T. Butler discussed the problem in considerable detail and suggested, with some hesitation, that 'at the accession of James II only at the outside one-seventh or one-eighth of the total area of the island remained in the possession of Catholics'.[4] His reasoning was founded on the report presented to the English parliament in 1699 by the commissioners appointed to inquire into the forfeited Irish estates. The total area returned by the commissioners (including the estates subsequently restored to their owners by the treaty of Limerick or otherwise) was approximately 1,100,000 Irish acres. This, on Petty's basis, would be almost exactly one-seventh of the total profitable area. Butler argued that as all the Irish Catholics had sided with James the estates of nearly all must have been forfeited, and that therefore the area recorded by the inquiry commissioners accounted for almost all the land in Catholic ownership at the outbreak of the war. In common with other writers on the subject, Butler confined his attention to the published report of the inquiry commission. That report provided a summary, in several respects misleading, of the full record presented by the commissioners to the English parliament. The full record makes it clear that a large number of Catholic estates were not included in the commissioners' figures. In particular, the majority of those landowners who were protected by the articles of Limerick and Galway had not been dispossessed of their estates at the conclusion of the war; as those estates had not been actually forfeited they were not taken into account by the commissioners.[5]

The most direct evidence for the restoration settlement is contained in the Books of Survey and Distribution, which record in detail all the land forfeited by Cromwell together with much of the adjacent unforfeited land which was measured along with it. The left-hand pages show the proprietors of 1641 with the names and areas of the lands which they held. The right-hand pages show the names of those to whom the lands

[1] Ibid., ii. 598.
[2] *Aphorisms relating to the kingdom of Ireland*, 1689.
[3] Lawrence, *Interest of Ireland*, 1682.
[4] Butler, *Confiscation*, p. 202.
[5] The statistics of the inquiry commission report of 1699 are set out in Appendix A, pp. 174-6 below. Butler's views are discussed more fully in my article 'Land owned by Catholics in Ireland in 1688' (*I.H.S.*, vii. 180-90).

were assigned at the restoration.[1] The books illuminate more clearly than any generalised description the complexities of the restoration settlement. Turning their pages we get an immediate presentation of how the settlement actually worked, and of how unequally it affected different types of Catholic families. Thus in the Meath book the left-hand pages show the old Catholic families of Norman or English origin in possession of four-fifths of the county in 1641. The restoration assignments on the right-hand pages show that less than half these lands were recovered. Fingall was restored in full, and Gormanston recovered everything except for a few lands assigned to Petty. Less prominent families, such as Baths and Cusacks, lost the greater part of their former holdings. Some names, such as Delafield, Missett and Sherlock, dropped out altogether. In areas where the Gaelic Irish were strongest in 1641 the proportion recovered at the restoration was considerably smaller. Thus in Tipperary the O'Dwyers and O'Glissanes lost all their 1641 possessions; in their place such names as Prittie and Purefoy appear in the restoration columns. In contrast, Butlers, Everards and Purcells recovered a great part of their former holdings. In general, the books show that the old families of the pale recovered almost half their former holdings, while with the conspicuous exception of Lord Clancarty the Gaelic Irish of Leinster and Munster were to a great extent eliminated. Considerable parts of Connacht and Clare continued to be Catholic strongholds.

Complete accuracy cannot be claimed for the measurements recorded in the books. These were taken from the Down survey for most of Ireland and from the Strafford survey for Clare, Galway, Roscommon and Mayo. The general tendency of these surveys was to underestimate the area. Petty believed that Ireland contained about eighteen million statute acres.[2] The Ordnance survey figure is more than twenty million. With considerable fluctuations in the accuracy of the measurement of individual lands this deficiency of rather more than ten per cent governs the figures for all the counties, whether measured by the Down or the Strafford survey. Another feature of the books is the division of land into profitable and unprofitable, which was made on a very arbitrary basis. In the area covered by the Down survey a comparatively small fraction of the land was classed as unprofitable, chiefly bog. In the

[1] The Books of Survey and Distribution were used as the official land records from the time of Charles II onwards. There are several sets, of which the most complete is the Quit Rent Office set, now in P.R.O.I. This set is in course of publication by the Irish MSS Commission; the vol. for Roscommon has already appeared, edited by Dr R. C. Simington.

[2] Petty, *Economic writings*, ii. 558.

Strafford survey a common practice was to decide that poor mountain land should be regarded as half or quarter profitable; the rest was shown as unprofitable. In spite of these deficiencies the Books of Survey and Distribution provide a remarkably complete record of the ownership of Irish land. The inaccuracies are no greater than we should expect from the primitive nature of the instruments employed.[1] There is no reason to suppose that they affect the relative proportion of lands held respectively by Catholics and Protestants.

By compiling lists of the areas assigned to each of the old families reinstated after the restoration, it is possible to make an estimate of the total area restored to Catholics. The sorting out of owners into Catholic and Protestant is facilitated by the numerous references to religious denomination which the books contain. There is also ample material in the records of the period for checking the religious affiliations of individual families. With very few (and clearly designated) exceptions, those who forfeited after 1641 and, still more so, those who followed James in 1688 were Catholics. Between 1641 and 1688 there were some defections from the Catholic ranks, such as Wesley of Dangan and Fitzpatrick of Castletown. They were, however, comparatively few, and were more than offset by Catholic purchases of land.

The Survey and Distribution books show the assignments made under the restoration settlement. They do not show the purchases which Catholics made on a considerable scale in the latter part of Charles II's reign and under James II. Particulars of a number of these purchases are available in the records of the Williamite forfeitures. The most notable of the estates thus acquired was that of Sir Patrick Trant, who among other purchases bought the large Clanmaliere estates in Leix and Offaly from Arlington, to whom they were granted at the restoration. Tyrconnell also acquired the greater part of his estate by purchase.

Analysis of the Survey and Distribution books, read with the records of the Williamite forfeitures, shows that in 1688 Catholics owned between a fourth and a fifth of the country. The number of Catholic owners was rather more than thirteen hundred. Their holding of profitable land, some 1,700,000 Irish acres, works out at forty per cent above Butler's estimate.[2]

The position created by the restoration settlement was unstable and

---

[1] Goblet, *La transformation de la géographie politique de l'Irlande*, i. 337-42, discusses the technical reasons for the inaccuracies of the survey.

[2] The figures do not include the 'private estate' granted to James as duke of York. An account of this estate is given in chapter viii, below.

satisfied none of the parties. Catholics, encouraged to hope for full re-instatement, were sorely disappointed with the share assigned to them. Ormond's policy of favouring families of Norman or English origin at the expense of the Gaelic Irish perpetuated the differences which had split the ranks of the Kilkenny confederacy. Even so, there were many of Norman or English stock who failed altogether to recover their possessions; others were only partially reinstated. Many of those who succeeeded in establishing claims experienced great difficulty in getting actual possession of the lands assigned to them. Petty's contentions with McGillicuddy and Fitzgerald of Ticroghan are typical of numerous disputes which arose between Cromwellian settlers and returning Catholics. The unequal operation of the settlement was to have much influence on the proceedings of the patriot parliament of 1689 and on the attitudes of rival Jacobite parties after the Boyne.

Protestant opinion was no less dissatisfied with the restoration settle-ment. Cromwellians showed a natural resentment at having to surrender portions of their holdings to former proprietors whom they continued to regard as conquered rebels. The Protestant attitude is summarised in a contemporary pamphlet: '. . . the victors not being permitted to enjoy what they had justly won by the sword, while the Irish were restored to what they had as truly forfeited by their cruel disloyalty, by which partial piece of justice the victors were indeed subdued and the conquered were in the conclusion victors'[1].

Petty, who was absolved from surrendering any part of his posses-sions, took a rather different view, and deprecated the desire of 'some furious spirits' that the Irish should rebel again that they might be put to the sword. He thought that the English had played for heavy stakes and had won a gamester's right to their estates.[2]

From the beginning of James's reign the maintenance of the settle-ment became a recurring theme in the correspondence of Petty and his friend and kinsman, Sir Robert Southwell. By August 1685 Petty found his Kerry troubles eclipsed by concern for the whole Irish settlement. Southwell anxiously inquired whether Petty had any particular reasons to believe the settlement in danger, and asked whether he could 'discover any new marks that the government is fond of a new scramble or to be pestered with some years' tinkering to frame a new settlement and put all trade, improvement and exchange in the meantime to a stand'.[3] In the summer of 1686 Petty had an interview with Tyrconnell, which he

[1] *State of the Papist and Protestant properties.*
[2] Petty, *Economic writings,* i. 154.
[3] *Petty-Southwell correspondence,* p. 140.

thus described in a letter to Southwell: 'he pressed me to speak of the settlement. I told him there were things in it against the light of nature and the current equity of the world, but whether it was worth the breaking I doubted.'[1] Southwell took comfort from the fact that 'the great man' had been heard to say that 'his own fortune was settled by the acts and that his majesty has no thought of parting with a foot of his estate in that country'.[2] Petty next went to Windsor, where he had 'private and ample conference' with the king, who told him 'expressly and voluntarily' that he would not break the settlement.[3]

A leading part in the agitation against the settlement was taken by Richard Nagle, writer of the 'Coventry letter'. Petty, however, did not give up hope and continued his efforts to influence Tyrconnell. In March 1687 he wrote to Southwell: 'I have given many notes to Thom Sheridan at my lord Tyrconnell's importunity, who pretends to write the history of Ireland. To what a good pass had I brought matters with that great man till Dick Nagle came over.'[4] Southwell in acknowledging a copy of the Coventry letter observed that the settlement 'like Saint Sebastian is stuck full of arrows'.[5]

Petty's last work was the *Treatise of Ireland*, presented to James in September 1687. The treatise refers to Protestant apprehensions that the settlement would be reversed, reflected in a drastic fall in land values and in the beginnings of a migration to England.[6]

From the entries in the Books of Survey and Distribution the relative strength in 1688 of the rival groups of landed proprietors, Catholic and Protestant, may be summarized as follows:

Protestants held almost the whole of Ulster and four-fifths of Leinster and Munster (excluding Clare). They also held the whole of Leitrim and nearly all Sligo. Catholics held nearly half the land beyond the Shannon. In the rest of Ireland, although the total area which they held was small, Catholic proprietors included a number of magnates who exerted great local influence and, after James's accession, were the cause of considerable apprehension to Protestants. The greatest of these was Lord Clancarty, who owned nearly the whole barony of Muskerry. Lord Antrim represented a Catholic stronghold in Ulster. Lords Slane, Galmoy, Mountgarret and others had considerable estates in Leinster. Sir Valentine

[1] *Petty-Southwell correspondence*, p. 215.
[2] Ibid., p. 213.
[3] Ibid., p. 234. The Windsor visit was in Sept. 1686.
[4] Ibid., p. 259. The Coventry letter, written from Coventry by Nagle to Tyrconnell on 26 Oct. 1686 criticised the Acts of Settlement and Explanation. The text is in Gilbert, *Jacobite narrative*, pp. 193-201.
[5] Ibid., p. 264.   [6] Petty, *Economic writings*, ii. 597.

INTRODUCTORY

Browne, whom James later created Lord Kenmare, had a large part of Kerry.

Although the Catholics were decidedly the weaker side, they were gaining in strength, partly by the gradual recovery of lost land, partly by new purchases. Except in the north, they had a strong enough nucleus of great landowners to enable them to take advantage of the political situation created by the accession of James. At the same time, there were a large number of expropriated persons pressing impatiently for the complete reversal of the settlement. They are referred to in a contemporary account as 'the old proprietors who evermore haunt and live about those lands whereof they were dispossessed, and cannot forbear to hope and reckon a day of repossession'.[1]

The course of the Williamite confiscation was chequered and confused. There were several changes of policy, and much of what was done was later undone. In particular the situation was complicated by the restoration, under articles or pardons, of forfeited land and by the parliamentary resumption of William's grants. The story falls into three main sections.

Firstly, there is the period of the war of 1689–91, during which forfeiture policy played an important part in the strategy of both sides. It was of particular significance in the negotiations which went on almost continuously during the last year of the war and which culminated in the treaty of Limerick. The relation between the land question and the conduct of the war is the subject of further discussion in the following chapter.

The second section covers the period up to 1699, when the English parliament appointed a commission to inquire into the administration of the Irish forfeitures. The commissioners reviewed the entire proceedings of the crown in relation to the forfeitures from 1690 onwards. Different sections of their report dealt with outlawries, adjudications under the articles of Limerick and Galway, pardons and royal grants.

The third section covers the period from the Resumption Act of 1700 to the completion of the trustees' sales in 1703. The English parliament, strongly objecting to the large grants which William had made to Bentinck, Keppel and other favourites, resumed all but a small fraction of the Irish forfeitures and ordered them to be vested in trustees. The trustees' administration involved the hearing of numerous claims preferred by interested parties, both Catholic and Protestant, and the sale of the resumed estates.

[1] R. Southwell, Some general hints of Ireland, 1684 (B.M., Eg. MS 917, f. 88).

20

2

THE WAR AND THE LAND, 1689-91

To James and William the Irish land question was a subsidiary matter; to their Irish supporters it was of major importance. From the beginning of the conflict it was recognized by both sides that the ownership of the land of Ireland was at stake. A virtual monopoly of the land would be the reward of complete victory for either side. In a negotiated peace religious liberty and the land would be the subjects of the hardest bargaining.

The repeal of the Acts of Settlement and Explanation had been pressed upon the reluctant James ever since his accession. The flight of the Protestants and their adherence to William made an immediate issue of the question. Louis XIV (or his secretariat) had a much clearer idea than James of the importance which the problem had for Irish Catholics. The first letter which he sent to d'Avaux, his ambassador in Ireland, gave a simplified version of the restoration settlement and urged that James should be persuaded, firstly, to return to Catholics the regicides' estates which had been granted to him, and, secondly, to forfeit the property of disloyal Protestants and grant it to Catholics. Louis recognized that it might not suit James to resume the property of all Protestants and thus alienate Protestant feeling both in England and in Ireland.[1]

D'Avaux gives a detailed account of the negotiations which led up to the Repeal and Attainder Acts of 1689. His letters show the steady opposition maintained by James to both measures. The most was made of loyal Protestants and of Catholics who had purchased from Protestant grantees.[2] According to d'Avaux James threatened to dissolve parliament if certain Catholics were not left in possession of their purchases, and several members countered with the threat that if they did not get satisfaction they would not follow James to the war.[3]

[1] *Négoc. d'Avaux en Irl.*, pp. 31-2.
[2] Ibid., pp. 34-5, 56-7, 63, 111, 129.
[3] Ibid., p. 192.

The acts as finally passed provided the basis for little short of a complete Catholic resettlement of Ireland. Heirs of 1641 proprietors were to recover their ancestors' estates in full, and bona fide purchasers were to be reprised by the forfeiture of property held by persons who had joined or abetted the rebels. James himself was to be reprised with the estates held in 1641 by Sir Robert King. Most Protestants whose title went back to 1641 were included in the Attainder Act. Thus in the event of a Jacobite victory the lands of the older-established Protestant proprietors as well as of those who held under the restoration Act of Settlement would have been available for distribution to Catholics.[1]

The Act of Repeal provided for the appointment of commissioners of claims, and this seems to have given James the last word. Almost immediately a proclamation was issued that there would be no court of claims for the present, 'lest some should neglect the public safety upon pretence of attending their private concerns'.[2] It is doubtful whether a regular court of claims was ever established. King has an appendix which professes to contain copies of orders for the restoration of estates. But only one instance is given, that of Ballyshannon, county Kildare. An order was passed by the governor of the county in May 1690, at the close of the Jacobite régime, to the effect that Luke Fitzgerald had proved before him that his ancestors were possessed in 1641 of the mansion house of Ballyshannon. The new holder, Francis Annesley, was therefore directed to hand over possession of the house.[3]

It is evident that there were also numerous instances of informal seizure of the property of those Protestants who had fled. In July 1689 the revenue commissioners issued orders for action to be taken against persons who had seized land on the pretext that the owner was absent in rebellion. Such lands were to be taken over by the lord lieutenant of the county pending further orders.[4] The revenue commissioners seem to have leased out some estates forfeited by the Act of Attainder, but the practice was later stopped on the ground that 'several officers on pretence of taking lands forfeited by the late Act of Attainder do follow the commissioners of revenue now in their circuit and thereby neglect to attend their commands'.[5] Ormond's correspondence refers to com-

[1] The text of the Jacobite acts of 1689 is given in the pamphlet *A list of . . . nobility, gentry and commonalty . . . attainted of high treason.*
[2] Proclamation of 30 July 1689 (*H.M.C., Ormonde MSS*, ii. 407).
[3] King, *State of the Protestants*, app. 24.
[4] N.L.I., Report on Nugent papers.
[5] Proclamation of 25 Apr. 1690 (*H.M.C., Ormonde MSS*, ii. 436.)

plaints that some of his tenants were compelled to pay rent to former proprietors on the strength of the Jacobite legislation.[1]

The evidence indicates that James and his government were by no means anxious to implement the Acts of Repeal and Attainder and tried as far as possible to restrain the natural eagerness of their dispossessed supporters. Little progress had been made for the formal transfer of land to the 1641 proprietors when the Jacobite defeat at the Boyne put any territorial reconquest out of the question. After that the Catholics' only hope was to save as much as possible of their existing estates and liberties.

On the Williamite side also the importance of the land question was recognized from the first, and diverse views on the subject were put forward. Some of the Protestant settlers in Ireland welcomed the conflict between William and James as providing an opportunity for depriving Catholics of their remaining lands and so securing Ireland for the Protestant cause. Others were more cautious and favoured a conciliatory policy which might induce landed Catholics to change their adherence from James to William without having recourse to arms.

On 9 January 1689 the lords and gentlemen of Ireland presented William with a paper recommending that he should summon the Catholics to surrender on a promise that they should enjoy their existing estates and 'be connived at in the private exercise of their religion by secular priests only'. Those who did not surrender within a time-limit should be proceeded against with the utmost severity. William was asked to lose no time in sending over sufficient force to reduce the obstinate.[2] On February 22 William issued a declaration which was generally in line with these proposals. It called on the Irish Catholics to surrender on the promise that they should keep their estates and continue to enjoy all the favour of the private exercise of their religion that the law allowed; an early session of the Irish parliament was also promised in which further indulgence to Catholics would be proposed. The declaration added that the estates of those who did not submit by April 10 would be forfeited and distributed to those who assisted William in reducing Ireland to its due obedience.[3] This declaration had practically no effect and it became clear that Ireland could not be reduced without the use of force.

The idea, evidently suggested by the precedent of 1642, that the land could be made to pay for the reduction of Ireland was early put forward

[1] Ormond to Valentine Smyth, 2 Sept. 1690 (N.L.I., Ormonde MSS, clvi. 45).
[2] *H.M.C. rep. 12*, app. vi. 184.
[3] *H.M.C. rep. 12*, app. vi. 164-5.

by Richard Cox, later lord chancellor. He is said to have presented each member of the convention parliament with a copy of his 'Aphorisms relating to the kingdom of Ireland', in which he made the point that the estates of the Irish Catholics were sufficient to defray the expense of reducing them to their duty. He estimated that such estates amounted to a fourth of the country and were worth £3,000,000.[1] The suggestion found favour with the English parliament and clauses applying the forfeitures to the cost of the war formed part of various abortive attainder bills.

In the summer of 1689 the 'English nobility and gentry of Ireland' apparently suspected that William's terms were going to be too easy, and submitted a manifesto urging that the leading rebels should be excepted from pardon, on the ground that Ireland would always be rebellious as long as considerable properties remained in the hands of the Catholic Irish. This manifesto was answered by a pamphlet which made the accurate forecast that if the leaders were excepted from pardon they would prevent their followers from submitting, with the result that William's forces would have to remain in the field all winter.[2] This pamphlet was followed by another, which argued that some sort of declaration was necessary not to make the 'whole Irish nation' desperate, but that the chief and most notorious rebels should be excepted and their estates applied to the relief of Protestants. The writer suggested that a distinction should be drawn between the Jacobite leaders. Lords Clancarty and Antrim should on no account be pardoned. The pardoning of influential but less intransigent opponents, such as Lords Brittas, Clanricarde and Nettervill, might be useful and cause internal jealousy.[3] Cox, at one stage, suggested that a distinction might be drawn between the Gaelic Irish and the old English, which would have the advantage of making it clear to the world that the quarrel was national and not religious.[4]

It is a nice question how far the passing of the Jacobite Acts of Repeal and Attainder influenced Williamite policy. Forfeiting the estates of unsuccessful 'rebels' was in any case part of the routine of Irish history; in particular the parallel between 1641 and 1688 was in everyone's mind. Even if no Jacobite parliament had met, it seems certain that there would have been just as keen a demand for Irish forfeitures. Strengthening the Protestant interest and financing an expensive war by the confiscation of opponents' lands were primary objectives for Williamites as

[1] Ware, *History of the writers of Ireland*, p. 209.
[2] *Reasons for his majesty's issuing a general pardon to the rebels of Ireland.*
[3] *A declaration for Ireland or no declaration?*
[4] T.C.D., MS I. 6. 10, p. 73.

they had been for parliamentarians; the desire for retaliation was a secondary consideration. In any case, the acts were only the last of a series of transactions, all of which Protestants considered to merit retribution.

King's *State of the Protestants* makes a great deal of both acts and has, via Macaulay, given the impression that they loomed very large in the scheme of things. From other sources it appears that the acts were taken calmly enough. The 'breaking of the settlement' had long been apprehended and cannot have come as much of a shock. There are several allusions to both acts in the pamphlets of the time, but there is little mention of them in the State Papers or other official records. The numerous Irish witnesses who appeared before the English house of lords from June to August 1689 to give evidence on the policy to be adopted for reducing Ireland and on the English attainder bill are not recorded as mentioning either act.[1]

Some use was made of the acts to strengthen the arguments of the more thorough-going section of William's supporters. Thus, while the repeal bill was still being debated in Dublin, a speaker urged the English commons to follow James's example and raise supplies by the seizure of Irish estates.[2] James's example was, however, only cited as a reinforcement of proposals that had been brought before the English commons some time before the Dublin parliament was convened. A Dublin newsletter, reporting with comparative coolness the passing of the Act of Repeal, remarked that its thirty provisions would very soon serve as a good precedent for the English.[3] A note of 1690 contains a suggestion of Dr Gorges, formerly Henry Cromwell's secretary and then Schomberg's, to turn the Irish Act of Attainder on themselves; each provision was to be used 'vice versa' against the Irish Jacobites.[4]

But references of this sort are not very conspicuous, and the legislation of the Dublin parliament seems to have counted for little in comparison with the much greater issues involved in the war as a whole. The two acts must have contributed to the general stiffening of the Protestant attitude against any settlement with the Catholics; they do not, however, seem to have been taken into special consideration in the framing of William's policy.

From the time that he was committed to the Irish expedition William's general policy appears to have been to offer the minimum of concessions consistent with bringing the war in Ireland to a rapid conclusion. It was

[1] *H.M.C. rep. 12*, app. vi. 137-44 and 229-35.
[2] Grey, *Debates of the house of commons*, ix. 348.
[3] R.I.A., MS 24, G. 2, p. 11.
[4] Ibid., p. 2.

of overriding importance to him to finish that war as soon as possible and switch his forces over to the continent. At the same time, if he could bring sufficient pressure on the Irish Jacobites to induce them to surrender unconditionally he would be able to make use of their forfeited estates to pay for the campaign and to reward deserving friends and helpers. It was not until that policy had been tried and had failed that William accepted the fact that the grant of comparatively favourable terms would be necessary to make the Jacobites submit.

The declaration of Finglas, issued a few days after the Boyne, promised pardon to those of the lower orders who surrendered. No such terms were offered to the 'desperate leaders of the rebellion' who were faced with the alternatives of continuing an apparently hopeless fight or throwing themselves upon William's mercy.[1] The declaration resulted in a limited number of submissions on the part of the elderly and unwarlike, but, in the words of a subsequent proclamation, it did not produce 'those effects of gratitude and obedience from several of our rebellious subjects which we justly expected'.[2] It was agreed by contemporaries, both Jacobite and Williamite, that the uncompromising nature of the declaration made the Irish Jacobites hold out from sheer desperation.[3]

William's failure at Limerick appears to have convinced him that he had made a mistake in demanding the unconditional surrender of the Jacobite nobility and gentry, and from the autumn of 1690 there was a marked change of policy. The new policy aimed at ending the war in Ireland by a negotiated settlement to be secured by the offer of comparatively generous terms to Catholic landowners. From the Williamite point of view this policy had the advantage of producing a division of opinion among the Jacobites. There was a distinct cleavage of interest between those who held estates under the restoration settlement and those who had failed to recover their ancestral property. During the winter of 1690–1 Ginkel, who commanded the Williamite forces in Ireland after William's departure, carried on a series of negotiations with the Irish peace party, which represented the landed interest. No direct result came of these negotiations, partly because of the vigorous action taken by Sarsfield as leader of the resistance movement, partly because the peace party itself had little confidence that a Protestant parliament in Dublin would ratify concessions offered by Ginkel to Catholic landowners.[4] By the summer of 1691 Bentinck, William's principal adviser,

---

[1] *London Gazette*, 10 July 1690.

[2] Mullenaux, *Journal of the three months' royal campaign*, p. 17.

[3] Gilbert, *A Jacobite narrative*, pp. 105-6; Burnet, *History of his own time*, iv. 99.

[4] An account of these negotiations is given in my article 'Williamite peace tactics, 1690-1' (*I.H.S.*, viii. 303-23).

became convinced that the military situation on the continent made it imperative to end the war in Ireland without delay. He wrote to Ginkel that if the Irish thought of surrendering, as there was some ground for hoping, he should not hesitate to offer them quite favourable terms.[1] Ginkel shared his view and succeeded in persuading the lords justices in Dublin that the issue of a proclamation offering generous terms provided the best hope of bringing the war in Ireland to an early conclusion. The lords justices were acutely aware of the opposition shown by influential Protestants in Ireland to the grant of terms which would enable the Jacobites to retain their lands. They also apprehended that the English commons would not relish losing the prospect of paying for the war out of the proceeds of forfeited Jacobite estates. Nevertheless the lords justices expressed their conviction that all the forfeited estates in Ireland were not worth the expense and hazard of another summer's war and that as there was a party among the Irish which was opposed to any negotiation it was necessary that the proclamation should leave no room for suspicion.[2] The drafting of the proclamation was the subject of much discussion and in the form finally approved its terms were considerably more restricted than those which Ginkel had proposed. This proclamation, dated 7 July 1691, offered pardon to those Jacobite officers who should surrender within three weeks and also deliver up any town, forts or garrisons in their charge or bring over their regiments or troops or a considerable portion of them. Similar terms were offered to the civilian inhabitants of Limerick or Galway who should be instrumental in procuring the surrender of those towns. The issue of the proclamation was the occasion of much Protestant criticism. The terms were described as far too favourable and it was alleged that the draft had been unanimously rejected by the Irish privy council.[3] The reaction in England was also unfavourable; William was informed that public opinion in London was highly critical of the leniency of the terms offered.[4] Ginkel was unmoved by the criticism and remained of opinion that it was advisable to finish the war in Ireland as soon as possible, if necessary by offering a general pardon; one month of war cost more than all the forfeitures were worth.[5]

The first considerable result to be achieved by the proclamation was

[1] Bentinck to Ginkel, 11/21 May 1691 (Japikse, *Correspondentie van Willem en Bentinck*, iii. 236).

[2] Sir Charles Porter to Sydney, 29 May 1691 (*Cal. S.P. dom., 1690-1*, pp. 393-4); lords justices to Nottingham, 29 May 1691 (ibid., pp. 394-5).

[3] T.C.D., MS I. 6. 10, pp. 149-51.

[4] Godolphin to William, 10 Aug. 1691 (*Cal. S.P. dom., 1690-1*, p. 481).

[5] Ginkel to Coningsby, 24 July 1691 (*H.M.C. rep. 4*, app., p. 322).

the surrender of Galway, the articles of which, signed on 21 July 1691, guaranteed their estates both to the garrison and to the townsmen.[1] These articles were also the subject of much criticism and Ginkel was reproached for having given Galway unnecessarily favourable terms.[2] From the beginning of the final siege of Limerick the question of a negotiated settlement assumed increasing importance. The Williamites were desperately anxious to end the war in Ireland before winter set in; the Jacobites had lost heart after Aughrim and a growing number of them were eager to secure tolerable terms before it was too late. The influence of the Irish peace party increased and that of the resistance movement declined, to the distress of the French whose policy was to prolong the war into the winter with the object of locking up William's forces in Ireland for another year. On September 16, the day on which he crossed the Shannon, Ginkel repeated the offer of the July proclamation and announced that it would hold good for another eight days.[3] On the eighth day, September 23, the Jacobites at last responded; Sarsfield and Wauchope came over to the Williamite camp and asked for terms.[4] Ginkel had already received a letter from William authorizing him to promise Sarsfield a reward if the negotiations were successfully concluded—a move which shows William's anxiety for an Irish settlement and his recognition of Sarsfield as the key figure. The offer of an estate had no attractions for Sarsfield, but he asked for the privilege of sending back some cargoes of wine and other goods from France on the return voyage of the ships which were to transport the Irish troops.[5] Ginkel fixed the quota at three hundred tons; the agreement was honoured and several of Sarsfield's cargoes, which had been seized by the customs, were released on William's orders.[6]

Keen bargaining took place over the conditions of the capitulation, and the articles of surrender were not signed until October 3. They guaranteed their estates to the garrison and citizens of Limerick and to the various forces still holding out in the west, provided that they submitted to William and did not accept the other alternative offered, that of going to France. Catholics in general were assured that their position

---

[1] *A particular relation of the surrender of Galway*, 1691.

[2] Bentinck to Ginkel, 3/13 Aug. 1691 (*Correspondentie*, iii. 249).

[3] Story, *Continuation*, pp. 219-20.

[4] Ginkel to lords justices, 23 Sep. 1691 (*H.M.C. rep. 4*, app., p. 323).

[5] Ginkel to George Clarke, 23 Sep. 1691 (Clarke corr., xii. 1010); Ginkel to lords justices, 28 Sep. 1691 (*P.R.I. rep. D.K. 56*, p. 396).

[6] *Cal. treas. papers, 1697-1702*, p. 114; *P.R.I. rep. D.K. 57*, p. 484; *Cal. S.P. dom., 1693*, p. 5.

would be no worse than it had been in the reign of Charles II.[1] These terms were strongly criticized from both the Jacobite and the Williamite sides. The Jacobite author of 'A light to the blind' commented that the Irish commissioners had agreed too easily with Ginkel. They should have insisted on the right of all Catholics to the free exercise of their religion, their temporal liberties and the restoration of the estates which they held in the reign of Charles II.[2] On the other hand the Dublin Protestants were quick to denounce the leniency of the terms granted to the Jacobites. Archbishop Narcissus Marsh confessed himself unable to understand why such conditions had been granted to a rebellious people that were not able to defend themselves.[3] Bishop Dopping of Meath, in the course of a sermon preached in Christ Church Cathedral, Dublin, dwelt on the faithlessness of the Irish and the imprudence of relying on their treacherous promises and submissions.[4]

The negotiations which took place during the final year of the war show the importance which the land question had for both sides. The terms finally granted represented a considerable modification of the earlier policy of wholesale confiscation. They had the effect of making the Williamite settlement much more of a compromise than it would have been if the Irish Jacobites had given up the struggle immediately after the Boyne. Apart from the estates restored or preserved to those who came within the terms of the articles, a number of pardons were given to those who had taken part in the negotiations or had submitted to the Williamite authorities.

[1] The negotiations are referred to in my article 'The original draft of the civil articles of Limerick, 1691' (*I.H.S.*, viii. 37-44). The question of the missing clause of the treaty is discussed in chapter v, below.

[2] Gilbert, *A Jacobite narrative*, pp. 176-8.

[3] Marsh's diary (*Irish Ecclesiastical Journal*, v. 148).

[4] T.C.D., MS P. 3. 7. William's disapproval of the sermon was expressed by Dopping's temporary removal from the privy council (*Cal. S.P. dom., 1691-2*, pp. 28 and 430).

3

CONFISCATION BY OUTLAWRY

The governments of James and William both regarded their opponents as guilty of the offence of high treason, which included levying war against the king in his realm and adhering to his enemies in his realm or elsewhere.[1] The Jacobite Act of Attainder had its counterpart in a series of abortive English attainder bills directed against the Jacobites in Ireland. Because of the dispute between William and his commons over the disposal of the estates concerned no English act of attainder was actually passed. Instead, outlawry proceedings were taken against a large number of individuals by legal process. Such process began with the finding of a bill of indictment by a jury and the issue of a writ of 'capias', or warrant, by the sheriff. If the accused was produced he was either bound over for further appearance or put on trial before a judge and jury. If after two writs of 'capias' the sheriff returned 'non est inventus', a writ of 'exigent' was issued which directed the sheriff to have the name of the accused called out on five successive county-court days, charging him to appear on pain of outlawry. If he did not appear by the last time of calling, he was said to be 'quinquies exactus' and was declared an outlaw. Such outlawry involved 'attainder by process, otherwise termed attainder by default or outlawry'. The majority of the Jacobites were outlawed or attainted in this way—both terms were used without apparent distinction. Attainder of treason rendered the offender liable to be hanged, drawn and quartered and to forfeit his lands and goods to the king; but the death penalty does not appear to have been inflicted on any of those who supported the Jaco-

---

[1] In 1584 the legal opinion was expressed that cases of treason committed abroad could not be tried in Ireland (Brady, *S.P. Ir. ch. Eliz.*, pp. 83-4, referred to by Edwards, *Church and state in Tudor Ireland*, p. 269). The opinion took no account of the Irish Act of Slander, 28 H. VIII, c. 7, under which the Williamite proceedings for foreign treason were taken (*P.R.I. rep. D.K. 17*, app., pp. 16-17).

bite cause in 1690–1.[1] The original case-records of these proceedings
were preserved in the iron chest of the court of king's bench in Dublin.[2]
They were destroyed when the record office was blown up in 1922. It is,
however, possible to piece together a considerable amount of information about the proceedings from the forfeiture records, the State Papers
and other sources. This information throws much light on the scope,
distribution and timing of the Williamite outlawries. It also serves to
correct some inferences which historians have drawn from the figures
cited in the inquiry commissioners' report.

The commissioners stated that the names of all the persons outlawed,
with their descriptions and the counties in which they were outlawed,
appeared in the first of the nine books which contained the full record of
the commission's investigations and were presented to the English parliament at the same time as the report.[3] The first book—the Book of
Outlawries—is in three sections showing, respectively, those outlawed
in England, those outlawed in Ireland for high treason committed there,
and those outlawed for foreign treason.

Outlawries in England. The fifty-seven persons who were outlawed in
England, were not, as Froude presumed, absentee Irish landlords. The
list includes the duke of Berwick, Lords Melfort and Powys, and a number of English and Scottish Jacobites who had no connection with Ireland
other than having gone there with James. The remaining names are
those of Irish Jacobites, Tyrconnell, Antrim, Sir Patrick Trant and a
number of others, most of whom are well known, although there are
several minor figures whom it is surprising to find in such a select list.[4]
The outlawry proceedings were held in England at a time when Dublin
and the Irish courts were still under the control of James. The list contains all but two of the names proposed for inclusion in the attainder
bill which was introduced in the English commons in June 1689, while
the Irish parliament in Dublin was engaged in passing a similar, but
much more comprehensive, measure.[5] Discussions between lords and
commons about the names to be included held up the English bill until
August 1689, when it was killed by the prorogation of parliament. It was
the first of the seven abortive attainder bills which were brought to vary-

[1] Jacob, *New law-dictionary* (1729), art. on Attainder, Attainted, Capias, Exigent,
Indictment, Outlawry and Treason. The English act of 1696 (7 and 8 Will. III, c. 3)
which introduced certain regulations favourable to the accused in treason cases did
not apply to Ireland.
[2] *P.R.I. rep. D.K. 17*, app., p. 13.
[3] *Commrs' report*, pp. 9–10. T.C.D., MS N.1. 3, ff. 1-70, contains a copy of the
Book of Outlawries. The figures are discussed in Appendix A, pp. 174-6, below.
[4] Froude, *Ire.*, i. 245. The list is given in full in *H.L.MSS*, n.s., iv. 17.
[5] *Commons' jn.*, x. 193.

ing stages of maturity in the first two of William's English parliaments. It was the only one to have such a limited character. The bill as sent up by the commons contained only twenty names; the lords struck out seven of them and in their place proposed four others, including Tyrconnell, Antrim and Richard Hamilton.[1]

It seems clear that the limited scope of this first bill was due to the fact that the Williamites still hoped that the Irish Jacobites would capitulate without a fight. The inquiries which the lords held during the summer of 1689 on the state of Ireland contain frequent references to the belief that Tyrconnell was inclined to make terms.[2] A pamphlet of September 1689, put the case for confining proceedings to a limited number of individuals. The writer thought that the readiest method of reducing Ireland was for William to make a further declaration offering such terms as would not make the Jacobites desperate, but that 'the chief and most notorious of the rebels' should be excepted; the lords and gentlemen of Ireland had provided the privy council with a list of these.[3]

When it became evident that Schomberg's arrival was not going to make the Irish Jacobites capitulate, English policy changed and subsequent attainder bills were much more comprehensive in character. The later bills were designed to attaint all those in rebellion in Ireland; the controversies which they excited related less to the comprehensiveness of the attainders than to the use to be made of the forfeited estates. As successive attainder bills failed to become law the action taken against the adherents of James was restricted to judicial proceedings. These proceedings, however wholesale and summary they might be, were considerably less thorough than an inclusive attainder act, such as the Cromwellian act of 1657,[4] would have been.

The first reference to judicial proceedings which we have is an address presented to William by the English commons in August 1689, on the prorogation day. The address asked him to issue a commission 'of oyer and terminer for the indicting of such persons as are or have been in rebellion in Ireland or elsewhere in order to their speedy conviction'[5]. Next we find from Luttrell's diary that in October bills were found at the sessions house in the Old Bailey against a number of Catholics 'for being in arms with King James'. Luttrell evidently considered the case of importance as he gives the names of fifty-three of those indicted, all

[1] *H.M.C. rep. 12*, app. vi. 228.
[2] Ibid., app. vi. 137-44.
[3] *Declaration or no declaration?*
[4] Firth and Rait, *Acts and ordinances of the interregnum*, ii. 1251-2.
[5] *Commons' jn.*, x. 269.

32

of whom are included in the list of fifty-seven recorded by the inquiry commissioners.[1]

The indictment included over thirty names in addition to those proposed for inclusion in the attainder bill; they were no doubt taken from the list supplied by the lords and gentlemen of Ireland. They included such prominent Jacobite peers as Clancarty, Galmoy, Gormanston and Limerick. Other well-known figures were Sir Richard Nagle and Sir Stephen Rice. Indictment was followed by further proceedings in the English court of king's bench. As those indicted were away in Ireland with James, it is to be presumed that writs of exigent[2] were issued and that names were called out on the prescribed five occasions. We get references to the outlawry proceedings in the Irish inquisition records and in several petitions. The inquisition held in Kerry on Sir Valentine Browne records that he was outlawed on the eve of St. Valentine's day, 1690, at the Guildhall, London.[3] A petition submitted by Simon Luttrell's wife mentions that Tyrconnell was outlawed at the king's bench in England on 'Monday next before the feast of St. Valentine in the first year of their majesties' reign'.[4] The inquisitions on Dudley Bagenal and Lord Bellew of Duleek give 12 and 18 February 1690 as the dates of outlawry. The record of these English proceedings was transmitted to Ireland in November 1690 when William's courts were established in Dublin.[5] All the subsequent judicial proceedings took place in Ireland.

High treason in Ireland. The lists of those indicted and outlawed for high treason in Ireland contain 2,603 names, assigned to twenty counties as well as to the cities of Dublin, Cork, Waterford and Kilkenny and the town of Drogheda. The twelve counties for which there are no lists include Clare, Limerick and the counties of Connacht; a small number of persons from those counties are included in the Dublin city lists. Tipperary also does not figure, as it had its own palatinate court under Ormond's authority, which failed to send in a return to the commissioners.

The arrangement of the lists corresponds closely with that of the bills of indictment which are summarized in the seventeenth report of the deputy keeper of the Irish public records; this throws considerable light on the chronology of the proceedings.[6] The summary gives the year and law term for most of the bills. It shows that the indictments began in the

---

[1] Luttrell, *Brief historical relation*, i. 593-4.
[2] The term is explained on p. 30 above.
[3] P.R.O.I., Transcripts of exchequer inquisitions.
[4] P.R.O.I., Wyche papers, petition book, pp. 29-30.
[5] P.R.O.I., Wyche papers, petition book, pp. 29-30.
[6] *P.R.I. rep. D.K. 17*, app., p. 16.

Michaelmas term of 1690 and that the great majority of them took place before the end of the war. Thus the statement starts with three bills for Meath, dated Michaelmas 1690; almost the last item is a fourth bill for the same county, dated Easter 1693. The statement for domestic treason given in the Book of Outlawries similarly starts with three lists for Meath containing in all 203 names; on the last folio of the statement is a fourth list for Meath, containing a single name, that of Joseph Morgan of Cockstown. A statement of persons indicted and outlawed for high treason in Ireland was sworn before Sir Richard Reynell, chief justice of the king's bench, in October 1691.[1] Comparison of this statement with the domestic treason lists in the Book of Outlawries shows that nearly all the persons included in those lists had been proceeded against by the end of the war. This accounts for the fact that the lists are confined to the area over which William had jurisdiction at that time and do not include the counties beyond the Shannon.

In the majority of cases the proceedings seem to have been conducted in the absence of those indicted. Their summary character is illustrated by the records of the Dunboyne peerage case.[2] Thus a writ of exigent was issued by the court of king's bench in November 1690 against James Butler of Dunboyne. The sheriff of Meath was to cause the writ to be 'executed from hustings to hustings till according to the law and custom of Ireland he be outlawed if he do not appear, and if he appear he be produced to answer for treason whereof he is indicted'. The sheriff replied that on 16 April 1691 at a hustings held at Galtrim Lord Gormanston and the other defendants were called out a fifth time and, not appearing, were named by judgment of the coroner as outlawed. The exchequer inquisitions for Meath give a number of names of persons declared to have been outlawed at Galtrim on 16 April 1691. 11 May 1691 was the date of many of the Dublin outlawries. Similar field-days seem to have been held at other places during the summer of that year. There is a good deal of variation between the county lists. Apart from Dublin city, which was supplied with victims from a wide catchment-area, the highest return was that from Westmeath, with 304 names. It was closely followed by county Cork, with 297. Queen's County has only twenty-one names; Longford and King's County do not figure at all.

There is much duplication in the Book of Outlawries. Thus Tyrconnell appears in twelve lists for high treason in Ireland, and many other names are shown several times over. It appears that juries liked to show their

[1] B.M., Harl. MS 7545.
[2] P.R.O.I. MSS.

34

patriotism by indicting leading Jacobites whether they were connected with the county or not. A county Cork list starts off with Tyrconnell and the earl of Limerick, neither of whom owned property in the county. The Londonderry list includes Lords Galmoy, Gormanston, Bellew and other prominent persons described as 'lately of Pennyburn mill'. This was the scene of a successful sally during the siege, and the indictment proceedings seem primarily to have been intended as a parting thrust from the defenders of Derry. All those named were the subject of outlawry proceedings in their own counties and the Derry indictments had no practical effect.

The usual charges were those of having held military or civil office under James since 10 April 1689, the date mentioned in William's first declaration. In framing the indictments use seems to have been made of James's army list, as appears from a petition of Folliott Sherigley to the Irish commons in which he refers to the service which he rendered 'in securing the muster rolls and books of entry of the Irish army after the rout at the Boyne, whereby the commanding officers who served in the Irish army were known and outlawed'.[1] But the outlawries were not confined to those who held military or civil office. Leslie quotes a series of questions proposed by the Dublin grand jury and answered by the judges on 21 November 1690. Among these were the following: 'whether popish freeholders, who raised and maintained soldiers in their houses for their sons or others, that submitted to their majesties' declaration [of Finglas,] took protection and did not violate the same, ought to be indicted for their former abetting of the rebellion? *Yes.*

'Whether an old proprietor that entered into possession by virtue of the late acts (of repeal and attainder) ought to be indicted or not? *Yes.*

'Whether popish freeholders, electors of parliament men, etc., who signed indentures of their election to the sheriffs and have committed no other crimes ought to be indicted of treason? *Yes.*'[2]

A large proportion of those who were summarily outlawed consisted of persons who were in fact absent as active adherents of James. But equally summary treatment was given to quite a number of the elderly or unwarlike who took protection and remained in the English quarters. The records provide numerous examples of the very rough justice meted out in such cases. Thus from a petition presented to the English commons in 1701 it appears that Richard Fagan of Feltrim had responded to William's original declaration by resigning his commission in James's army and retiring quietly to his home, where in August 1690

---

[1] *Commons' jn. Ire.*, ii. 126 (29 Nov. 1695).
[2] Leslie, *Answer to . . . the State of the Protestants*, pp. 26-8.

35

some rapparees killed him for submitting to William. After his death he
was outlawed by a Williamite court in Dublin for non-appearance and
his estate was forfeited.[1] The English parliament was sufficiently moved
by this story to grant his brother a hundred pounds a year out of the
forfeited estate.[2] The same set of petitions contains a complaint from
Michael Chamberlain that, although he had submitted on the declaration of Finglas and got his appearance registered by the lord mayor, he
was thrown into prison. While in prison he was indicted of high treason,
'and by a proceeding altogether new and unheard of before' the sheriff
who had him in custody returned him 'non est inventus'; whereupon he
was outlawed and his estate seized.[3] Parliament refused to take any
action in his case, which may have been due to the fact that he was one
of James's judges. Another case was that of Peter Nottingham, an old
man of eighty-seven, who was indicted of high treason. 'Having by
chance notice thereof he surrendered himself in order to his trial, and
prayed that in regard to his great age he might be speedily either tried
or bailed, but both were refused to him; he was thrown into a gaol and
there continued in a most lamentable and necessitous condition without
very necessaries of life, and whilst there under the strictest confinement
was outlawed for high treason without ever being brought to answer for
himself.'[4]

Although most of the proceedings seem to have been of a summary
character, we have records of quite a number of persons who presented
themselves before the judges and were bound over to appear for trial at
some future date. Lists of such cases are contained in the statement
sworn before Sir Richard Reynell, to which reference has already been
made.[5] In April 1692 the lords justices reported that the court of king's
bench would be full of 'notices and applications of those who were
under protection and being indicted of high treason had appeared on the
capias and exigent and so prevented their outlawry; before the reduction of Limerick it was thought fit to use these people with great tender-
ness'. As further instructions had not come from England the king's
counsel had refrained from prosecuting them.[6]

The policy decided upon for such cases appears to have been one of
masterly inactivity. When a fresh set of lords justices arrived in 1697,
they found that, as for some years a stop had been put to indicting and

[1] Annesley MSS, xx. 95.
[2] 1 Anne, c. 47 (private act).
[3] Annesley MSS, xx. 153.
[4] Ibid., xx. 68.
[5] B.M., Harl. MS 7545, referred to on p. 34 above.
[6] Cal. S.P. dom., 1695 (addenda), p. 184.

outlawing, 'a great part of the Papists' were either indicted and not yet
tried or not yet indicted though liable to be so. Notices were therefore
given to those who had been indicted and had from term to term appeared on recognizances to be ready to stand their trial.[1] Most of these
were still untried in 1699, when the inquiry commissioners took a number of statements on the subject. Thus William Cook of Painstown told
them that he was indicted in county Carlow at Michaelmas 1690, and
bound over to appear at the king's bench in Dublin; he had since been
summoned to attend the court at regular intervals, but had not yet been
either tried or discharged. Patrick Wall of Ballinakill was similarly indicted in 1690 and continued to appear at the king's bench for several
years; he succeeded in obtaining a trial at Carlow summer assizes in
1699, at which he was acquitted. Pierce Bryan of Queen's County
appeared for thirty-three successive terms at the king's bench without
being either tried or discharged.[2] The crown clerk of Tipperary supplied
the inquiry commissioners with a list of sixty-six persons indicted for
high treason in April 1691 and not since tried or outlawed.[3]

Virtually all those who remained unconvicted in 1699 appear to have
escaped outlawry altogether. The inquiry commissioners had hopes of
adding to the forfeitures by convictions being obtained in fresh or outstanding cases. The storm caused by the Act of Resumption seems to
have been sufficient to put this out of the question. In their first report
the trustees admitted that there was no prospect of fresh forfeitures as
juries were determined to acquit in spite of the evidence.[4] In 1700
Methuen, the chancellor, summed up the situation by saying that 'everybody of sense sees that any future prosecutions, against whosoever they
are, will have very little effect'.[5]

The records indicate that most of the sentences of outlawry for high
treason in Ireland were passed before the end of the war. Extremely few
of the dates of outlawry given in the inquisitions are later than 1691.
Those who succeeded in obtaining bail or avoiding indictment at that
time were in most cases able to escape actual outlawry, although they
had to endure a good deal of trouble and anxiety. The last name in the
Dublin city lists of outlawry for high treason in Ireland is Nicholas
French of Abbert, county Galway. From a petition which he preferred
it appears that he had brought a suit in 1693 against Denny Muschamp,
who had retaliated by getting him indicted at Kilmainham 'in a time of

[1] *Cal. S.P. dom., 1699-1700*, p. 402.
[2] Annesley MSS, xxiii. 54-5.
[3] Ibid., xxvii. 113-14.
[4] *H.L.MSS*, n.s., iv. 208.
[5] *Cal. S.P. dom., 1700-2*, p. 102.

peace when none were indicted'. French's story was accepted and a pardon granted.[1] A bill of indictment was returned from Kerry at Michaelmas 1692. This corresponds to the Kerry list which is given on the last folio of the statement for high treason in Ireland in the Book of Outlawries and forms almost the last item of the statement. It contains only three names. The list does not include the Knight of Kerry, who had fought at the Boyne, but did not come within the articles of Limerick. Proceedings were started against him, but the jury threw out the case.[2]

The lull in proceedings for domestic high treason lasted from the surrender of Limerick till the end of 1697. In the following two years there seems to have been a considerable amount of activity in prosecuting persons in Connacht who were neither indicted nor protected by articles, and also in bringing to trial persons who had been indicted in the English quarters during the war and had ever since remained on recognizances. The calendars of State Papers contain a number of petitions from those adversely affected by such proceedings. This renewal of activity does not seem to have met with William's approval; we find some cases in which he asked why prosecutions were being revived.[3]

Remarkably few results were achieved by this renewal of treason proceedings. The principal field for fresh action was in Connacht where there had been no indictments at all for high treason in Ireland. Some twenty Connacht names were included in the Dublin city lists of outlawry, but there remained a large number of Connacht landowners neither indicted nor protected by the articles of Limerick or Galway. This had been pointed out by the lords justices soon after the conclusion of the war in a letter in which they referred to those concerned in the rebellion and not comprised in any articles; 'living remote in Connacht, where the enemy's quarters were, they have not yet been prosecuted'.[4] Connacht, however, was still enough of a Catholic stronghold to protect those who were prosecuted for domestic treason. The majority of the jurymen were Catholics who refused to indict their co-religionists. The inquiry commissioners complained bitterly that Connacht seemed scarcely reduced to his majesty's obedience, Protestant freeholders not being more than one in fifty and the juries being composed of articlemen who acquitted those presented for trial.[5] One of their witnesses deposed

---

[1] *Cal. S.P. dom., 1698*, pp. 243-4.

[2] T.C.D., MS N. 1. 3, f. 48; William Brewster to Sir William Trumbull, 24 Nov. 1696 (*H.M.C., Downshire MSS*, i. 711).

[3] *Cal. S.P. dom., 1699-1700*, pp. 292, 323.

[4] Ibid., *1695 (addenda)*, pp. 184-5.

[5] *Commrs' report*, p. 24. Articlemen was a term applied to persons admitted to the articles of Limerick or Galway.

that he had been on the jury at the last Galway assizes when nearly forty persons were prosecuted for their part in the rebellion. Seven of the jurors were Catholics and two were converts. They acquitted all the prisoners except one against whom the evidence was overwhelming. That case was ingeniously met by one of the jurors withdrawing with the result that the trial could not proceed and the prisoner was bound over.[1] Another witness referring to the same case remarked that such jurors would not find the prisoner guilty, for they 'did not look upon it to be treason to be in arms and fight against Protestants for King James'.[2]

It is perhaps more remarkable that so many of those who had been continued on bail in various counties of Leinster and Munster eventually avoided conviction, either by acquittal or by lapse of the proceedings. The inquiry commissioners recorded their impression that Protestant freeholders 'through length of time or by contracting new friendships with the Irish, but chiefly through a general dislike of the disposal of the forfeitures' were reluctant to find any persons guilty of the late rebellion.[3] There was, of course, a strong section of Protestant opinion which maintained that the Irish had been much too leniently treated at the capitulation of Limerick, and which was anxious to deprive as many Catholics as possible of their property. In 1695 the Irish commons expressed the view that 'the Papists, who are equally guilty of the rebellion with those that are already outlawed, and not included in any articles or agreement or pardoned, be outlawed or attainted by act of parliament, and that those who have appeared or shall appear upon the exigents may be put upon their trials'.[4] But enthusiasm must have been considerably lessened by distaste for William's grants to Bentinck and Keppel, and by the apprehension that the English parliament was going to resume such grants as Irish Protestants had received. Furthermore, forfeitures incurred several years after the end of the war would have affected vested interests acquired by Protestants in the form of leases, mortgages and purchases. Considerable anxiety was expressed by the Irish commons during the debate on the bill for confirming the outlawries, and a committee was appointed to consider methods of preserving to Protestants such rights and interests as might be affected by the bill.[5]

The 'new-found friendship with the Irish' is illustrated by a number of

[1] Annesley MSS, xxiii. 138.
[2] Ibid., xxiii. 123.
[3] *Commrs' report*, p. 23.
[4] *Commons' jn. Ire.*, ii. 144 (13 Dec. 1695).
[5] *Commons' jn. Ire.*, ii. 167 (12 Aug. 1697).

cases in which applicants for pardon offered evidence that they were on good terms with their Protestant neighbours. The relations between country gentlemen of different religions seem often to have been better than one would have supposed from the corporate actions of the Irish parliament. An example of a Catholic who escaped conviction as a result of the representations of his Protestant neighbours was Thady Quin of Adare. The story is given in a lengthy report submitted by the attorney-general in 1699. In February 1698 Thady Quin was adjudged not to be within the articles of Limerick. This led to several attempts being made to indict him for high treason. Proceedings were brought in three counties. In two the jury returned a finding of 'ignoramus'; he was indicted in a third county, but admitted to bail by the court of king's bench. Thereupon 'the high sheriff, grand jury and others of the Protestant gentry and clergy of the county of Limerick' preferred an address to the chief justice that Thady had not plundered or oppressed any Englishman or Protestant, but had done his best to protect his Protestant neighbours during the Jacobite regime. As a result of these representations the case against him was withdrawn.[1]

The virtual restriction of effective proceedings for domestic treason to the period of the war and to the English quarters enabled a large number of Catholics in Connacht and Clare to retain their property without being adjudged within the articles of Limerick or Galway. The number of those on the hither side of the Shannon who escaped outlawry without the protection of the articles was much smaller, but still appreciable.

Foreign treason. The foreign treason lists given in the Book of Outlawries are for all counties except Meath and Tipperary and contain 1,261 names. More than a hundred of these had already appeared in the lists for high treason in Ireland, and a good many others are returned for more than one county. Most of the proceedings for foreign treason appear to have taken place in 1696. In February of that year commissions of inquiry were issued for every county and county borough except Tipperary.[2] Inquisitions were then taken and returns made of those held to be concerned in treason beyond the seas. We have a record of the inquisition held in Drogheda on 27 March 1696 by which Bartholomew Gernon and fifteen others were found to have withdrawn allegiance from the king and the late queen and to have levied war against them on 20 February 1693 with other persons numbering about ten thousand, some of whom were subjects of the king of France, with the object of

[1] Dunraven, *Memorials of Adare*, pp. 181-5.
[2] *P.R.I. rep. D.K. 17*, app. p. 16.

invading Ireland.[1] The inquisitions were followed by writs of exigent and the calling out of those named. Sentences of outlawry were passed on those who did not appear at the third time of calling. From a copy of the writ of exigent sent by the clerk of the crown to the sheriff of Waterford on 12 June 1696 we find that Balthazar Sherlock, Walter Galway and others were found by inquisition to have aided and abetted the king of France, and that after having been called out in three successive months and not appearing they were declared outlawed.[2] About a third of the names were returned from Connacht and Clare. Evidently juries could more easily be persuaded to find against those who had actually left the country, few of whom had any landed property to forfeit. Conspicuous among those outlawed for foreign treason who had estates to lose were Lord Mountleinster in Galway and Walter Bourke and Henry O'Neill in Mayo.

Here again we find some examples of extremely rough justice. The first name on the Dublin city list of outlawries for foreign treason is that of Jane Levallin, spinster. In 1689 Jane was an orphan three years old; on the outbreak of the war her grandfather sent her over to France. During her absence she was outlawed for high treason 'supposed to be committed by her in parts beyond the seas'.[3] Her case was put before the English commons during the debate on the resumption bill, but rejected.[4] She then engaged the services of Dr Davenant, the well-known tory pamphleteer. This resulted in the passage of a private act for the reversal of her outlawry and the restoration of her forfeited estate.[5] Dr Davenant's services were not cheap. He was summoned by the English lords to explain why he had taken a bond of a thousand pounds from Jane to get her bill through the house of lords; 'the question being put whether it was a crime in the doctor it passed in the negative'.[6] Another hard case was that of Mary Vernon, who was sent to France as a consumptive girl of thirteen and had remained there with relations as her father had died. During her absence she was outlawed for foreign treason.[7] In her case also a private act was passed for reversal of the outlawry and restoration of the estate.[8]

Sir Lawrence Esmonde was sent to France for education in 1689,

[1] N.L.I., Report on Verdon papers.
[2] P.R.O.I., transcripts. Three callings seem to have sufficed for foreign treason, as compared with five for domestic treason.
[3] Annesley MSS, xx. 60.
[4] *Commons' jn.*, xiii. 309.
[5] 1 Anne, c. 56.
[6] Luttrell, *Brief historical relation*, v. 175.
[7] Annesley MSS, xx. 162.
[8] 1 Anne, c. 61.

when he was twelve years old. He returned in 1692 with a pass, and found that he had been indicted for high treason alleged to have been committed in Ireland. Queen Mary ordered the prosecution to be stayed and he was left in peace till 1699, when a second indictment was brought against him on the ground that he had acted as an officer in France.[1] William gave orders that the prosecution should not be proceeded with, but meanwhile the trustees for the Irish forfeitures had interested themselves in the case.[2] Accordingly William thought that nothing could be done but to tell the trustees the circumstances and inform them of the orders which the queen had previously passed in Esmonde's favour.[3] The trustees persisted, but the proceedings were terminated by one of the jurors withdrawing with the result that no verdict could be given.[4] By that time the period prescribed by the Act of Resumption for treason proceedings had elapsed. The large Esmonde estate thus escaped forfeiture.

A number of historians have presumed that the figure of nearly four thousand outlawries related to landowners.[5] Butler has discussed this question in some detail. His conclusion is that as the total number of Catholic landowners in Ireland could hardly have exceeded thirteen hundred the outlawed persons were certainly not all landowners.[6] The disparity between the total number of outlawries and the number of outlawed landlords is strikingly brought out by the second of the books accompanying the inquiry commissioners' report. This book—the Book of Forfeitures—gives particulars of the estates forfeited, including those restored under articles and by royal favour. The total number of estates recorded is only 457.

Examination of the lists of outlawries shows that the names fall into a number of categories. Besides landowners there are younger sons, tenants, traders and representatives of a variety of other occupations. There are many cases in which several members of one family were outlawed. Thus the Westmeath lists show four members of the family of Fox of Moyvore outlawed for high treason in Ireland and a fifth member of the same family outlawed for foreign treason. Many of those whom the lists describe as gentlemen are given addresses on other men's estates. Some of these were leaseholders, others were representatives of old families who had been dispossessed. The lists also contain a number of

[1] Cal. S.P. dom., 1699-1700, pp. 292-3.
[2] Ibid., 1700-2, pp. 87-9.
[3] Ibid., p. 173.
[4] Annesley MSS, iv. 199.
[5] Ranke, History of England, v. 207; Froude, Ire., i. 245; Curtis, Ire., p. 275.
[6] Butler, Confiscation, p. 220.

persons described as merchants and yeomen. There are quite a few artisans, and a Cork list contains some boatmen. A considerable number of priests are included; among them are the Catholic archbishops of Armagh and Tuam.

In considering why so many landless persons should have been outlawed it must be taken into account that the penalties of outlawry were not restricted to the forfeiture of freehold property. Unexpired leases, mortgage claims and personal property were all the subject of inquisition proceedings. Some of the inquisitions take account of such minor items as bolsters and pewter dishes. The order given to the bailiff of Kilkenny in 1694 for the seizure of outlawed persons' property includes such articles as blankets, rugs and 'two French hats'. Another item is a hundred barrels of beer from the Irish college.[1]

We do not hear of death sentences being passed on any of those included in the outlawry lists. In a letter of 1693 instructions were given to the lord-lieutenant that there were to be no executions without the queen's special order.[2] The 'act to hinder the reversal of outlawries' contained a provision which maintained the king's power of pardoning 'so as to save the life only of an outlawed person'.[3]

The hasty and irregular character of many of the outlawry proceedings was a source of considerable anxiety to those who had received grants or taken leases of the forfeited estates. A number of outlawries were reversed by pardons and others were challenged on legal points. The legality of outlawry after death was a particular point on which disputes arose. The opinion of the celebrated Sir Bartholomew Shower was obtained on the illegality of the indictment brought against Sir Valentine Browne, Lord Kenmare, after his death, which took place in August 1690.[4] A warrant was issued for the reversal of the outlawry on this ground, but it was then discovered that he had already been outlawed in England. William refused to permit the reversal of the English sentence.[5] The outlawry of Richard Fagan of Feltrim was challenged in the courts on the same ground, but the judges confirmed its validity.[6]

In transmitting the bill for confirming outlawries and attainders the lords justices explained that legislation of this character was absolutely necessary, as no outlawry was free from errors which were sufficient to reverse it and defeat the crown's title. In particular the law had been

[1] P.R.O.I., Haydock papers.
[2] Ibid., Wyche papers, 1st series, i. 73.
[3] 9 Will. III (Ire.), c. 5, s. 21.
[4] *Cal. S.P. dom., 1694-5*, p. 4.
[5] *Cal. treas. bks*, x. 1417.
[6] *Cal. S.P. dom., 1694-5*, p. 38.

interpreted as permitting the attainder of those who had died in rebellion, but many such attainders had recently been challenged.[1] The bill provided for attainder in such cases on a finding by inquisition that the deceased had died or been killed in rebellion. A certain number of such findings are given in the inquisition proceedings. Many of those concerned were already included in the outlawry lists, but a few additional forfeitures were obtained by this means. In its original form the bill caused anxiety to Protestants who feared that their interests might be adversely affected by it. Their protests led to an amendment to the effect that the provision for the attainder of those who had died in rebellion applied only to Catholics, and that the rights of Protestants who had inherited or purchased the property of such Catholics should not be liable to forfeiture.[2] Protestants also expressed their objection to another clause of the bill by which reversions of entailed estates were to be forfeited. This provision was accordingly made the subject of a separate bill, which was rejected *nem. con.*[3] Protestants who had purchased or lent money on reversions were naturally opposed to legislation of this nature. The inclusion of a similar provision in the English Act of Resumption was one of the reasons for its unpopularity in Irish Protestant circles.

[1] *Cal. S.P. dom., 1697*, pp. 243-4.
[2] 9 Will. III (Ire.), c. 5, ss 3, 4.
[3] *Commons' jn. Ire.*, ii. 176 (25 Aug. 1697).

4

THE TREATY OF LIMERICK AND
THE CONFISCATION

T he treaty of Limerick failed to secure to Catholics the religious
safeguards for which they had hoped as the chief reward of their
stubborn resistance. But the second of the civil articles, with the
corresponding provisions of the articles of Galway, had the effect of
restoring their estates to a considerable number of Catholic landowners.
Still more were secured in the possession of estates which lay in the
Irish quarters and had not been forfeited. Under the articles a number
of the outlawries were reversed and pardon guaranteed to those who
had not been outlawed by the end of the war. The scheme of the articles
provided the officers of the Irish army with the alternatives of going to
France and forfeiting their estates, or of staying at home and securing
the possession of their estates by submission to William. Sarsfield and
Lord Galmoy were the most prominent of those who elected to go to
France. The majority of those who owned land remained in Ireland.

As the articles of Limerick and Galway constituted the major check
to the processes of outlawry and forfeiture, it is necessary to examine in
some detail how they were implemented and what effect they had on the
land question. The inquiry commissioners of 1699 were supplied with
lists of the adjudications under the articles. These lists, which give particulars of 1,283 claims, comprise the third and fourth of the nine books
which accompanied the report of the commission. They provide our
only substantial source of information on the subject although they can
be supplemented by a number of scattered references to individual cases.
The lists give the name and address of each claimant, the articles
(Limerick or Galway) under which the claim was made, the decision and
the date of the order.[1] The most striking characteristic of the lists is the

[1] T.C.D., MS N. 1. 3, ff. 101-51. The statistics relating to estates restored under the
articles are discussed in Appendix A, pp. 174-6, below.

high proportion of claims allowed. In fifteen cases the claimants were adjudged not to be within the articles; one case was endorsed as still in dispute; the remaining claims were all admitted, a few of the entries being duplicated.

The successful claimants included representatives of almost all the leading Jacobite families. There were twelve peers—Antrim, Clanricarde, Dillon, Dunboyne, Dunsany, Fitzwilliam of Merrion, Gormanston, Iveagh, Kingsland, Louth, Mountgarret and Westmeath. The families of the pale were well represented with twenty-eight Fitzgeralds, twenty-two Nugents and lesser numbers of other well-known names. Claims were by no means restricted to the old English. Numerous MacNamaras and O'Briens from Clare appear in the lists. There are several Kellys from Connacht and Reillys from Cavan. Other representatives of well-known Gaelic families were Donough and Cornelius McGillicuddy of the Reeks and Morgan Kavanagh of Borris. The lists include Captain John Connell of Ballymagallinagh,[1] great-grandfather of the Liberator, and Garret Nagle of Shanballyduff, grandfather of Edmund Burke. Almost all the claimants seem to have been Catholics, although the pressure of the penal laws caused a great many of them to conform to the established church in the course of the eighteenth century. A Protestant exception was Sir Thomas Crosby of Ballyheigue, who sat in the Dublin parliament of 1689 and was one of those outlawed in England.

William showed a commendable anxiety to implement the articles as quickly as possible. Early in January 1692 a letter from the lords justices mentioned that the king had directed the privy council to proceed to the examination of persons claiming the benefit of the articles of Limerick. In the same letter they said that to prevent dissatisfaction they had already restored their estates to about sixty persons who seemed to be undoubtedly entitled to the benefit of the articles; if subsequent examination showed that any of these were not so entitled they could easily be dispossessed.[2] On 11 January 1692 a proclamation was issued in Dublin calling on those concerned to prefer their claims. A later proclamation prescribed that each claimant under the articles of Limerick or Galway should produce three witnesses, one of whom was to be a Protestant; it was explained that the latter requirement was quite reasonable, as several Protestants had remained in Limerick and Galway throughout the war.[3] The first hearing took place on 6 April 1692.[4]

[1] The modern Ballynabloun, bar. Iveragh, co. Kerry.
[2] *Cal. S.P. dom.*, 1695 (*addenda*), p. 174.
[3] *Dublin Intelligence*, 26 Mar.–2 Apr. 1692.
[4] Ibid., 2–9 Apr. 1692.

No adjudications, however, were given till April 20, when Sir Patrick Barnwell and Thomas Peppard were declared within the articles of Limerick. Claimants considered the conditions imposed to be unduly onerous. A statement of Catholic grievances, submitted in 1693, protested against the stipulation about witnesses and also against the demand that successful claimants should enter into recognizances of a thousand pounds each before being given back their estates. Articlemen were further aggrieved by an order of December 1692, under which many of them were imprisoned for three weeks.[1]

The third of the books accompanying the report of the inquiry commissioners contains the adjudications given in 1692 and 1694. Authority was given in 1693 to Sydney as lord-lieutenant to hear claims with his council, but he does not seem to have acted on it. There was a gap in the hearings until fresh authority was given to a new set of lords justices in April 1694. The book records 491 claims, of which seven were rejected and one is endorsed 'still in dispute'. One claimant was adjudged within the articles of both Limerick and Galway, and another adjudged not to be within the articles of Galway. The rest of the claims recorded in the book relate exclusively to the Limerick articles. Adjudications under the articles of Galway were held up on account of a disputed interpretation of those articles which will form the subject of further discussion.

The Public Record Office of Ireland has a series of lists showing claims put down for hearing on certain dates in 1694.[2] A similar series for other dates in the same year is preserved in the National Library of Ireland.[3] The lists consist of the claimants' names and addresses, evidently in the hand of a clerk, and notes which are in another hand, possibly that of William Palmer, the deputy clerk of the council, who kept the minutes. The notes show that the principal point at issue in disputed cases was whether the claimant had ever 'taken protection' from the Williamite authorities. The second article of Limerick contained a proviso excluding from benefit those who had taken protection (e.g. by voluntary surrender under the terms of the declaration of Finglas, which offered a guarantee of life and personal property but not of real estate). This proviso was attributed to the initiative of Richard Cox, who was convinced that many persons had taken protection from the Williamite authorities after the Boyne and had subsequently gone over to the Irish quarters. He wrote to this effect to the lords justices at the time of the negotiations for the surrender of Limerick and succeeded in getting such

[1] *Cal. S.P. dom., 1693*, pp. 443-5.
[2] P.R.O.I., Wyche papers, 1st series, iii. 1-2; 2nd series, 106-18.
[3] N.L.I., MS 174.

persons excluded from the articles.[1] The notes on the 1694 claims contain a number of references to this question of protection. Thus in the list of cases fixed for 14 July 1694 against the name of James Barrett of Curraghaneily there is a note 'second sitting after Michaelmas to prove protection'. In the list for November 19 James Barrett is again shown with the note 'proved in protection' and the order 'not within'. A considerable number of names are marked 'non app.' (did not appear) and no decision is recorded, although in some cases the decision would certainly have been against the claimant. Thus, in the list for 18 June 1694, the names of George Darcy of Plattin and John Archer of Riverstown are endorsed 'took protection', while that of James Hackett of Ballytown is endorsed 'in France'. In a number of cases the king's counsel appears to have made unsuccessful attempts to prove that claimants had taken protection. A note against the name of Richard Reddy of Kilmurry records that a fortnight was given to the king's counsel to prove that he had taken protection. Similar notes were made against the names of John Purcell of Crumlin, Thomas Nevill of Rathmore and several others who are shown in the book of adjudications as coming within the articles.

We have a considerably fuller record of one of the claims. This is the case of Edmond Blanchfield of Blanchfieldstown, who is shown in the book of adjudications as adjudged within the articles of Limerick on 27 November 1694, with the further endorsement 'still in dispute'. Notes of the evidence recorded in the case have been preserved—the only example of such evidence which we have.[2] The court heard a number of witnesses, including one who gave his evidence in Irish through an interpreter. From the depositions it appears that immediately after the declaration of Finglas, while William was still at Finglas, a friend of Blanchfield's obtained a protection for him and sent it to him. Before it arrived Blanchfield had already left his home near Kilkenny and had gone off to county Cork. When the protection was forwarded to him he sent it back to a neighbour, asking him to use it to save Blanchfield's stock from the depredations of William's army. The protection was actually so used by the neighbour and by Blanchfield's seventeen-year-old daughter, who had remained to guard her home. The court found that Blanchfield had proved himself to have been on the relevant date in that part of county Cork which was in the Irish quarters. A note was made that he was adjudged within the articles unless the king's counsel could prove that he had taken protection. On the evidence recorded it is

---

[1] Ware, *History of the writers of Ireland*, p. 213.
[2] P.R.O.I., Wyche papers, 1st series, i. 114.

somewhat surprising that the court should have had any hesitation about deciding against the claim. The case was the subject of dispute and had not been decided at the time of the inquiry commission of 1699.

In 1701 the matter came before the trustees for the Irish forfeitures, and the discussion which then took place throws further light on the proceedings. Palmer, the deputy clerk of the privy council, was called on to give evidence. He read out the minutes of the case, from which it appeared that six members of the court had found for Blanchfield and three against him. Palmer maintained that he must have received orders to enter the claimant as adjudged within the articles or he would not have done so; when the court was divided in opinion the minutes and the rule passed on them were always read out. However, no certificate had been issued to Blanchfield. From Palmer's evidence it appears that Sir Cyril Wyche, one of the lords justices who had found against the claimant, declared that he would never sign the certificate. In 1697 Blanchfield had preferred an appeal to William, praying that the lords justices should be ordered to certify his adjudication. When this appeal was referred to Ireland a note was added to the original record that one of the lords justices had been against the adjudication and another for it. In 1698 William had ordered a fresh hearing of the case. There were various postponements, but it appears that Blanchfield was again adjudged within the articles; the decision, however, was not given till 13 September 1699, a few days after the last day allowed by the act for the confirmation of the articles of Limerick. Blanchfield again applied to William, who ordered that he should be allowed to refer to the minutes taken at the council board and to the orders passed on them. William, in fact, seems to have done his best for Blanchfield without being able to make his intervention effective as against the authorities on the spot. Unluckily for Blanchfield, Wyche, who had been the adverse lord justice, was again concerned with the case as chairman of the trustees. The trustees' finding was that there was no adjudication entitling Blanchfield to the benefit of the articles. His estate was accordingly forfeited and sold.[1]

The question of defining the Irish quarters was raised in the case of Peter Trant of Dingle, whose name occurs in the list of claims put down for 29 November 1694. The case was endorsed 'respitt. whether Dingle was in the Irish quarters'. The case was decided in favour of the claimant and less than a month later he was adjudged within the articles. A curious objection was raised to the claim of Sir James Cotter that he had infringed the articles by resuming possession of his estate without

[1] Annesley MSS, xi. 180-6.

authority. The matter was referred to Cox, on whose report Cotter was admitted to the benefit of the articles. Representations against this decision were made to the English commons, and the matter was discussed in a report presented by a committee in 1694,[1] but Cotter remained in possession of his estate. The Irish commons also turned their attention to Cotter on the ground that he had maliciously ordered Edward Denny's house at Tralee to be burned. As the articles of Limerick included an indemnity for acts committed during the war Cotter would ordinarily have been protected against a claim for damages. The commons, however, resolved to prepared heads of a bill to withdraw the indemnity in this particular case. The proposal went no further and Cotter's rights under the articles remained unimpaired.[2] Another case about which representations were made to the English commons was that of Lord Antrim. It appears that Antrim was established on a hill outside Limerick and was not in the town at the time of the capitulation. Protests were made to the commons against the decision by which his occupying the hill with a few men surrounded by a small ditch was 'adjudged to be a good garrison'.[3] Antrim's case was later the subject of discussion when the Irish parliament ratified the articles of Limerick without the 'omitted clause', a vexed question which will be examined in the following chapter. An interesting case was that of Colonel Daniel O'Donovan of Banelaghan, county Cork, who went to France with the Jacobite army but later came back to Ireland. On his return he reported to the Williamite authorities and was ordered to surrender to the high sheriff of Cork. He was proceeded against for treason but admitted to bail; the case was kept pending until his claim to be admitted to the benefit of the articles of Limerick was granted, on 7 December 1694. The explanation for this exceptional treatment appears to lie in the fact that he had shown reluctance to go to France and before he left Ireland had inquired about the prospects of serving William in Flanders.[4]

The first series of adjudications, in which the tribunal consisted of the privy council, continued until the end of 1694. After that there was a break of almost three years during which no claims under the articles were heard. The delay seems to have been due to the controversy over the ratification of the articles by the Irish parliament. The adjudications did not legally depend on any act of parliament. There was, however, much controversy over the interpretation of the articles,

---

[1] *Commons' jn.*, xi. 56.
[2] *Commons' jn. Ire.*, ii. 280 (28 Nov. 1698).
[3] *Commons' jn.*, x. 830.
[4] N.L.I., Report on O'Donovan papers.

and in particular over the omitted clause, which extended them to persons under the protection of the Irish in certain counties. Capel, who became lord deputy in 1695, was violently anti-Irish and the hold-up in the adjudications may be attributed to his influence. The treaty of Limerick was thoroughly disliked by a considerable section of Protestant opinion. This point of view was frankly expressed in a letter written by Bonnell, the Irish accountant-general, to Harley immediately after the conclusion of the war. 'Had the Irish been totally reduced by the loss of all their estates, this country would have been looked on by the English as a secure place and many would have flocked here.'[1] Capel drew round him a party of the noisier Protestants, who were particularly bitter against Porter, the lord chancellor. Porter had been one of the signatories of the articles, and as a lord justice in 1692 and as chancellor in that year and in 1694 was prominently associated with the adjudications. He was accused of showing undue favour to Catholics, and was described by one of his opponents as a danger to the country.[2] William appears to have been personally in favour of a liberal interpretation of the articles. After Porter's death he is said to have regretted the loss of a good chancellor and to have observed that 'the root of animosity against him was for little else than his supporting the articles of Limerick'.[3]

The Irish parliamentary proceedings for the ratification of the articles were largely concerned with the omitted clause, which will be the subject of discussion in the following chapter. The act as passed ratified the second article of Limerick as applying only to (a) the inhabitants of Limerick and of the other garrisons which were in Irish possession on 3 October 1691, and (b) the Irish officers and soldiers then in arms who were not prisoners of war and had not at any time previously enjoyed the protection of the Williamite authorities for themselves or their families or goods. The act conferred pardon on all persons already adjudged or to be adjudged within the second or third articles.[4]

After the passing of this act hearings began again. In place of the privy council a new tribunal was appointed, consisting of nine judges, three each from the courts of king's bench, exchequer and common pleas. The fourth of the books accompanying the inquiry commissioners' report contains particulars of the 791 adjudications given by the judges between 27 October 1697 and 1 September 1699. The latter was

---

[1] *H.M.C. rep. 14*, app. ii. 479.
[2] *H.M.C.*, *Buccleuch MSS*, ii. 425-6.
[3] Southwell to Cox, 26 Dec. 1696 (Ware, *History of the writers of Ireland*, p. 218).
[4] 9 Will. III, c. 2. The third article referred to merchants who were abroad at the time of the capitulation but returned within eight months.

THE TREATY OF LIMERICK AND CONFISCATION

the final date prescribed by the act for admitting claimants to the benefit of the articles. Eight claims were rejected by the judges and the rest allowed. The inquiry commissioners made several criticisms of the court of claims constituted by the judges. They commented that in many cases the articles were 'expounded too beneficially', and that claimants received their adjudications before the expiry of the prescribed period of fourteen days. They apprehended that a great many persons had thus been restored to estates that 'upon a review would be found to belong to his majesty'. They also remarked that more adjudications were given since the commencement of the inquiry commission than had previously been given since the articles were drawn up.[1] The last point is not far short of the truth. The list of adjudications shows that about six hundred claims were decided between 1 June and 1 September 1699. On the latter date—the last day available for admitting claimants—seventy-five claims were allowed.

Cox, who was one of the judges concerned, emphatically repudiated the charges made by the commissioners. 'What is but common justice they may call favouring the Irish and a lessening of the forfeitures, and we cannot help that. We got nothing but trouble and censure by that court of claims, and if the justice we administered there will distinguish us and preserve us from the destroying angel when he comes to punish the oppressions and perjuries, notorious and public, committed against the claimants it is all the reward we desire or expect.' The commissioners had criticized the court for hearing nearly a hundred cases in a day at short notice. Cox explained that some busybodies in Kilkenny had indicted some poor tradesmen, which had caused a panic in the counties of the west and brought several hundred claimants up to Dublin. The judges found that many of them had no landed property and, after consulting the government, told them that the authorities had no intention of troubling landless men and that they might go home. The claimants, however, protested that indictments might at any time be brought against them unless they had adjudications. The court therefore gave adjudications to a total of 3–400 landless claimants on the evidence of one or two witnesses in each case. Landowners were usually required to produce three or four witnesses.[2]

One of the unsuccessful claimants was Thady Quin of Adare. He was proved to have been within the walls of Limerick at the time of the capitulation. However, the 'king's managers' (counsel for the crown) produced evidence that in 1690, during the first siege of Limerick, he had

[1] *Commrs' report*, p. 13.
[2] *H.M.C. rep. 14*, app. ii. 611-12.

been in the Williamite quarters in the company of several Protestant gentlemen. It was thus inferred that he had taken protection and was thereby excluded from the benefit of the articles.[1] As already mentioned, the authorities were later induced to drop the outlawry proceedings in his case.

Charles Geoghegan of Moycashel, another unsuccessful claimant, got the emperor to intercede on his behalf with William, who called for a report on the case. From this report Geoghegan appears to have claimed that on 3 October 1691 he was colonel of an infantry regiment in the garrison of Ennis, and that he had never taken protection from the Williamite authorities. Against this the king's managers produced several witnesses 'both Protestant and Papist of a fair and a good reputation', including some officers of the late Irish army, who deposed that Geoghegan had taken protection after the Boyne and that his regiment had been disbanded. Evidence was given that after the first siege of Limerick had been raised Geoghegan had gathered together 'a huge number of loose, idle persons, commonly called rapparees, in no way concerned in the army, and had infested and laid waste as much as in him lay the country, so that he was pursued even by the Irish army and fled from them'. It was also deposed that Ennis was never a garrison and that no part of the Irish army was ever kept there apart from some few wounded and sick who lay there for the recovery of their health. Geoghegan was allowed time to produce evidence to rebut these charges. Among his witnesses was Lord Dillon, who could only depose that he had heard that Geoghegan had been in arms but had not actually met him. The case was given a number of hearings, and the judges took several days to read their notes and consider their verdict, which was given unanimously against the claim. The emperor's intercession seems to have been made after the expiry of the period prescribed for the admission of claims, and the lords justices strongly advised against the reopening of the case.[2] The decision was upheld and Geoghegan's estate was subsequently sold by the trustees.

A number of the claims adjudged in 1699 seem to have been preferred earlier and allowed to remain dormant. The list of claims put down for hearing on 12 July 1694 contains six names marked 'non app.', all of which appear in the adjudications of 1699.[3] The inference is that the claimants were left undisturbed and took no steps to prosecute their

---

[1] Dunraven, *Memorials of Adare*, p. 181. See also p. 40 above.
[2] Lords justices to William Blathwayt, 25 Oct. 1699 (B.M., Add. MS 9,716, pp. 98-9).
[3] N.L.I., MS 174.

claims until they were alarmed into further proceedings by the activity associated with the forfeitures inquiry and by the time-limit fixed by the act for the confirmation of the articles.

The claims of David Nagle of Carrigacunna and Pierce Nagle of Annakisky were put down for hearing on 19 November 1694. Against each an endorsement was made that further time was given to the king's counsel to prove the claimant in protection and that the cases were adjourned until the second sitting after Christmas.[1] No sittings are recorded after that Christmas and thereafter the privy council ceased to be the tribunal for hearing claims. The next we hear of these two cases is in 1699, when David Nagle was adjudged within the articles of Limerick and Pierce Nagle's claim was disallowed. Thomas Broderick told the inquiry commissioners that David Nagle had taken protection and then had gone over to the enemy. Broderick had made it his business 'without the prospect or expectation of a penny profit' to send witnesses to Dublin to prove the protection. He had refused Nagle's offer of half his estate if he would 'surcease prosecution and only be passive in the matter'. Broderick added that when he heard that the credit of some of the crown witnesses was impaired by Nagle's evidence he wrote to the crown solicitor offering to send up further witnesses who would put the matter past dispute. The court was divided on the question of allowing further evidence. It finally refused to do so and admitted Nagle to the benefit of the articles.[2] He was the grandfather of Nano Nagle, foundress of the Presentation Order.

Most of the claims heard by the judges seem to have been admitted without much ado. The record naturally tends to be fuller in the few cases over which disputes arose. From the material available we get the general impression that the proceedings were reasonably fair and that in contested cases sufficient opportunity was given to claimants to bring evidence in support of their claims.

[1] P.R.O.I., Wyche papers, 2nd series, 115.
[2] Annesley MSS, xxiii. 66.

5

THE MISSING CLAUSE OF THE TREATY

The controversies which arose over the treaty of Limerick centred to a remarkable degree on the celebrated 'omitted clause', which brought within the scope of the second article all those that were under the protection of the Jacobite forces in the counties of Limerick, Cork, Clare, Kerry and Mayo. After the signed copy of the treaty had been despatched to William it was reported to him that a clause consisting of the words 'and all such as are under their protection in the said counties' had been agreed to and incorporated in the rough draft, but had inadvertently been omitted from the fair copy. The letters patent of 24 February 1692, which ratified the Limerick articles, detailed the circumstances of the omission and declared that the clause should form part of the articles.[1] In the prolonged dispute which arose it was argued that the clause was an interpolation rather than an omission, and that the Irish Jacobites had fraudently obtained a valuable concession after the terms of the treaty had been agreed. There are numerous contemporary references to this controversy which throw much light both on what happened in the course of drafting the treaty and on the attitude subsequently adopted by William and his advisers. At the same time, a number of points remain obscure and there is much that is enigmatic about the whole proceedings.[2]

A prominent part in the drafting of the articles was taken by George Clarke, who was secretary at war for Ireland and acted as Ginkel's civil adviser. In his autobiography, writen in 1720, Clarke referred in some detail to the question of the omitted clause. On 27 September 1691 the

---

[1] The text of the letters patent is given in Curtis and McDowell, *Irish historical documents*, p. 175.

[2] Accounts of the omission of the clause are given in Murray, *Revolutionary Ireland and its settlement*, pp. 239-40; and Butler, *Confiscation*, pp. 222-6; but there is much material to which they have not referred and which brings fresh information to bear on the question.

Irish Jacobites had sent to Ginkel the terms which they proposed for the capitulation.[1] Clarke says that 'these being very large it was thought better to send them a draft of the terms we would grant them than to retrench and alter theirs'. On September 28 Sarsfield came to Ginkel's camp to discuss the draft. He was accompanied by Sir Toby Butler and others. Clarke goes on to say that the first question which Sir Toby asked was what was meant by the title 'Articles granted by Lieutenant-General Ginkel, commander-in-chief of their majesties' forces, to all persons now in the city of Limerick or in the Irish army, that is in the counties of Clare, Kerry, Cork and Mayo and other garrisons that are in their possession'. Clarke answered that they meant to grant terms to those who were in a condition to offer opposition. Sarsfield then said that he would 'lay his bones in these old walls rather than not take care of those who stuck by them all along'. The second article was therefore construed to extend to all those under the protection of the Irish in the counties referred to.

Clarke pointed out that he had made particular mention of the matter as the words, though at first agreed to, were omitted by mistake in transcribing the copy of the articles which was signed; the mistake was not found out until the following day when Ginkel's son had already left for England with the 'original or a copy to be laid before their majesties'. Clarke added the following comment: 'this occasioned a great deal of trouble, for when we came to England M. Ginkel, Major-General Talmash and I gave certificates or depositions of what passed and that which was left out by mistake was granted to the Irish under the broad seal of England and, as I take it, by act of parliament in Ireland. For I sent over the very original draft of the articles from which the signed copy was made to Lord Chancellor Porter in order to satisfy the parliament there, where many were averse from doing the Irish that piece of justice and aspersed Lord Coningsby, who was one of the justices that signed the articles, as if by his means the broad seal had been obtained to give the Irish a favour that was never intended them at the time of the treaty; whereas in reality it was the first thing insisted upon by them and agreed to by us; and further I have reason to believe that if it had not been for that lord [i.e. Coningsby] the general's son had been sent for back and the words that were left out inserted.'[2]

Clarke's recollection was, of course, at fault as regards the Irish parliament ratifying the omitted clause. He may have confused the act of 1697, which ratified the second article of Limerick without that clause,

[1] *Diary of the siege and surrender of Limerick*, p. 16.
[2] *H.M.C., Leyborne-Popham MSS*, p. 280.

with the proceedings of 1695, when an attempt was made in the Irish commons to impeach Porter—an attack which was largely directed against Porter's policy of implementing the articles in a liberal manner. Clarke had presumably sent over the draft of the articles in 1695 to assist Porter in his defence. The latter successfully justified his conduct and the commons resolved that his explanation was satisfactory.[1]

From another collection of Clarke's papers it is possible to trace how the form of the articles was changed during the various stages of the negotiations. The collection includes a paper in Clarke's writing which he endorsed as follows: '28 September 1691. Explanation of the articles. Memorandum. This is the original minute of what was settled by the General Ginkel and the commissioners from Limerick who were empowered to treat about the surrender of the city.'[2] The explanation extended the benefit of the first article (which in drafting became the second) to all that were under the protection of the Irish in the counties of Clare, Kerry, Cork and Mayo.

In the same collection there is another paper, which according to an endorsement in Clarke's hand is the original draft of the articles. Clarke's endorsement adds that in transcribing the fair copy which was actually signed Payzant, the clerk, left out the words 'and all such as are under their protection in the said counties'. The draft is in a clerk's hand with interlineations, which Clarke says in his endorsement are in the hand of Sir Toby Butler. The clerk's draft is in accordance with the terms settled on September 28 and includes the words 'and all such as are under their protection'.[3] From internal evidence it may be inferred that the clerk's draft was written on September 28, and that the clause was a settled part of the agreement several days before the lords justices arrived on October 1. This becomes a relevant matter in considering the account which Coningsby later gave of his recollection of the drafting of the articles.

The draft is in the form of articles granted by Ginkel, and contains an undertaking by Ginkel that they would be ratified within forty-eight hours by the lords justices. It appears that on September 29 the French and Irish insisted that the lords justices should sign the articles at the same time as the other signatories. To this may be attributed an addition to the heading of the draft in Clarke's hand coupling the lords justices with Ginkel, and a further addition in Butler's hand of the names

---

[1] *Commons' jn. Ire.*, ii. 109 (25 Oct. 1695).

[2] B.M., Eg. MS 2,618, ff. 165-6.

[3] B.M., Eg. MS 2, 618, ff. 161-3. The text is given in my article 'The original draft of the civil articles of Limerick, 1691' (*I.H.S.*, viii. 37-44).

Porter and Coningsby. The last paragraph is crossed out and a paragraph added in Clarke's hand that the lords justices and Ginkel would jointly undertake to get their majesties to ratify the articles. The heading was completely changed in the final version, but the draft of the articles themselves, as amended by Sir Toby Butler, was incorporated word for word, with the exception of the omitted clause. Oddly enough, the draft does not include the provision for the debts of Colonel John Browne of Westport, which seems to have been incorporated at the last minute.[1] There are various other additions; thus the county of Limerick was added to the four counties named in the draft. The lords justices, Porter and Coningsby, arrived on the evening of October 1 and the following day was spent in prolonged discussion. The Jacobite officers are said to have stayed with the lords justices and Ginkel until midnight, 'by which time all the difficulties which arose in settling the articles being agreed they were concluded and ordered to be fair drawn for signature.'[2]

The articles were signed on October 3 and the Williamite forces occupied the Irish town on October 4. The next development is described in a statement given to the inquiry commissioners in 1699 by Sir Donough O'Brien, who had apparently contrived to remain in county Clare throughout the war without taking either side. He was in Limerick at the time of the negotiations, and told the commissioners that he first saw the text of the articles when the Irish town had been surrendered and the English town was still held by the garrison. He was then in the company of Sir Stephen Rice and Sir Toby Butler when a copy of the articles was read out. Sir Donough expressed the view that the terms did not comprise the inhabitants of the five counties. Sir Toby Butler replied that this was impossible and, taking the rough draft out of his pocket, said that the inhabitants of the five counties were included in the draft terms. Sir Toby then went off to Ginkel and the lords justices and later reported that they had assured him that the omission was a mistake and would be rectified.[3] Sir Toby seems to have asked Clarke for an attested copy of the original draft. The lords justices did not approve of this and the papers contain an order of 7 October 1691, written in Clarke's hand and signed by Porter and Coningsby, directing Clarke not to give out 'foul drafts' of the articles or show to anyone copies of letters which the lords justices had written on the subject either before or after the articles were

---

[1] Browne, who was one of the signatories of the treaty, claimed that goods earmarked for the payment of his Protestant creditors had been commandeered by Sarsfield and Tyrconnell. The articles provided for the levy of a cess on each restored estate for the payment of these debts.

[2] *Diary of the siege and surrender of Limerick*, p. 17.

[3] Annesley MSS, xxiii. 95.

signed.[1] Clarke sent a copy of this order to Sir Toby; he added that as the lords justices and the general had already sent to the king for leave to rectify the omission they thought it inconsistent with the respect they owed to his majesty to give an attested copy of the articles before they received the king's answer.[2]

In 1697 Coningsby gave his version to the English lords justices. He said that when he and Porter reached Limerick they found that Ginkel and the Irish had drawn up a 'long scroll' which the lords justices did not like. So Coningsby himself and George Clarke sat up all night over a fresh draft, which formed the text of the articles which were actually signed. Coningsby denied that the clause was in his draft or intended to be there. He said that when the question of inserting it was first brought up in the English privy council it met with opposition, until at last it was agreed upon in the cabinet and the king then declared his pleasure in council that the clause should be included in the articles.[3] Coningsby's version does not tally with Clarke's copy of the draft, in which, as we have seen, the body of the articles remained substantially in the form prepared before Coningsby and Porter arrived in Limerick.

Three conclusions can reasonably be drawn from this evidence:

(1) that the Irish Jacobites attached much importance to the clause;

(2) that the clause was incorporated in the terms drawn up before the arrival of the lords justices, remained in the final draft and was omitted from the fair copy which was actually signed;

(3) that there was a section of English Williamite opinion in Ireland which from the first was opposed to the restoration of the omitted words.

This leads on to the question whether the omission was accidental or was the result of secretarial sabotage. The latter suggestion finds some support in the fact that Nottingham, the secretary of state, said he never received the first letter which Porter wrote to him about 'the mistake in the copy of the capitulation.'[4]

It might have been expected that the question of the omitted clause would have been treated as finally settled by the letters patent which ordered the insertion of the missing words. The clause, however, was to be the subject of prolonged controversy. It was next referred to in an address presented to William by the English commons in March 1693. 'And as to the additional article which opens so wide a passage to the

[1] B.M., Eg. MS 2,618, f. 169.
[2] Ibid., f. 168.
[3] *Cal. S. P. dom.*, *1697*, pp. 269-70.
[4] Nottingham to Porter, 24 Oct. 1691 (*Cal. S.P. dom.*, *690-1*, p. 551).

Irish Papists to come in and repossess themselves of the estates which they forfeited by their rebellion, we most humbly beseech your majesty that the articles of Limerick with the said addition may be laid before your commons in parliament, that the manner of obtaining the same may be inquired into; to the end that it may appear by what means the articles were so enlarged and to what value the estates thereby claimed do amount.'[1] A report presented to the English commons in 1694 by a committee referred to claims made 'by virtue of the additional article, said to be agreed to but omitted in the perfected articles'. The committee estimated that at least half the claims fell within this category, and inquired what would be the effect of allowing the additional article.[2]

The dispute over the clause intensified when the bill for confirming the articles was passing between Ireland and England under the provisions of Poynings' law. The trend of the correspondence between the authorities concerned was that on the merits the additional clause ought to be included, but that if it was included the Irish parliament would object and throw the bill out altogether. The objection raised by some of the Irish lords to the omission of the clause seems to have taken the authorities by surprise; in a number of letters the view was expressed that public opinion seemed to have become so favourable to the Catholics that the clause might after all have been included.

The bill came over from Ireland with the clause omitted. Shrewsbury, the secretary of state, wrote to Blathwayt, the secretary for war who was in Holland with William, that he had deferred sending the bill to the king until the omission was cleared up. He expressed the view that without the clause the bill might 'possibly not so exactly agree with all that was promised under the great seal as his majesty's strict justice would incline him to wish'. On the other hand, Shrewsbury added, if an addition was made to the bill in accordance with the amendment of the articles it might prove very prejudicial to the king's interest. The general opinion was that if the clause were included the bill would be thrown out. Even if it passed, the estates of many notorious offenders would be covered, and nothing would be more certain to alter the 'good disposition of the gentlemen of Ireland'.[3] The same day Shrewsbury wrote to Methuen, the Irish chancellor, that the English council had held up the bill as they had received no explanation of the omission of the clause and had been informed from Ireland that the bill was entirely in accord-

[1] *Commons' jn.*, x. 843.
[2] Ibid., xi. 56.
[3] *H.M.C., Buccleuch MSS*, ii. 508.

ance with the articles as passed under the great seal.[1] Methuen made the disingenuous reply that the words were overlooked in the draft of the bill; as the point was never mentioned in the Irish council he had seen no reason to refer to it in transmitting the bill to England, although he was very well aware of the omission. He expressed the opinion that the bill would be more acceptable without the clause, but that if it was put in out of regard to the king's honour he thought that the bill would pass the Irish parliament.[2]

Winchester, one of the lords justices, wrote to Shrewsbury that he thought the additional words were as much part of the second article as any, if they had been inserted at first, but he questioned how they were obtained. He suggested that the king knew best how far his honour was engaged.[3] Galway, the other lord justice, told Shrewsbury that he had always understood that the additional article was objected to both by parliament and by the English privy council. He thought that if the clause were included much confiscated land and even estates granted by the king would be disputed. If, however, it was thought that the honour of the king was engaged, he would do his best to get the bill through parliament with the additional clause.[4]

The English lords justices decided that the matter should be referred to William, saying that the clause had apparently been omitted from apprehension that the bill would not pass if it were included; Protestants in Ireland having a general dislike of the powerful position in which Catholics had been left in the five counties concerned and throughout Connacht.[5] Shrewsbury later wrote to Lord Galway that the point had been judged 'too tender' to determine without the direction of the king, who best knew how he had been prevailed upon to add the disputed words and how far his honour was engaged.[6]

Meanwhile the debates on the bill for the confirmation of outlawries appeared to point to a body of opinion more favourable to the Catholic position than the authorities had expected. Galway wrote to Shrewsbury that since that debate he could no longer trust his judgment; he now thought that the additional clause might facilitate the passage of the

---

[1] *H.M.C., Buccleuch MSS*, ii. 509-10.
[2] Ibid., ii. 518.
[3] Ibid., ii. 517.
[4] Ibid., ii. 517. The record of forfeitures and grants does not support this opinion so far as Mayo and Clare are concerned. Possibly Galway thought that claims might be made that parts of Cork were under the protection of the Irish at the conclusion of the war. Much land in that county had been the subject of forfeitures and grants.
[5] *Cal. S.P. dom., 1697*, p. 271.
[6] *H.M.C., Buccleuch MSS*, ii. 532.

articles bill instead of hindering it. He was convinced that the bill would pass in whatever form the king decided.[1] A formal letter to the same effect was sent a week later by the lords justices to Shrewsbury, saying that they found opinion in Ireland so much more favourable to the Catholics than they had expected that perhaps the bill would encounter no difficulty even if the additional clause were inserted.[2]

William, however, had already directed that the bill should be approved without the additional clause, and this was to prove decisive.[3] There was a considerable party in the Irish lords, including Bishop King of Derry, which was not in favour of omitting the clause. The house, on the motion of Lord Orrery, resolved to ask the lords justices what reasons they had given for transmitting the bill to England without the additional words. The lords justices replied that such a request was unprecedented; they would only say that they did not transmit the bill until they had laid before the king all the difficulties involved—this was hardly an accurate version—and that it was his majesty's pleasure that the bill should be passed as it was. By a narrow majority the house resolved that the answer was satisfactory and that the bill should pass into law. Seven temporal peers and seven bishops protested against this decision on the grounds, inter alia, that the bill omitted the material words 'and all such as are under their protection in the said counties', which had been declared by royal letters patent to be part of the second article. The protesters added that several persons who had been adjudged within the articles would now be barred. They considered that as the omitted words were of such importance and had been confirmed by the king after solemn debate in council they should not have been omitted without express reason.[4] This protest caused much surprise in England. Shrewsbury wrote to Methuen that nothing was more surprising than to see an Irish house of parliament making difficulties over a bill because it was not sufficiently favourable to Catholics; that bishops should lead the opposition was 'wonderful to the last degree'.[5]

It is certainly remarkable that so many members of an exclusively Protestant house of lords should have expressed such views. Winchester attributed to Lord Drogheda a leading part in the opposition and suggested that he was associated with the duke of Ormond, whose proxy he held.[6] This suggests that the opposition was directed against the whig

[1] *H.M.C., Buccleuch MSS*, ii. 536-7.
[2] *Cal. S.P. dom., 1697*, p. 331.
[3] Ibid., p. 325.
[4] *Lord's jn. Ire.*, i. 633-7.
[5] *H.M.C., Buccleuch MSS*, ii. 567.
[6] Ibid., ii. 557 and 583.

clique which had been predominant in the Irish administration since Capel's regime. It was also remarked that several of the temporal lords concerned were recent Protestants who retained some sympathy with their former co-religionists. Three of those who signed the protest against the articles bill fell within this category. King's attitude is summed up in a letter which he wrote to Southwell in December 1697, explaining why he had voted against a bill for the disarming of Catholics. 'I did observe men of no religion, nay that scoffed at all religion, very eager for this bill, and I thought that it was hard that such should impose upon men that had some, though an ill one, and to put it into the power of such men to ruin men merely for having conscience I could not consent to.'[1]

The bill for confirmation of the articles of Limerick received the royal assent in September 1697. In the following month the English privy council seems to have tried to work the omitted clause into a bill for preserving the king's person. Winchester wrote to Shrewsbury that he regretted that the council should have added to the bill a clause to save Lord Antrim and other Catholics from incurring any loss as a result of the act for the confirmation of the articles of Limerick. Winchester thought that the inclusion of the clause might harm the security bill.[2] Actually that bill was thrown out by the lords, apparently because of the oath which its terms imposed upon Catholics.[3]

It is extremely difficult to determine what was the practical effect of the omission. From a letter of Vernon's it appears that the omission of the clause was believed to affect Lord Antrim in particular.[4] It will be remembered that Antrim's camp outside Limerick had been treated as a garrison for the purposes of the adjudication.[5] If that interpretation was maintained he would be unaffected by the omission of the clause; it was not disputed that garrisons were entitled to the benefit of the articles. Objection had, however, already been taken to the finding that Antrim's camp constituted a garrison. The omitted clause may have been his second line of defence. In any case Antrim's adjudication was not affected.

While the bill was under discussion Cox expressed the view that if the additional clause were not included all the Irish in Kerry and in the quarters of the Irish in the counties of Cork, Limerick and Mayo might forfeit the estates which they had hitherto held under the authority of

[1] B.M., Add. MS 21,506, p. 107.
[2] *H.M.C., Buccleuch MSS*, ii. 568.
[3] *Lords' jn. Ire.*, i. 664-5.
[4] *Cal. S.P. dom., 1697*, p. 268.
[5] See p. 50 above.

THE MISSING CLAUSE OF THE TREATY

the clause.[1] On the other hand the lords justices and council of Ireland wrote about the same time that the bill confirmed the second article in the sense in which it had been understood so far and submitted to by the Irish in the claims already decided.[2] As the council were responsible for all the adjudications given up to that time they should have been in a position to know the facts. The statement that no regard had been paid to the omitted clause in the claims already decided seems to be at variance with the house of lords protest, which stated that several persons had been adjudged within the articles who would now be barred. Cox's view could be reconciled with that of the lords justices and council on the supposition that a number of persons had been continued in the possession of their estates on the strength of the additional clause without being formally adjudged within the articles. On the whole, the evidence seems to show that this was the position.

It has already been mentioned that adjudications were held up for almost three years from the end of 1694, while discussion proceeded on the question of the bill for the confirmation of the articles. In the meanwhile a large number of claims had mounted up. In April 1697 the clerk of the privy council submitted a demand to be paid for copying out 1,150 claims and 400 rules.[3] A possible explanation of the varying accounts, therefore, would be that a number of persons had claimed under the disputed clause and that these claims were kept pending. If they were not outlawed they would remain in possession of their estates.

In October 1697, after the bill for the confirmation of the articles had passed into law, Methuen wrote to Shrewsbury that he had deliberately omitted the additional clause from the bill as it was obnoxious to Protestants; but that it was still in the king's power to make the clause good as much as if it had been included in the bill.[4] What significance is to be attached to Methuen's suggestion? Are we to conclude that there was a tacit agreement not to launch prosecutions against those who had up till then been left undisturbed on the strength of the additional clause? Certainly there was no spate of fresh forfeitures after 1697 in the areas concerned, nor do we hear of prosecutions in those areas. The Connacht prosecutions of 1699, on the failure of which the inquiry commissioners commented, seem all to have taken place in Galway, which was not one of the five counties mentioned in the second article of Limerick.

The problem primarily relates to Mayo and Clare. Little of Cork and

[1] *H.M.C. rep. 14*, app. ii. 586.
[2] *Cal. S.P. dom., 1697*, p. 245.
[3] *Cal. treas. bks*, xii. 111.
[4] *H.M.C., Buccleuch MSS*, ii. 562.

Limerick remained under Irish control by the end of the war, and the Williamite forces had made considerable inroads into Kerry. There were a large number of Catholic landowners in Mayo and Clare who neither forfeited nor were adjudged within the articles. In Mayo the number of articlemen was remarkably small. Up to 1697 there were only seven claims adjudged from the county. Six of the claimants can be identified as military officers who would not come under the protection clause. If those who would have qualified under that clause were in practice not deprived of their estates, one would expect all those who forfeited in Mayo and Clare to have been killed or taken prisoner or else to have gone to France. We have not the material to be specific about the first categories, but it is of some significance that more than nine-tenths of the area forfeited in either county belonged to persons who were outlawed for foreign treason. Presumably all these went to France.

From a comparison of the adjudications with the forfeited estates no adjudications appear to have been reversed as a result of the omission of the clause. It is also significant that, although a number of protests were made from time to time by Catholics that the articles were being infringed in various ways, the omitted clause does not specifically figure in any of them. This raises the presumption that Catholics were less severely affected by the omission than might have been expected from the arguments brought forward in the course of the controversy.

Taking the evidence as a whole, it is perhaps possible to infer that William's government, having appeased the more militant Protestants by omitting the disputed clause, was not anxious to take action which could be represented abroad, and particularly at the court of the emperor, as a clear breach of faith.

6

THE GALWAY SURRENDER

During the war of 1689–91 particular importance was attached by both sides to Galway, whose leading inhabitants were large landowners in the county and inclined to put the preservation of their property before their allegiance to James. A number of them had bought lands which were held under the restoration Act of Settlement, and the repeal of that act by the Jacobite parliament of 1689 had aroused their resentment and shaken their loyalty. In the autumn of that year d'Avaux reported to Louis that he was extremely anxious about the Galway situation, as there were many Catholic malcontents in the town whose property was adversely affected by the repeal of the Act of Settlement.[1] About the same time Schomberg was writing to William about the prospects of negotiating the surrender of Galway with the governor of the town.[2] During the winter of 1690–1 Denis Daly, a leading Galway landowner who had been one of James's judges and a vigorous opponent of the Act of Repeal, took a prominent part in the negotiations with Ginkel and held out hopes of getting the town to surrender; as a result he was imprisoned on Sarsfield's orders.[3] The Williamites appear to have regarded Galway as the most promising field for the policy of securing a negotiated settlement by the offer of favourable terms to Catholic landowners. In the summer of 1691 the lords justices informed Ginkel that they had ordered the naval commander at Kinsale to sail for Galway with authority to offer advantageous terms to the townsmen, by which they would retain their houses and lands.[4] One of the Dublin officials told Ginkel that he was confident 'that the town of Galway

[1] *Négoc. d'Avaux en Irl.*, p. 533.
[2] Schomberg to William, 6 Oct. 1689 (*Cal. S.P. dom., 1689-90*, p. 286).
[3] O'Kelly, *Macariae excidium*, pp. 105-6.
[4] Lords justices to Ginkel, 6 July 1691 (Clarke corr., viii. 698). The naval expedition did not reach Galway till after its surrender to Ginkel (Story, *Continuation*, p. 174).

would give up upon promise of half of that six and fifty thousand pounds a year which is the value of their property in land'.[1]

Ginkel reached Galway on July 19, a week after Aughrim. He at once sent a trumpeter to Lord Dillon, the governor, offering the terms of the proclamation of July 7 if the town would surrender before artillery had to be used.[2] The first reply was that Galway would be defended to the last, but next morning Dillon asked Ginkel for a safe-conduct for emissaries who were to negotiate the capitulation of the town. The conditions of surrender were the subject of keen bargaining; the emissaries returned several times to the town for consultations and agreement was not reached until late that night. The argument chiefly turned on whether the benefit of the articles should be extended to those inhabitants of Galway who were not actually in the town at the time. Denis Daly took a leading part in the negotiations; his services were duly acknowledged by Ginkel, who gave him a promise that he and his heirs should enjoy their estates without forfeiture 'as the Protestants of Ireland enjoyed theirs'.[3]

The articles, which were signed on July 21, bore the marks of hasty drafting and their terms are by no means clear. According to the official Williamite account 'the garrison and townsmen that remain have the benefit of the lords justices' proclamation which gives them their estates and liberties, and those who have a mind to depart are to be conducted safe to Limerick'.[4] But the ninth article, which promised that 'all and every' of the garrison and officers as well as the townsmen should enjoy their estates real and personal, made no distinction between those who remained and those who went to Limerick. The eighth article extended a general pardon to the townsmen but did not specify that pardon was to be granted to those of the garrison who did not elect to go on to Limerick. No oath of allegiance to William, such as was required in the case of Limerick, was prescribed in the Galway articles.[5]

Ginkel was severely criticized for having given unduly favourable terms to Galway, and the articles were the subject of controversy for several years during which no claims were heard. Two years after the surrender of the town Sir Roebuck Lynch, Sir Walter Blake, Sir John Kirwan and others submitted a representation that they were entitled to the benefit of the articles of Galway and had preferred their claims to the privy council but that the hearing of their applications had been

[1] Israel Fielding to Ginkel, 5 July 1691 (Clarke corr., viii. 689).
[2] For the proclamation of 7 July 1691 see pp. 27-8 above.
[3] H.L. MSS, n.s., iv. 30.
[4] A particular relation of the surrender of Galway, 1691.
[5] The articles of Galway are printed in Harris, Life of William III, app., pp. 73-4.

postponed.[1] The delay seems to have been due to a dispute over the wording of the eighth and ninth articles, under which pardon and the enjoyment of estates were guaranteed. The objection had been raised that the articles ought not to include those freemen and townsmen who were not actually in Galway at the time of the capitulation. The records which refer to this dispute throw light on the events which led up to the surrender and, in particular, on the negotiations which Ginkel conducted with leading persons of Galway town and county. Ginkel himself shows up well. He seems to have adopted a generous attitude towards those with whom he negotiated, and in later years proved ready to intervene with William on their behalf. The record brings out the importance which the negotiated surrender of Galway had for the Williamite cause. There was, however, much opposition to any leniency being shown to Galway. To this may be attributed the restricted interpretation placed upon the terms of the articles, and the criticism of what were regarded as unduly liberal methods of adjudication.

On 23 April 1697—the reason for the inordinate delay does not appear—William decided at a meeting of his privy council that the articles were to be construed as extending only to those who were in the town when it surrendered.[2] This ruling caused considerable alarm among the claimants. Lord Galway wrote to Shrewsbury that Catholics were collecting money to send a deputation to William and to his allies, the Catholic princes, to get the explanation of the Galway articles changed, and to quash the bills for the confirmation of outlawries and for the ratification of the articles of Limerick. Lord Galway expressed the hope that if the deputation presented itself William would assure it that all promises would be honoured.[3] Shrewsbury replied that he hoped the deputation would have no effect on the king, as his royal word would be made good, although not in the sense given to it by the applicants. He thought that even if the Catholic princes intervened they would be too late to be effective.[4]

In August 1697 Arthur French, who was mayor of Galway at the time of the capitulation, went over to the continent to enlist Ginkel's support against the restrictive interpretation of the articles. Ginkel wrote to Blathwayt, William's secretary, that the drafting of the eighth and ninth articles had given him particular trouble, and that it was a long time before he could bring himself to agree to them. He was in-

[1] P.R.O.I., Wyche papers, 2nd series, 119.
[2] Annesley MSS, xxvii. 159.
[3] *H.M.C., Buccleuch MSS*, ii. 485.
[4] Ibid., ii. 489.

duced to do so by the consideration that prolonging the siege would have put him in a difficult position, as he would have had to use his heavy artillery for a further eight to ten days to make a breach in the walls. He had therefore agreed to the wording proposed and had also given particular assurances to four or five of the citizens who were not then in Galway; one of these was Judge Daly's brother, to whom he had given a protection to keep him from going off to Limerick.[1]

The inquiry commissioners seem to have directed particular attention to showing that William's interpretation of the Galway articles was not strictly kept, and that various claims had been improperly admitted. They recorded evidence that Robert Dillon of Clonbrock had been seen in Iar Connacht during the siege, and that bribery was used to suppress the evidence that Dillon was not actually in the town of Galway.[2] Robert Dillon's son Luke frankly admitted that Palmer, the registrar of the court, had demanded £86, which his father had succeeded in beating down to £66. 6s. Luke expressed the opinion that his father had incurred nearly £1,500 in charges and expenses in connection with his claim.[3] The adjudication was not disturbed and we find the family, which had by then conformed, in receipt of a peerage at the end of the eighteenth century.

Robert Shaw, the town clerk of Galway, told the commissioners that after the articles had been signed the gates were opened to admit Charles Daly of Carrownekelly, Oliver Martin of Tulira and others who were all adjudged within the articles.[4] Arthur French, the then mayor, corroborated this statement, but explained that these were persons to whom Ginkel had given assurances when the articles were being drawn up. French said that they were in Ginkel's camp during the negotiations but had entered the town before it was handed over. Ginkel's letter to Blathwayt was actually produced in evidence in the case of Oliver Martin, whose case is marked 'within the articles nisi', dated 8 July 1699. Although the adjudication is not recorded as having been confirmed, Martin's estate was recorded as restored under the articles. He was evidently of considerable service during the negotiations. It appears that the service was remembered at the time of the anti-popery acts, in the second of which it was provided that the estate of Oliver Martin might be inherited by primogeniture.[5] Arthur French also admitted that just before the surrender of the town he entered the names of Robert Dillon

[1] Annesley MSS, xxvii. 153.
[2] Ibid., xxiii. 22.
[3] Ibid., xxiii. 210.
[4] Ibid., xxiii. 103.
[5] 8 Anne, c. 3, s. 39.

and Richard Martin in the roll of freemen with the intention of bringing them within the terms of the articles, but that they were never actually sworn.[1]

The thirteenth article provided that officers belonging to any of the regiments in Galway who were not themselves present should have the benefit of the articles, provided that they submitted to the governor of Galway within three weeks. The terms of this article were invoked to support the claim of Lord Bophin, Clanricarde's brother. Bophin, who was colonel of an infantry regiment, was taken prisoner at Aughrim. The regiment formed part of the garrison of Galway, and Ginkel expressly agreed that Bophin should be entitled to the benefit of the articles. Ginkel actually wrote to William asking that Bophin, who had been taken over to England, should be released. He was not however released in time to make his submission within the prescribed three weeks. At the end of the war he returned to Ireland, took the oath of allegiance and was allowed to remain for several years in the peaceful enjoyment of his estate. About 1697 he heard that the court had expressed the opinion that his case did not come within the articles. He therefore applied to Ginkel, who confirmed that he had promised that Bophin should be included.[2] A king's letter was therefore sent to the lords justices on 2 April 1698, asking them to inform the court that Bophin was 'particularly intended and declared to be comprised and comprehended within the said articles'.[3] In spite of this support Bophin's troubles were not over. The solicitor-general gave his opinion that the terms of the king's letter were not sufficient warrant for the court to find Bophin within the articles.[4] Methuen, the chancellor, told the inquiry commissioners that he did not think that the lords justices had ever communicated the king's letter to the judges. Methuen himself had advised Bophin that he had no prospect of succeeding in his claim.[5]

Bophin decided not to prosecute his claim under the articles, but to ask for pardon. Here his chief difficulty was that his estate had been granted to Albemarle, who was in the powerful position of king's favourite. It was arranged that a bill should be introduced in the Irish parliament to reverse Bophin's outlawry and to enable him to raise £9,000 on his estate. The money was ostensibly intended for the payment of debts, but evidence was given that £7,500 was to be paid to Albemarle, leaving £1,500 as pickings for those who had been inter-

[1] Annesley MSS, xxiii. 112.
[2] Ibid., xx. 1-10.
[3] Ibid., xxvii. 161-3.
[4] Ibid., xxiii. 139
[5] Ibid., xxiii. 144.

mediaries in the negotiations.[1] The Irish parliament disliked the proposal and rejected the bill nem. con.[2] Finally, Bophin prevailed on the English parliament to pass a private act reversing his outlawry and putting the estate in the hands of trustees for the benefit of his children. The terms of the act required him to pay £25,000 and to bring his children up as Protestants.[3]

Ginkel and William's government generally seem to have tried to honour the understanding reached with the Galway landowners. They were, however, subject to considerable pressure from those Irish Protestants who were not in official positions and do not seem to have appreciated the advantage which the surrender of Galway gave to the Williamite forces. Many of the witnesses who appeared before the inquiry commission criticized the admission to the articles of those who were evidently not besieged within the walls of Galway but engaged from outside in active negotiations with Ginkel.

The controversy over the Galway articles is well brought out in a speech made by Cox, who was one of the judges, at the hearing of six claims under the articles. Five of the claimants, Patrick Blake of Kiltullagh, Richard Blake of Ardfry, Walter Blake of Drum, Robert French of Tulla and George Staunton of Galway, were aldermen or burgesses of Galway, but had been out in the country while the town was invested by Ginkel. They came by permission to Ginkel's camp, and assisted in arranging the capitulation and in drawing up the articles. Ginkel then told them to go into the town and assured them that they would get the benefit of the articles. The sixth claimant was Sir John Kirwan, a former mayor of Galway who had sent Ginkel a message that he need not wait for his heavy artillery as the town would capitulate at the first appearance of his army. Kirwan was imprisoned in the town on suspicion of corresponding with Ginkel. He contrived to escape and 'went off in his own ship and, not daring to trust himself in Limerick and not knowing where else to go, he put the evil day off as far as possible and went to France'. When Ginkel heard the story he promised that if Kirwan returned within six months he would be included in the articles. William confirmed the promise and Kirwan duly returned and presented a petition for pardon. An endorsement was made on the petition that no pardon was necessary as Kirwan was entitled to the benefit of the articles.

---

[1] *Commrs' report*, pp. 11-12.
[2] *Commons' jn. Ire.*, ii. 298 (17 Jan. 1699).
[3] 1 Anne, c. 39. The trustees reported that only £10,185 had been paid by 25 June 1703 and that the balance was to be paid within a year (*H.L. MSS*, n.s., v. 250). The balance was not paid in time and there was talk of forfeiting the estate. Eventually, a further act (7 Anne, c. 29) was passed, extending the time for payment.

He accordingly remained in undisturbed possession of his estate until the case came up for adjudication.

After the six claims were heard the first judge to speak gave his opinion against admitting the claimants to the benefit of the articles. His objection was evidently based on William's decision that the articles did not apply to freemen and inhabitants of Galway who were not in the town at the time of the capitulation. Cox spoke next and argued that the intention had been to exclude only 'titular freemen and mere natives who were not inhabitants of Galway', whereas these claimants had houses in the town. He used considerable eloquence on their behalf and stressed the point that they had received specific assurances from Ginkel. A note at the end of the speech records that the rest of the court was won over by Cox's plea. The names of the six claimants are entered in the list of adjudications as admitted to the articles on 31 August 1699.[1]

Altogether seventy-eight claims were admitted under the articles of Galway. The claimants included representatives of most of the 'tribes', Blakes, Bodkins, Kirwans and others; there were fourteen Frenches and thirteen Lynches. Between them the successful claimants owned a large part of the county, and the articles were of great importance in maintaining the influence of the old-established Galway families.

[1] B.M., Add. MS 38,153, ff. 18-20.

7

ROYAL PARDONS

In addition to the land restored under the articles of Limerick and Galway a considerable area was restored by royal pardon to forfeiting persons who were not included in the articles. Among those pardoned were representatives of several celebrated families. A number of the pardons are also of interest as illustrating various aspects of the war of 1689–91. The names of those pardoned were recorded by the inquiry commissioners in their fifth book—the Book of Pardons and Reversals.[1]

Several of those restored by royal pardon were persons who had submitted after the Boyne on the terms offered by the declaration of Finglas. That declaration held out no promise that those who submitted would be allowed to keep their land. But later developments, and in particular the guarantees given under the articles of Limerick and Galway, made it appear unreasonable to maintain so uncompromising an attitude towards all those who had submitted at an early stage, while those who had kept up a troublesome and stubborn opposition were allowed to remain in possession of their estates.

This point of view was expressed by Bonnell, the Irish accountant-general, shortly after the capitulation of Limerick. Remarking on the fact that a considerable number of the Jacobites were enabled to keep their estates under the articles, he observed that others, who had submitted after the Boyne and had since remained peaceful, were outlawed and had lost their estates. 'This is such a wondrous inequality that it can hardly be that even a settlement should be founded on it. . . . What will these men hereafter say for losing their estates now for adhering to King James while he was among them and submitting to King William as soon as King James left them, when yet they see so many others enjoy

---

[1] *H.L. MSS*, n.s., iv. 28-32. For the statistics of the book see appendix A, pp. 174-6, below.

their estates who stood out above a year longer?"[1] A similar view was expressed by the Jacobite, Bevil Higgons: 'those Irish who were the most forward to fling themselves into the English protection as soon as they had an opportunity have fared the worst and lost their estates, only for submitting to the civil authority. Whereas others, who held out to the very last and were the occasion of shedding much blood by a prolongation of the war, are all indemnified by articles. By this example posterity will be instructed to hope for more safety and better quarter by a desperate resistance than an early submission.'[2]

Candidates for pardon were selected in a somewhat arbitrary manner, and by no means all those who submitted after the Boyne succeeded in recovering their estates. One of the successful applicants was Richard Talbot of Malahide, who submitted to William on 9 July 1690 at Finglas. He had accepted the post of auditor-general under James, but represented that he had only done so to recompense himself for the loss of the Malahide customs, a hereditary perquisite of which he had been deprived.[3] Oliver Grace, who had been chief remembrancer under James, submitted on 10 July 1690. He was indicted in the Michaelmas term of that year, but not outlawed; on his surrender to the sheriffs he was admitted to bail and obtained the queen's order for the stay of further proceedings.[4]

Several members of the 1689 parliament appear in the list of those pardoned. Matthew Hore of Shandon, county Waterford, claimed to have opposed the bill for the repeal of the Act of Settlement.[5] John Galway claimed that he had been elected by the votes of the Protestants of Cork and had never voted against them or their interests.[6] Robert Longfield represented that he 'having been a member of the late pretended parliament at Dublin did not intermeddle in, or give any vote for, the repeal of the Acts of Settlement and Explanation'. He was clerk of the quit-rents and immediately after the Boyne had delivered over the papers of his office and submitted.[7] Longfield's pardon was the subject of a complaint to the English commons that he was 'a Protestant turned Papist' and 'being under no articles but what he made for himself came over to England and returned with some letter or order to reverse his

---

[1] James Bonnell to Robert Harley, 3 Nov. 1691 (*H.M.C. rep. 14*, app. ii. 479-80).
[2] Quoted by Ralph, *History of England*, ii. 307.
[3] *Cal. S.P. dom., 1693*, p. 9. The warrant for Talbot's pardon was transcribed by Harris, Collectanea, x. 211.
[4] *Cal. S.P. dom., 1698*, p. 40.
[5] Ibid., *1693*, p. 129.
[6] Ibid., *1691-2*, p. 189.
[7] Warrant of pardon, 5 Aug. 1692 (Harris, Collectanea, x. 8).

outlawry'.[1] The Book of Pardons records the observation that Long-field's pardon was obtained by the king's favour without any merit appearing.

Charles White of Leixlip owed his pardon to the intervention of the emperor, although it is not clear how the latter came to be interested in the case. The lords justices took umbrage at not being consulted before the issue of the warrant for the reversal of White's outlawry. They also took exception to the emperor's intervention on the ground that this might encourage others to make application to foreign princes, which might tend to 'public inconvenience'.[2] However, they later withdrew their objections on a report from the solicitor-general that White, as governor of Kildare and a member of James's privy council, had been very kind to Protestants.[3] White lost no time in making his submission. There is still extant a letter from his wife, written the day after the Boyne, in which she asks for protection and explains that her husband would himself have written 'but that he is very ill with the gout in his hands and feet'.[4]

Pardon was also given to a number of persons who were irregularly outlawed. Thus Luke, earl of Fingall, was included in the list of out-lawries although he had died several years before the war. His son Peter was a minor and had not been in Ireland during the war. Lord Balti-more's pardon was given on the ground that 'he was never in the rebellion nor for many years in Ireland'. Several other cases are recorded in the Book of Pardons of persons who were outlawed by mistake although they were not in Ireland during the war.

Lord Cahir's pardon was granted on the ground that he had complied with the original declaration which William had made in February 1689, promising pardon and the enjoyment of their estates to those who submitted by April of that year. Cahir had accordingly given up his commission in James's army and retired into private life within the time prescribed. Unfortunately for him his private business took him to Cork where he was involved in the siege, taken prisoner and committed to the tower of London. It was then proposed to send him to France under a scheme for the exchange of prisoners. He explained his position and was permitted to remain a subject of William and Mary.[5]

The lists of pardons and reversals include two earls of Tyrone. Richard Power, the first earl, defended Waterford and after its sur-

[1] *Commons' jn.*, x. 830.
[2] *Cal. S.P. dom.*, *1694-5*, p. 102.
[3] Ibid., p. 135.
[4] Mrs White to Lord Drogheda, 2 July 1690 (R.I.A., MS 24. G. 3, p. 40).
[5] *Cal. S.P. dom.*, *1691-2*, pp. 219-20.

render proceeded to Cork, where he was taken prisoner. He was sent to the Tower and died soon afterwards. His outlawry was reversed to save the title of his son John, who was brought up as a Protestant and took William's side. John, the second earl, died in 1693. The next heir was his brother James, who was pardoned on the ground that his father had forced him to remain in Waterford during the siege and that after the surrender of the town he had not followed his father to Cork, but had gone off to William's camp, submitted and received a promise of pardon.[1] The third earl died in 1704 and the next heir, John Power of Monylargy, petitioned the Irish parliament for a reversal of his outlawry. His petition was not granted although he had offered to bring up his son as a Protestant and had produced certificates to show that, as mayor of Limerick during the siege, he had been conspicuous for his kindly treatment of the Protestants in the city.[2]

Lord Bellew of Duleek was in the garrison of Limerick at the time of the capitulation and was thus entitled to the benefit of the articles. He was, however, in bad health and was advised on medical grounds to go to France. He received Ginkel's permission to do so. Some months later, when his health was restored, he called on Ginkel in Brussels and obtained a certificate which eventually enabled him to secure a pardon.[3] Unfortunately his estate had already been granted to Sydney, and the inquiry commissioners noted that the pardon was not granted until Bellew had promised to waive his claim to £3,000 mesne profits.

Another Bellew mentioned in the Book of Pardons was John Bellew of Barmeath, county Louth. The note against his name relates that he was outlawed by his own consent to prevent the enemy having any suspicion of the services he was doing for their majesties in the Irish quarters; he was pardoned in pursuance of a promise previously made to him by the government. The story behind this was given to the inquiry commissioners by a witness who told them that in May 1691 Porter had sent Bellew into Connacht with instructions to 'do some considerable service', promising that if he should be outlawed in his absence it would be reversed and he should have the king's pardon. Presumably the considerable service was to prepare the way for a negotiated conclusion of hostilities on the lines of the proclamation of July 1691. Porter later told the witness that he had been well satisfied with Bellew's performance, and that the outlawry had been deliberately proceeded with to avoid any suspicion that Bellew was engaged on William's ser-

[1] *Cal. S.P. dom., 1697*, p. 122.
[2] *The humble petition of John Power esq., commonly called Lord Power.*
[3] Warrant, dated 18 Mar. 1697, in Harris, Collectanea, x. 263.

vice in the enemy's quarters.[1] The ruse was less successful than appears from this account, as the suspicions of the Jacobites were in fact aroused and Bellew was 'clapped into prison where he remained till the battle of Aughrim'.[2] Lord Kinsale was also imprisoned by the Jacobites. During the first siege of Limerick he had tried to cross over into William's camp with the object of submitting. Later he managed to escape and took the oath of fidelity to William in July 1691.[3] A pardon was given to Theobald, the seventh Viscount Dillon, who was killed at Aughrim. It was obtained on behalf of his son Henry, the eighth viscount, who was included in the articles of Limerick but apprehended that his title to the family estates might be endangered by the outlawry of his father.[4]

Richard Martin, the great-grandfather of 'Humanity Dick', obtained a warrant of pardon on the grounds that he had submitted on the terms of the proclamation of July 1691 and had brought over a considerable portion of his troop with their horses and arms, and also that during the war he had protected the Protestants from ruin.[5] He went to England to make direct application for the pardon and this seems to have given offence to the Irish government. Capel referred back the case on the ground that the warrant had been issued without any inquiry having been made in Ireland. The attorney-general observed that Martin was 'one of those many persons in Connacht who were not indicted nor outlawed, though as guilty of the late rebellion as others who were outlawed'.[6] The decision to pardon Martin was upheld and Shrewsbury wrote back to Capel that he should proceed with the case.[7] The inquiry commissioners gave some attention to the proceedings. The former high sheriff for county Galway told them that on the day before the English army arrived in front of Galway Richard Martin had come to him 'with seven men on serviceable horses' and had asked in consternation what he should do, as the Irish would certainly hang him if they found him. The sheriff accordingly took him to Ginkel.[8] When his claim to pardon was being examined Martin produced documents signed by Ginkel, and also a certificate signed by Colonel Richard Coote that he was constantly in the general's tent before Galway while the articles

[1] Annesley MSS, xxiii. 100.
[2] *Cal. S.P. dom.*, *1693*, p. 133.
[3] Ibid., *1691-2*, p. 141.
[4] Ibid., *1693*, p. 116.
[5] Ibid., *1694-5*, p. 410.
[6] Ibid., pp. 506-7.
[7] Ibid., *1695*, p. 17.
[8] Annesley MSS, xxiii. 23.

were being drawn up and that he was of material service in the negotiations.[1]

A curious sequel was the issue of letters patent in 1698, granting manorial rights to Richard Martin in respect of his estate of Clare, county Galway. The Irish commons protested vigorously. An address was presented to the lords justices to the effect that the commons, 'being sensible of the many inconveniencies which do, and may, happen to this kingdom by the grant of manors and other royalties and privileges to Papists', prayed for the cancellation of the letters patent.[2] The lords justices reported the case to England saying that, as Martin's estate was 'an entire tract of land of about thirty miles extent in a remote part of the province of Connacht, inhabited for the most part, if not wholly, by Papists', it was apprehended that the creation of a manor might be a hindrance to the levying of crown dues and an obstruction of justice so far as Protestants were concerned. The commons had framed heads of a bill for dissolving all manors in the hands of Catholics, but the bill had not been returned from England. They had therefore presented an address against Martin's grant as being 'the most dangerous by reason of its great extent and its situation in a remote part of the kingdom on the sea-coast, which in case of a foreign war would give the inhabitants an opportunity of corresponding more securely with his majesty's enemies'.[3] It does not appear that the English government paid any attention to these protests, and several successive Martins were lords of the manor of Clare.

The inquiry commissioners expressed the opinion that many of the pardons had been obtained by giving gratifications to persons who had abused the royal compassion. They found, however, that when they came to examine the question they met with difficulties 'too great to be overcome', as most of the transactions had taken place in private and with persons outside Ireland. They therefore contented themselves with recording a few particular cases in which they were satisfied that gratifications had been given.[4] Several of the entries recorded in the Book of Pardons mention the name of Margaret Uniack, an intimate of Sydney's. Sir John Morris of Knockagh is noted as having paid £500 to her and her uncle. She is said to have received £100 from Harvey Morris and £200 from John Kerdiff. The list of reversals includes the name of Thomas Uniack of Youghal, who sat in the 1689 parliament and appears

---

[1] *Cal. S.P. dom., 1694-5*, p. 507.

[2] *Commons' jn. Ire.*, ii. 299 (17 Jan. 1699).

[3] Winchester and Galway to Vernon, 4 Mar. 1699 (P.R.O.I., Phillipps MSS, Irish correspondence and king's letters, 1697-1782, p. 78).

[4] *Commrs' report*, pp. 10-11.

to have been the lady's father. The evidence recorded by the commissioners contains a number of allegations that pardons were obtained by bribery. Richard Martin was said to have complained of the heavy expense of preferring his application in England, and Robert Longfield was said to have remarked that his pardon cost him 'his hat full of guineas'.[1]

The policy of granting pardons was the subject of criticism from both the English and the Irish parliaments. The English commons presented an address to the king in March 1693, in which among other grievances reference was made to the reversal of outlawries against 'several rebels' in Ireland not within the articles of Limerick, 'to the great discontent of your Protestant subjects there'. The commons demanded that no outlawries in Ireland should be reversed or pardons granted except on the advice of parliament.[2] The Irish commons resolved in 1695 that the 'countenance and favour' shown to Catholics were among the causes responsible for the miseries of Ireland. They directed the crown clerk to lay before the house a statement of all outlawries reversed together with an account of the authority by which the reversals had been ordered.[3]

In 1697 the Irish parliament passed an act 'to hinder the reversal of several outlawries and attainders'.[4] The act provided that, notwithstanding any pardon, no outlawry or attainder should be reversed after 27 July 1697, except in accordance with the articles of Limerick and Galway. The act also provided for the attainder of Catholics found to have 'died in rebellion'. A limited number of named individuals were excepted from the provisions of the act. They included Lord Athenry and Lieutenant-colonel John Kelly of Skryne, who were comprised in the articles of Bophin, concluded in August 1691, when the garrison of the island surrendered on terms to the Williamites. Another of those exempted from the provisions of the act was Henry Crofton of Longford, county Sligo, who was comprised in the articles of Sligo. Crofton came of a Protestant family but seems to have been brought up as a Catholic by his mother, who was a daughter of O'Conor Don. He was high sheriff for county Sligo in 1687 and sat in the 1689 parliament. One of his sons was the celebrated General Henry Crofton of Spain.[5] A saving clause was also provided for Nicholas Taafe, second earl of Carlingford, who was killed at the Boyne. The clause was included for

---

[1] Annesley MSS, xxiii. 37 and 102.
[2] *Commons' jn.*, x. 842.
[3] *Commons' jn. Ire.*, ii. 69 (23 Sept. 1695).
[4] 9 Will. III, c. 5.
[5] Crofton, *Crofton memoirs*, pp. 134-6.

the benefit of his brother Francis, the third earl, who was a general in the emperor's service and had taken no part in the Irish war.

The name of Patrick Sarsfield also occurs in the list of exemptions. This was not the earl of Lucan, as Butler has supposed,[1] but his father, Patrick Sarsfield the elder, who had died in May 1690. It was surmised that the outlawry recorded in his name was really intended for his more famous son. If it were not reversed it might have prejudiced his grandchild Charlotte, whose mother was the illegitimate daughter of Charles II.[2] The Sarsfield estate was claimed on Charlotte's behalf, firstly against Patrick the younger who took possession of it after his brother's death, and secondly against the crown which seized it as a forfeiture. Charlotte gained a vigorous advocate by her marriage to Agmondisham Vesey, son of the archbishop of Tuam. Vesey's claim was later rejected by the trustees, but he succeeded in obtaining an English act of parliament which allowed him to buy the estate from the trustees at a low valuation.[3]

A clause in favour of Edward Geoghegan of Castletown, Westmeath, represented an attempt to do justice to an unfortunate victim of the war. Geoghegan had held no office, military or civil, under James. He took protection from the Williamite authorities after the Boyne and lived peacefully at home until 'he was fallen on by a party of Captain Poyntz's soldiers, by whom he was shot through the body, stripped of all his substance, and both he and his family most barbarously used'.[4] As a result of this treatment he took refuge in the Irish quarters and was on that account outlawed. He obtained a pardon in 1696 but the order was frustrated by Wolsely, who had been one of the most active of William's commanders and had received a grant of Geoghegan's estate. The case became part of the Porter-Capel feud, Porter taking Geoghegan's side and Capel taking Wolsely's.[5] Wolsely succeeded in holding up the pardon on the ground that it referred to Geoghegan as 'gentleman', whereas he had been styled esquire in the outlawry record. One of Wolsely's allies represented to Shrewsbury that, although Geoghegan had been 'used severely enough', the officer commanding the party had 'certain intelligence of Geoghegan's constant entertaining the rapparees and giving them notice from time to time of our men's marching, and at the time when he fell on him sixteen rapparees were in his house; this was

---

[1] Butler, *Confiscation*, p. 228.

[2] *Cal. S.P. dom., 1697*, p. 263. William Sarsfield, elder brother of the earl of Lucan, married Mary, daughter of Charles II and Lucy Walter, and sister of Monmouth.

[3] 1 Anne, c. 57 (private act). An account of the case is given in chapter xii, below.

[4] Warrant in Harris, Collectanea, x. 304.

[5] Capel to Shrewsbury, 4 Dec. 1695 (*H.M.C., Buccleuch MSS*, ii. 272); Porter to Vernon, 28 Aug. 1696 (*Cal. S.P. dom., 1696*, p. 365).

not denied, but it was said that he entertained them from fear, not out of any love'.[1] Geoghegan had still not received his pardon when the Act of Resumption was passed in 1700; the act contained a saving clause in his favour. Shortly afterwards a fresh pardon was issued; the warrant gave Geoghegan the proper style of esquire and recorded that Wolsely's executors had no ground of objection to urge against the reversal of the outlawry.[2]

The Irish act deprived the king of the power to pardon persons who had been actually outlawed and were not the subject of a saving clause. Pardons, however, could still be given to persons who had not been outlawed, and the list includes a certain number of pardons of this class which were given after 1697. Thus George Browne of the Neale and his son John were pardoned in June 1698. Neither had been indicted or outlawed, although George had been sheriff of Mayo and John had been taken prisoner at Derry.[3] Other pardons given after 1697 were those in favour of Martin Blake of Moyne, who had been imprisoned by the Jacobites for corresponding with William's army,[4] and Francis Forster of Rathorpe, who had brought over part of his troop in accordance with the terms of the proclamation of 7 July 1691.[5]

[1] Thomas Broderick to Shrewsbury, 4 Dec. 1695 (*H.M.C.*, *Buccleuch MSS*, ii. 272-3).
[2] Harris, Collectanea, x. 304.
[3] Harris, Collectanea, x. 286; *Complete baronetage*, ii. 419.
[4] *Cal. S.P. dom., 1698*, p. 244.
[5] *H.L. MSS*, n.s., iv. 30.

8

'THE EXORBITANT GRANTS
OF WILLIAM III'

For the greater part of William's reign he and his English commons were engaged in a prolonged struggle for the right to dispose of the forfeited Irish lands. The contest, although it was regarded by both parties as of particular importance, was only part of the larger campaign for political control which was fought out between king and parliament. Its course was marked by the same ups and downs as the larger issue. At the outset William was subjected to continuous parliamentary pressure on the Irish land question. In the middle of his reign, while the Junto kept parliament under control, William had matters very much his own way, and took the opportunity to make grants of Irish lands on the grand scale to a number of his favourites and advisers. From 1699 parliament gained the upper hand. The Act of Resumption constituted a humiliating setback for the king and an assertion of parliamentary authority in a field in which the royal prerogative had appeared to be firmly established. The attitude of the commons seems to have been determined primarily by financial considerations, but xenophobia and dislike of courtiers were also important factors.[1]

The first attainder bill, which had reached an advanced stage of development when parliament was prorogued in the summer of 1689, involved only a small number of named individuals, whose estates were to be applied to the relief of Irish Protestants. Six subsequent bills, which attained varying stages of development between the autumn of 1689 and the summer of 1694, provided for the attainder of Irish Jacobites generally and for the application of their estates, or the greater part of them, to meeting the expenses of the reduction of Ireland. In the autumn of 1690 the committee of ways and means estimated that a

---

[1] The title of the chapter is that of a pamphlet which appeared in 1703.

million pounds could thus be raised.[1] The same figure recurs periodically in later estimates. When the fourth attainder bill was in the committee stage the court party succeeded in carrying a clause which reserved part of the Irish forfeitures for the king's disposal. This clause was, however, thrown out on the second reading,[2] and the bill as sent to the lords provided that the forfeited estates should be applied 'towards the charge of the present war'.[3] A foreign observer remarked that the object of the commons was to prevent courtiers securing grants for themselves and to ensure that gratifications were not given to foreigners.[4] The lords were still engaged in discussing this bill when William requested parliament to adjourn, at the same time giving his well-known pledge: 'I do likewise think it proper to assure you that I shall not make any grant of the forfeited lands in England or Ireland till there be another opportunity of settling that matter in parliament in such manner as shall be thought most expedient'.[5]

William's pledge was given in circumstances of acute financial stringency. The Irish war had been prolonged beyond his expectation and was costing too much. In particular, the problem of paying the troops presented difficulties. Godolphin, a commissioner of the treasury, advised William in February 1691 that the army should receive a quarter of its arrears in cash and three-quarters in debentures secured on the Irish forfeitures. 'What better or more public use can be made of those lands than to satisfy the arrears of that army which brought them under the subjection of England?'[6] William replied that the proposal suited him provided that a proportion of the land was left to be disposed of by himself.[7] Shortly afterwards Godolphin wrote that enough cash had been sent to meet four months' arrears of pay. 'For the remainder of their arrears there are very few of them that will not be very glad to take assignments of debentures on the forfeited lands, so that I hope you will find that the army will be pretty well enabled to go cheerfully into the campaign.'[8] The debentures were duly issued. Later, with the granting away of the lands on which they were secured, they became a drug on the market. Finally, they formed an important part of the complicated

[1] *Commons' jn.*, x. 445.
[2] Ibid., x. 512.
[3] Ibid., x. 524.
[4] F. Bonnet to Brandenburg court, 31 Oct. 1690, quoted in Ranke, *History of England*, v. 204.
[5] King's speech to lords, 5 Jan. 1691 (*Cobbett's parliamentary history*, v. 652-3).
[6] *Cal. S.P. dom., 1690-1*, pp. 242-3.
[7] Japikse, *Correspondentie van Willem en Bentinck*, iii. 211.
[8] *Cal. S.P. dom., 1690-1*, p. 328.

financial arrangements of the Act of Resumption and were bought up by speculators who used them to purchase lands from the trustees.

There was to be acute controversy over the question whether William had, or had not, broken his pledge. His defenders maintained that the king could not be held to his promise after the following session of parliament, which lasted from 22 October 1691 to 24 February 1692. Against this it was urged that the question was continually being raised in one form or another, and that William could not have supposed that parliament had allowed its case to lapse by default.[1] It would probably be fair to say that there was no clear breach of the actual pledge, but that William was not prepared to go beyond the bare letter of his undertaking and showed considerable adroitness in using his prerogative to adjourn and prorogue parliament in such a way as to prevent the passage of various bills relating to the Irish forfeitures. As time passed and parliament still failed to secure the passage of legislation on the subject, William's confidence grew and his Irish grants became larger and more numerous. He is certainly open to the criticism that the army was fobbed off with unsecured debentures and that the bills for its transport to Ireland remained unpaid, while enormous areas of Irish land were being granted to favoured individuals. As Davenant put it: 'no doubt it has heretofore been injurious to the reputation of a prince to be urged by clamorous debts, to suffer many thousands of miserable persons to want what is their due, to have his troops unpaid and his seamen in vast arrears'.[2]

Between the giving of the pledge in January 1691 and the conclusion of the following session of parliament in February 1692 only one warrant was issued for the grant of Irish land, and the case could plausibly be excluded from the terms of the pledge. The warrant, issued in April 1691, was for the grant of letters patent to Sydney in respect of the forfeited estates of Lord Bellew and Dudley Bagenal. To forestall criticism the warrant stated that the lands had previously been granted to Sir John Trevor and others in trust for Sydney, although such trust had not been specifically expressed.[3] This seems to have been the case. In the summer of 1690 Southwell wrote to Nottingham that the king had ordered him to draw up a grant of the forfeited estates of Bellew and Bagenal to Sir John Trevor and two others, whom he presumed to be but trustees.[4] It thus appears that Sydney, whom William had known

[1] *Jus regium* puts the case for William; Davenant, *Discourse upon grants and resumptions*, puts the commons' case.
[2] Davenant, *Discourse upon grants and resumptions*, p. 401.
[3] *Cal. S.P. dom., 1690-1*, p. 341.
[4] *H.M.C., Finch MSS*, ii. 445.

and liked at the Hague, had lost no time in putting in his claim for Irish land.

In December 1691 orders were passed that Henry Luttrell should be given a 'custodiam' of his brother Simon's estate.[1] This order followed with significant promptness upon a promise made by Ginkel at the time of the surrender of Limerick. It appears, however, from a petition of Henry Luttrell that shortly after the order was passed in his favour a general order was passed countermanding the granting of custodiams.[2] The latter order seems to have been due to parliamentary criticism, although William could no doubt have maintained that the recipient of a custodiam held his land on a care and maintenance basis and acquired no prescriptive rights. At a later stage Henry was given, first a custodiam, and then an outright grant of Simon's estate.

During the winter session of 1691–2 another Irish forfeitures bill passed the commons. This prescribed that the forfeited estates should be applied 'to the use of the war'. A clause reserved a third part of the forfeitures for disposal by their majesties 'to such military officers and soldiers who actually served in the wars in Ireland in person since 13 February 1689, and to no other person whatsoever'.[3] This met the claims of William's military commanders, but excluded mere courtiers and such civil advisers as Bentinck. The grants to Sydney and to Henry Luttrell came under consideration during the passage of the bill. An odd clause was passed directing that Sydney should surrender before 1 May 1692 the estates which had been granted to him, but providing that he might within six months be given other lands of equal value.[4] Apparently the object was to assert the authority of parliament without incurring the odium of depriving Sydney of all his Irish expectations. At the same time the house rejected a clause which provided that, if Simon Luttrell did not submit in accordance with the articles of Limerick, any grant made by the crown to Henry should be good in law.[5]

This bill met the fate of its immediate predecessor. Before it had passed the lords William first adjourned and then prorogued parliament, with the result that all pending legislation lapsed. Five days after the adjournment a warrant was issued granting the forfeited estates of Lords Limerick and Slane to Ginkel, who by common consent had the strongest claim on the royal bounty.[6] Two days later a much more con-

---

[1] *Cal. S.P. dom., 1691-2*, p. 28. A custodiam is a temporary grant.
[2] Ibid., p. 156.
[3] *Commons' jn.*, x. 664.
[4] Ibid., x. 659.
[5] Ibid., x. 663.
[6] *Cal. S.P. dom., 1691-2*, p. 158.

troversial warrant was issued. It was passed in favour of Henry Guy, secretary of the treasury, and two others, and granted them in trust the estates of the late King James.[1] This was the first stage of the notorious grant of the 'private estate' to William's mistress, Elizabeth Villiers, later countess of Orkney. As the most controversial of William's grants it will be reserved for more detailed treatment hereafter.

The winter session of 1692–3 gave further opportunity to the commons to consider the question of the Irish forfeitures, and much time was devoted to hearing evidence about the mismanagement and corruption of the forfeiture commissioners. The general theme was that the army remained unpaid while civil servants embezzled the proceeds of the forfeitures and great men applied for grants. The commons presented a lengthy address to the king on Irish grievances, which included the following request: 'and forasmuch as the reducing of Ireland hath been of great expense to this kingdom we beseech that according to the promise your majesty hath been pleased to give us no grant may be made of the forfeited lands in Ireland till there be an opportunity of settling that matter in parliament in such manner as shall be thought most expedient'.[2] William replied that he would always have great consideration of what came from the house of commons and would take great care that what was amiss should be remedied.[3] He did not, however, consider this guarded statement as binding him to continue his previous pledge. Parliament was adjourned in March 1693 and during the following months a number of three-year custodiams were granted. The recipients included Henry de Ruvigny (Viscount Galway), Lieutenant-general Talmash and Rudolph Kien, page of the bed-chamber.[4]

The Irish forfeitures were the subject of discussion and of further abortive bills during the parliamentary sessions of 1693–4 and 1694–5. These bills made even less progress than their predecessors. During the following three years, broadly speaking, the whig ministers had the commons under control, and William was in a strong enough position to make grants of the Irish forfeitures on his own lines without effective interference from the parliamentary opposition.

The sixth of the books accompanying the inquiry commissioners' report was the Book of Grants, which contained particulars of the seventy-six grants and custodiams then in force.[5] These were recorded

[1] *Cal. S.P. dom., 1691-2*, p. 164.
[2] *Commons' jn.*, x. 843.
[3] Ibid., x. 848.
[4] *Cal. S.P. dom., 1693*, pp. 113, 198.
[5] *H.L. MSS*, n.s., iv. 32-8.

as amounting to 636,807 acres, almost nine-tenths of the area forfeited
and not restored to the original proprietors. In a number of instances
two or three successive grants were made to the same individual. Some
of the grants were of house property or forfeited debts. Only forty-four
individuals were recorded as having received grants of land.

Outstanding among the grants were those in favour of Viscount
Woodstock, Bentinck's son, and of Keppel, earl of Albemarle. Woodstock was granted Clancarty's estate, recorded as amounting to 135,820
acres. In 1695 the gentry of county Cork had offered to make a joint
purchase of the estate for £60,000.[1] The proposition was laid before
William by Shrewsbury, who wrote back to Ireland that the king
'relishes very well what you propose about Lord Clancarty's estate and
is abundantly convinced much more is offered than ever he shall make
of it in the method it is in'.[2] Unfortunately for the gentlemen of Cork
their project got no further. About the same time the English commons
protested vigorously against the grants which had been made in Den-
bighshire to Bentinck, now earl of Portland. There was strong talk of
an act of resumption and William, bowing before the storm, made a
conciliatory reply: 'I have a kindness for my lord Portland which he has
deserved of me by long and faithful services, but I should not have given
him these lands if I had imagined the house of commons could have been
concerned; I will therefore recall the grant and find some other way of
showing my favour to him'[3]. The next mention we get of the disposal of
Clancarty's estate is in a letter of 1697 from Blathwayt to Lowndes,
secretary of the treasury, conveying the king's orders that a warrant
should be prepared for the grant of the estate to Portland.[4] The warrant
was issued accordingly, but shortly afterwards was replaced by another
warrant granting the land to Lord Woodstock, Portland's son and heir.[5]
Presumably William hoped that less attention would be attracted if the
grant was made, not to Portland himself, but to his less conspicuous
son. Objections had already been made in Ireland to the grant. One of
the lords justices reported that Francis Annesley was preparing to make
an issue of the forfeitures with particular reference to the grant of
Clancarty's estate to Portland.[6] Joost Keppel, earl of Albemarle, who
had ousted Portland from the first place among William's favourites,
was recorded as receiving a grant of 108,633 acres from the Irish for-

[1] *H.M.C., Buccleuch MSS*, ii. 264.
[2] Ibid., ii. 282.
[3] *Cobbett's parliamentary history*, v. 978-86.
[4] *Cal. treas. bks*, x. 86.
[5] *Cal. S.P. dom., 1697*, pp. 371, 463.
[6] *H.M.C., Buccleuch MSS*, ii. 522.

feitures. This area included the estates of Lord Clare and a number of other forfeiting proprietors.[1]

The case of the English commons largely depended on the charge that William had been grossly deceived by his servants in Ireland about the value of his grants. The inquiry commissioners maintained that the traffic in forfeited estates had principally operated to the advantage of middlemen who had cheated both William and the grantees and made fortunes by 'fishing in these forfeitures'. Their report sums up the situation in the following terms: 'indeed the whole management has been so intricate as it were designed to be kept a mystery; which has proved sufficiently advantageous to these men, though much to his majesty's detriment, who by this means has been deceived in the value of his grants and in many cases has given much more than he intended'[2].

The enormous grants made to Bentinck and Keppel and the lesser, but still very substantial, grants made to Zuylestein and other foreigners greatly accentuated the xenophobia and dislike of courtiers which were in any case habitual with the landed gentry. From the beginning of 1698 we find frequent complaints in the English commons and threats of an act of resumption. Similar sentiments among the Protestants of Ireland are illustrated by a story which Bishop King has about the grant made to the marquis of Puissar. The deaf archbishop of Armagh, catching only the last syllable of Puissar's name, remarked: 'what, has the czar of Muscovy gotten a grant of forfeitures? 'Tis very strange, he has not been a week in England and must he come in for a grant? Must we provide for all foreigners?'[3]

Other foreigners among the grantees were de Ruvigny, Viscount Galway, and Ginkel, earl of Athlone, who received respectively 36,148 acres and 26,480 acres. Galway was a Huguenot of distinction who left France not long after the revocation of the edict of Nantes. He entered William's service and played a leading part in the concluding stages of the Irish war, forfeiting his French estates as a result. After the war he became commander-in-chief in Ireland and subsequently a lord justice. In 1692 he wrote to William, reminding him of a promise that he should get something of the order of £25,000 in compensation for what he had lost in France. He asked for Sir Patrick Trant's estate and suggested that he might be made 'keeper' of it if William was not prepared to make an outright grant.[4] The suggestion was approved and a custodiam of

[1] *Cal. treas. bks*, xi. 437-41; xii. 321-7.
[2] *Commrs' report*, p. 25.
[3] King to Southwell, 12 Jan. 1698 (T.C.D., MS N.3. 1, p. 157). The allusion is to Peter the Great's visit.
[4] *Cal. S.P. dom., 1691-2*, pp. 550-1.

Trant's estate was given to Galway for three years. At the expiry of the period the lands were granted to him to hold 'as freely as Sir Patrick Trant held them before his forfeiture thereof'.[1] Galway established at Portarlington a settlement of Huguenots, whose future was soon threatened by the Act of Resumption. However, a private act of parliament was passed confirming the settlement and making provision for the salaries of the Huguenot minister and schoolmaster.[2] The Huguenots flourished in Portarlington for many years and evidences of the French settlement have survived into modern times.

Ginkel had made an even greater contribution to the Williamite cause and was considered to have fairly earned his grant of Irish land. It was confirmed by an act of the Irish parliament.[3] An important constitutional point thus arose when the grant was set aside by the English Act of Resumption. Ginkel's was the only grant to be confirmed in this way, although some other grantees attempted to get similar acts passed for their greater security. Several bills were prepared but not brought before the Irish parliament.

Sixty per cent of the area granted out of the Irish forfeitures was divided among seven foreigners. The remainder of the grants were shared by thirty-seven individuals, of whom several had distinguished themselves in the Irish war and others were office-holders in the Irish government. Others again were Protestant relatives of forfeiting proprietors; thus Charles, earl of Abercorn, who had turned Protestant, was given the forfeited estate of his Catholic brother Claud.

Among the grants given for war services were those made to Baker and Roche, the reward of services rendered during the siege of Derry. Both grants were maintained by a saving clause in the Act of Resumption. John Baker, son of Henry Baker who died during the siege as governor of the city, was granted the estate of Nicholas Gernon in county Louth. He was unfortunate in his grant, as another member of the Gernon family succeeded in establishing a deed under which the estate was settled on him. Baker petitioned the commons for relief but does not seem to have obtained redress at the time.[4] After the winding-up of the trust a private act was passed for recompensing John Baker and his family, and some years later a further act was passed for their relief.[5] Roche was granted the estate of James Everard in county Water-

[1] Ibid., *1693*, pp. 112-13; ibid., *1696*, p. 182.
[2] 1 Anne, c. 92; *Ir. rec. comm. rep., 1821-5*, pp. 378-9.
[3] *Commons' jn. Ire.*, ii. 135 (7 Dec. 1695).
[4] *Commons' jn.*, xiv. 314-15.
[5] 2 and 3 Anne, c. 48; 6 Anne, c. 19.

ford and a number of ferries in various parts of Ireland.[1] This was the reward of his enterprise in swimming up the Foyle, carrying a message from Major-General Kirk to the garrison, and again returning in the same way to Kirk's camp. Kirk had offered a reward of three thousand guineas for the feat and the grant seems to have been made in lieu of cash payment. Roche complained that the ferries had brought him no gain but endless trouble. William accordingly ordered that he should receive a further grant of lands in Cork and Meath.[2] This grant had not passed the great seal when the Act of Resumption became law. The trustees therefore held that it was not covered by the saving clause and treated the lands as vested in themselves. Roche succeeded in obtaining a private act by which he was to receive £3,269. 7s. 7d. out of the proceeds of the forfeited estates. He got only one-third of the amount in cash and a subsequent act assigned the balance in debentures.[3]

Gustavus Hamilton, who defended Enniskillen, received a grant of 3,482 acres. The inquiry commissioners noted that the grant was made for his 'great and early services in the war in Ireland and for his wading in the Shannon and storming the town of Athlone at the head of the English grenadiers'. Another Enniskillen man who received a grant was James Corry, who was given the Fermanagh estate of Cuconnacht Maguire. There was considerable controversy over this grant. The commissioners remarked that it was given on the grounds that his house had been burned and that he had at his own expense supplied the garrison of Enniskillen with provisions and materials worth £3,000. 'But inquiring into the merits of this gentleman it appeared to us that he gave no assistance to the men of Enniskillen, and that in the town of Enniskillen he publicly declared he hoped to see all those hanged that took up arms for the prince of Orange, and his house was burned by the said garrison.'[4]

Among the grantees were Thomas Prendergast and Francis de la Rue, who were implicated in the conspiracy to assassinate William in 1696 and turned king's evidence. Both grants were protected by a saving clause in the Act of Resumption. Prendergast, who was an Irish Jacobite, gave Bentinck the first information of the plot and later repeated the story to William. His information led to the arrest of the conspirators and his evidence to their conviction. He received a grant

[1] *Cal. S.P. dom., 1694-5*, p. 177.
[2] *Cal. treas. bks*, xv. 213.
[3] *Commons' jn.*, xiv. 251; *Cal. treas. bks*, xxiii, part 2, p. 318. The acts were 2 and 3 Anne, c. 45, and 6 Anne, c. 27.
[4] *Commrs' report*, pp. 17-18.

of the estate of Roger O'Shaughnessy of Gort.[1] Conforming to the established church, he became a baronet and a member of parliament and finally died of wounds received at Malplaquet. His grandson became the first Viscount Gort. The O'Shaughnessys disputed the grant on the ground that part of the property had been settled on Roger O'Shaughnessy's younger brother. The latter and his heirs succeeded in retaining possession of the disputed land for many years. When the case came before a jury in 1731, Prendergast's son asked for a transfer on the ground that he 'could not expect any equality or indifferency from any jury to be returned in county Galway by reason of the influence that the family of O'Shaughnessy held in that county'.[2] The transfer was refused and the jury found in O'Shaughnessy's favour. In 1755 the litigation was still going on and the Irish commons resolved to 'proceed against all such as shall promote, encourage or assist in carrying on the said suits, as persons endeavouring to lessen the Protestant interest of this kingdom'.[3] De la Rue was granted a number of scattered lands, making a total of 3,900 acres. He seems to have been a rather seedy French adventurer. He did not live long to enjoy his grant, as he was killed in a gambling brawl in a London coffee-house in 1701.[4] The trustees subsequently discovered that most of the land granted to him had never come into his possession. Part was protected by the articles of Limerick; part was affected by the loss of the minutes containing particulars of the inquisitions.[5]

One of the largest items in the Book of Grants was 77,291 acres granted in 1696 for a thousand years to the earl of Bellamont. Bellamont was Richard Coote, who had from the first been a vigorous supporter of William and had held the post of treasurer and receiver-general to Queen Mary. He was later governor of New York where he was involved in some unhappy negotiations with Captain Kidd, the celebrated pirate.[6] His grant consisted of the Kenmare estate, but was not so valuable as might be supposed. The patent was for a grant of all the estates of Sir Valentine Browne, commonly called Lord Kenmare, and of his son Sir Nicholas, except for the lead mines on Ross Island, for a thousand years at a peppercorn rent. The grant, however, was conditional on Bellamont forthwith making over the estate to trustees who were to pay him £1,000 a year, the surplus going to the crown; the trustees were to

---

[1] *Cal. S.P. dom., 1697*, p. 129.
[2] *Parliamentary cases, 1730-5*, nos 212-13.
[3] *Commons' jn. Ire.*, v. 285 (11 Dec. 1755).
[4] Luttrell, *Brief historical relation*, iv. 211.
[5] *H.L. MSS*, n.s., iv. 211.
[6] Macaulay, *History of England*, iii. 702-6.

manage the estate under the orders of the Irish government.[1] Difficulties at once arose over the payment of the income. The estate had been leased by the revenue authorities in Ireland to Francis Burton for £1,000 a year (which turned out to have been reduced to £774), and Queen Mary had ordered £400 a year to be paid from the proceeds to the wife of Sir Nicholas Browne.[2] In 1697 a warrant was issued to the lords justices to pay Bellamont £2,000 in cash on the ground that the estate was so encumbered that he was not able to receive his annual income from it.[3] Burton's lease expired in 1699, and a royal warrant was issued in that year to the lords justices to direct that the estate should be leased for not more than twenty-one years at the best rent obtainable; the surplus income, after satisfying the claims of Bellamont and Lady Kenmare, was to go to the crown.[4] The inquiry commissioners observed that the lords justices had disregarded the terms of the warrant and had leased the estate for sixty-one years to two members of the Irish parliament, Blennerhassett and Rogers, for at least £1,000 less than its true value.[5]

The most controversial of William's grants was that made to his mistress, Elizabeth Villiers, who was given the 'private estate'. This estate was granted to the duke of York (who later became James II) by section 194 of the Act of Settlement. It represented the equivalent, after the various restoration 'reprisals', of the lands granted under the Cromwellian settlement to the regicides. Petty had estimated its area at 120,000 acres, but by William's reign it was considerably less. Some lands had been disposed of by James to Tyrconnell and others; some were granted on paper only and James had never succeeded in getting possession of them. Particulars of the estate were recorded, not in the Book of Grants, but in the ninth of the books accompanying the inquiry commissioners' report. The lands thus shown amounted to 95,649 acres spread over sixteen counties. The gross income was estimated at almost £26,000 per annum. James had charged the estate with £3,000 per annum during the lives of two of his mistresses, Arabella Churchill and Susannah Bellasis. William scrupulously honoured the commitment. The rest of the revenue was available for Elizabeth Villiers, whose income would be further increased after the deaths of James's mistresses.

Elizabeth Villiers had come to the Hague as maid of honour to Mary. She was no beauty; according to Swift she 'squinted like a dragon'. But

[1] *Cal. treas. bks*, xi. 95.
[2] *Cal. treas. bks*, xiv. 297.
[3] *Cal. S.P. dom., 1697*, p. 159.
[4] *Cal. treas. bks*, xiv. 297.
[5] *Commrs' report*, pp. 26-7.

she seems to have been extremely intelligent and a good conversation-
alist. She became something of an Egeria to William. Her political
abilities are exemplified in some persuasive letters which she wrote to
Shrewsbury, urging him to take office in William's government.[1] In
later life she struck up a firm friendship with Swift, whose correspondence contains several of her letters. He described her as the wisest
woman he ever saw, and observed that her advice had for many years
been followed in the most important affairs of state. He qualified his
eulogy with the comment that she spelled 'like a Wapping wench'.[2]

There was a general air of mystery about the disposal of the private
estate, and there are numerous indications of opposition from various
quarters to its grant to Elizabeth Villiers. The first warrant directed that
the estate should be put into the hands of Henry Guy, secretary of the
treasury, for conveyance in such manner as the king might direct.[3]
Shortly after the issue Guy wrote to the Irish chancellor that the private
estate was not to be conveyed in the manner directed, and that the seal
was not to be affixed to the document until further orders.[4] Guy appears
to have had scruples about his trust and to have apprehended that parliament might make awkward inquiries. As Guy was himself a member of
parliament he would be obliged to give an answer on the spot; if no
member of parliament was concerned in the trust time might be gained
before an answer need be given.[5] Guy's scruples were temporarily overcome, but in the following year he and his fellow trustees obtained leave
to resign their trust to 'Mr. Topham, who has the reputation of an
honest man and is one . . . whom the persons concerned think they may
rely on'.[6]

Elizabeth Villiers's name did not appear in the orders until after the
queen's death. Even then care was taken to draw as little attention as
possible to the dimensions of the grant. A warrant was issued granting
to Elizabeth Villiers, spinster, the town and lands of Knockingen, containing 135 acres, together with all castles, manors, and towns in which
James, duke of York, had any estate of inheritance in Ireland on 5 February 1685.[7] Two of the Irish lords justices, Wyche and Duncombe,
refused to execute the warrant and the transfer was not effected until
Capel took over as lord deputy. Capel wrote to Shrewsbury that his

---

[1] H.M.C., Buccleuch MSS, ii. 57-8.
[2] Swift, Prose works, ii. 383 ,392; Correspondence of Jonathan Swift, ii. 409; v. 301.
[3] Cal. S.P. dom., 1691-2, p. 164.
[4] Cal. treas. bks, ix. 1642.
[5] Cal. S.P. dom., 1691-2, p. 405.
[6] Godolphin to William, 18 Aug. 1693 (Cal. S.P. dom., 1693, p. 275.)
[7] Cal. S.P. dom., 1694-5, p. 441.

former colleagues had refused to transfer the estate from Topham to Elizabeth Villiers, though they had transferred it from Guy to Topham, well knowing for whom it was in trust: 'I am told they value themselves now in refusing to pass this grant, which has caused the more notice to be taken of it, and indeed some impressions against it'[1]. Wyche's attitude is of interest in view of his later position as trustee for the forfeited estates.

There was considerable doubt about the legal position of the estate. In 1695 the Irish law officers expressed the opinion that it was not crown property: '. . . after the duke of York's accession to the crown that estate was never put in charge in the exchequer, but managed and kept as a private and particular estate, so as no title yet appeareth on record in the crown to those lands'[2]. It could not properly be regarded as a forfeited estate as James was not attainted. William appears to have assumed that he was entitled to take it over from James in the same way as he took over the crown, and for the same reason, that James had surrendered his rights by departure. Elizabeth Villiers seems to have been anxious to strengthen her legal position. Sir Richard Levinge, in the course of an opinion given in 1695, observed that she had sufficient grounds for pressing for an act of parliament declaring the private estate to have been vested in the crown at the time of her grant.[3] There are indications that the princess Anne considered that she had an interest in her father's estate and was by no means satisfied that it should have been granted to Elizabeth Villiers. When the bill for the confirmation of outlawries had been before the Irish parliament in 1697, Winchester wrote to Shrewsbury that Drogheda and a great many of the bishops were 'possessed with a notion that the princess was mightily against this bill and that this bill would confirm my lady Orkney's grant'.[4] After Anne's accession there seems to have been a general expectation that parliament would grant her the private estate, 'that being her proper inheritance'.[5] When Elizabeth Villiers was advised to have her title secured by an Irish act, William had been reluctant to have the matter ventilated in this way, but consented to the preparation of a bill if it was thought necessary.[6] The Irish chancellor reported that there was particular hostility in parliament to any bill

[1] H.M.C., Buccleuch MSS, ii. 187.
[2] Ibid., ii. 188.
[3] Ibid., ii. 189.
[4] Ibid., ii. 534. Elizabeth Villiers married Lord George Hamilton in Nov. 1695. Soon after he was made earl of Orkney.
[5] Bishop King to Southwell, 28 Mar. 1702 (B.M., Eg. MS 917, f. 183).
[6] H.M.C., Buccleuch MSS, ii. 187.

for the confirmation of the grant and no such measure was actually brought forward.[1]

This grant was the chief point of contention among the inquiry commissioners in 1699. It aroused bitter controversy in the parliamentary debates which followed on the commission's report. It has since been cited on various occasions as an example of royal profligacy. Karl Marx referred to it as exemplifying the private moral character of 'this bourgeois hero', William the third.[2] Froude referred to it as the 'worst case' among William's grants, and made the curious comment that the lady's sole claims to consideration were that her father had been knight marshal of Charles II's household and that her mother had been governess to the princesses.[3] Macaulay called it an unfortunate grant and took a good deal of trouble to explain it away.[4]

[1] Ibid., ii. 482.
[2] Marx, *Capital*, ii. 801.
[3] Froude, *Ire.*, i. 247.
[4] Macaulay, *History of England*, iii. 716-17.

9

THE COMMISSION OF INQUIRY, 1699

Willliam's third English parliament, which had been kept in fair control by the Junto of whig ministers, became markedly more troublesome after the treaty of Ryswick was concluded in September 1697. The coming of peace left members free to concentrate on the deplorable state of the national finances and on the various factors which were thought to be responsible for it.

Considerable time was devoted to the discussion of William's land grants. A report on a commons debate of December 1697 refers to a speech of Jack Howe, at this time a violent tory, who spoke of the 'unreasonable grants in Ireland' which had been made 'contrary to the king's proviso'. Howe proposed a general act of resumption, saying that if ever there was cause for such a bill it was then, 'which seemed to relish very well with many people'.[1] In February 1698 leave was given by the commons to bring in a bill for 'vacating' all grants of estates or other interests forfeited in Ireland since 13 February 1689, and for appropriating them to the use of the public.[2] Commenting on the proceedings an observer remarked that the 'current ran so strong that there was no opposing it, and consequently little was said on the court side'. The opposition proposed to raise a large sum of money either by selling the estates to the highest bidder or by obliging the holders to pay a certain number of years' purchase. Stress was laid on the point that the commons had previously addressed the king on the subject of the Irish forfeitures and had received 'very gracious answers' from him.[3] The tactic employed by the court party was to play for time by carrying the scrutiny even further and obtaining leave to introduce bills vacating all

[1] James Sloane to Sir Joseph Williamson, 21 Dec. 1697 (*Cal. S.P. dom., 1697*, p. 522).
[2] *Commons' jn.*, xii. 50.
[3] R. Yard to Williamson, 8 Feb. 1698 (*Cal. S.P. dom., 1698*, pp. 77-8).

grants made by Charles II and James II.[1] During the session particular grants made by William came under examination and the house demanded details of the lands given to Albemarle, Puissar and others.[2] Montague, as a lord of the treasury, incurred severe criticism for having himself received a grant of debts due to Tyrconnell, Sir Patrick Trant and others.[3]

Towards the close of the session the administration seem to have thought that some compromise was desirable. To a tory proposal that there should be a tax of five years' purchase on grants Montague replied that some such way of raising money might be adopted and that the grantees could be recompensed by having their grants confirmed by act of parliament.[4] A bill on these lines was prepared by Lowndes, the secretary of the treasury, who suggested that up to £600,000 might be raised by the measure, and that the grantees would have no real grievance as parliamentary ratification of the grants would appreciate the value of their estates.[5] The bill, however, had only reached the committee stage when parliament was first adjourned and then dissolved.

The next parliament was even more truculent. Tories and 'malcontent whigs' formed an alliance against the ministerial whigs. The line of cleavage was between the court party and the opposition, or country party; the latter was in a majority in the commons and in a minority in the lords. It was thus only possible for the majority party in the commons to push through anti-court legislation by making the fullest use of its control of the purse-strings. Towards the close of the session a clause was 'tacked' on to the supply bill empowering seven commissioners to take account of the Irish forfeitures.[6] Tacking was a device used to push through a measure distasteful to the lords or the crown by coupling it with a bill for the grant of indispensable financial aid. It was again employed in the following year to carry the Act of Resumption.

There was much controversy over the tacking clause. Burnet commented that 'in the debates a great alienation discovered itself in many from the king and his government, which had a very ill effect upon all things both at home and abroad'.[7] The lords did their best to resist the clause. They appear to have countered with a compromise proposal that

[1] *Commons' jn.*, xii. 90.
[2] Ibid., xii. 106.
[3] *Cal. S.P. dom., 1698*, p. 94.
[4] Ibid., p. 184.
[5] Ibid., p. 242.
[6] *Commons' jn.*, xii. 651.
[7] Burnet, *History of his own time*, iv. 399.

the grantees should pay four years' purchase and have their grants confirmed by parliament.[1] The commons rejected the proposal and insisted on their original bill, which then passed the lords with nine peers protesting. These peers, some of whom were tory and some whig, took their stand on the ground that the clause for inquiry into the forfeitures was foreign to the supply bill and would more appropriately have been the subject of an independent bill. 'The tacking of a clause of that nature is contrary to the ancient method of proceedings in parliament—and highly prejudicial to the privileges of the peers and the prerogative of the crown.'[2]

The method adopted for choosing the inquiry commissioners was to have lists of seven names 'put into glasses by way of balloting'. The commissioners selected were Lord Drogheda, John Trenchard and five members of the Irish commons, Francis Annesley, Sir Francis Brewster, James Hamilton of Tullymore, Henry Langford and Sir Richard Levinge.[3] Six of the commissioners were thus members of the Irish parliament, and Trenchard, as a graduate of Trinity College, Dublin, had some acquaintance with the country. The Irish commissioners had all been in conflict with the administration at one time or another. They appear to have been selected by the opposition in the expectation that they would produce a report which would whole-heartedly condemn the official handling of the Irish forfeitures. Trenchard, a whig writer of extreme views, had recently come into prominence with a pamphlet, *A short history of standing armies in England*, which had been largely responsible for the drastic reduction of William's armed forces. He, in particular, could be relied on to produce a report which would be highly unpalatable to the court.

In the event the commissioners formed an ill-assorted team and after much wrangling and disputation split into majority and minority groups. Annesley, Hamilton, Langford and Trenchard formed the majority. Drogheda, Brewster and Levinge formed a dissenting minority. Some modern historians have referred to the majority as tories and to the minority as whigs.[4] There is no evidence for this classification, which seems to spring from Archdeacon Coxe.[5] In fact, the majority seems to have consisted of two tories and two whigs, and the minority

[1] Luttrell, *Brief historical relation*, iv. 509.

[2] *Lords' jn.*, xvi. 453.

[3] *Commons' jn.*, xii. 657. *D.N.B.* has articles on Brewster, Drogheda, Levinge and Trenchard.

[4] Turberville, *The house of lords in the reign of William III*, p. 202; Feiling, *History of the tory party, 1640-1714*, p. 337.

[5] *Private and original correspondence of . . . Shrewsbury*, pp. 602-3

of two tories and one whig.[1] Trenchard, who took a leading part in the drafting of the majority report, was a violent whig. Levinge, one of the signatories of the minority protest, was a consistent tory. He had been speaker of the Irish commons and solicitor-general till 1695, when he was replaced in the former capacity by Robert Rochfort and in the latter by Alan Broderick, both prominent whigs. He was on the worst terms with Capel, the whig lord deputy.[2] In Anne's reign he took a prominent part on the tory side in Irish politics. It is curious that he should have been selected as a member of the inquiry commission as he had personal grounds for opposing a strong report. He had purchased from Albemarle for the moderate sum of £1,000 over 1,500 acres in Westmeath, the forfeited estate of Walter Tuite.[3]

All the evidence indicates that the line of cleavage was pro- and anti-court, not whig and tory. Feeling ran high. The majority commissioners neglected no opportunity to discredit the government's administration of the forfeitures and to paint a lurid picture of neglect, corruption, favouritism, and partiality to Papists. The dissenting minority did their best to obstruct the designs of the majority. Ralph summed up the position thus: 'of these commissioners, which were seven in all and all presumed to be anti-courtiers, four were disposed to put every circumstance to the torture with a view to inflame the report, and three were for the court under the pretence of candour and moderation'[4].

In the ballot the highest number of votes had been given to Francis Annesley, who sat for Downpatrick in the Irish commons. He belonged to the well-known family, of which Lord Anglesey was the most prominent seventeenth-century representative. His son became Lord Annesley of Castlewellan. A considerable part of what we know about the transactions of the inquiry commissioners and, in a much greater degree, of the trustees under the Act of Resumption is derived from the Annesley manuscripts, copies of the proceedings taken by Francis Annesley and preserved at Castlewellan. The manuscripts, to which numerous references have already been made, include a book of the depositions taken by the inquiry commissioners in 1699 and a book of letters written and received by them in the same year.[5] Annesley was a barrister of the Inner Temple and one of Bishop King's counsel in his case against the Irish

---

[1] Majority—tories, Annesley and Langford; whigs, Trenchard and Hamilton. Minority—tories, Drogheda and Levinge; whig, Brewster.

[2] *Cal. S.P. dom., 1695*, p. 119.

[3] *Ir. rec. comm. rep., 1821-5*, p. 379.

[4] Ralph, *History of England*, ii. 833.

[5] Annesley MSS, xxiii and xxvii. The descriptive catalogue (*Anal. Hib.*, xvi. 359-64) wrongly describes the latter volume as trustees' letters, 1699.

Society. Langford, another of the inquiry commissioners, was also one
of the bishop's counsel in the same case. King and Annesley became
very friendly, and a considerable number of their letters to one another
have been preserved in King's correspondence. Soon after Annesley
was briefed in the case King wrote to him to say how pleased he was to
have found someone on whose 'skill, prudence and integrity' he could
so entirely depend.[1] Annesley was also a friend of Southwell, who was a
close friend and regular correspondent of King's. Soon after the appointment of the inquiry commission Southwell wrote to King: 'I hope our
worthy friend Mr Annesley is in safety with you. I know not a better man.'[2]

King's attitude to the inquiry is of interest. He had disapproved of
the methods adopted for the disposal of the forfeited lands. His letters
contain a number of derogatory references to courtiers, and in the
previous year he had written to Annesley that 'the Irish lands go every-
where but where they should.'[3] To another correspondent he observed
that a violent faction 'have gotten all the forfeitures of Ireland into their
hands and they manage them, and by them all that have interest in
them, as best serves their private advantage; this makes good men
jealous of them'.[4] Nevertheless, King was opposed to the inquiry,
partly because it had been ordered by the English parliament, but chiefly
because much of the land granted by the crown had since been sold by
the grantees to purchasers in Ireland. King made the following comments: 'The design of the commission is to break all our legal securities
to gratify England, which will use the forfeitures so as to do as much
mischief in Ireland as they can, and if they either sell them by cant or
make them a fund to raise a sum of money they will take away all the
ready money in Ireland and we shall not recover in twenty years. . . .
The commissioners are under a dilemma. If they do execute it (i.e. their
commission) faithfully they hurt the kingdom (of Ireland) by giving a
handle to destroy our propriety and carry away our money, and if they
do not the roguery of the late managers will not appear and they will
be riveted in their places. The last consideration has ill-nature on its
side and therefore I believe will prevail.'[5]

The Irish objection to an English parliamentary inquiry was certainly
associated with the controversy stirred up by Molyneux's famous
treatise, *The case of Ireland's being bound by acts of parliament in England stated*, which had been published in the previous year and had been

---

[1] King to Annesley, 28 Oct. 1697 (T.C.D., MS N. 3. 1, p. 115).
[2] Southwell to King, 30 May 1699 (T.C.D., King MSS).
[3] King to Annesley, 16 July 1698 (T.C.D., MS N. 3. 1, p. 248).
[4] King to Clifford, 14 Dec. 1697 (Ibid., p. 139).
[5] King to Southwell, 15 June 1699 (N.L.I., MS 2055).

greeted with enthusiasm in Ireland and indignation in England. The inquiry into the Irish forfeitures, and even more so the Act of Resumption, made it clear how little respect the English parliament had for colonial assertions of constitutional independence. The theory that Ireland was subject to the king, but not to the parliament, of England was not easily reconciled with the new position brought about by the revolution of 1688, which established parliament, and not the king, as the ultimate authority in England. The action taken by the English parliament in respect of the Irish forfeitures is a particularly good example of the manner in which parliament's control of the king involved the exercise of its authority over Irish affairs.

When the commissioners reached Ireland they met with a hostile reception from the Irish administration, who naturally sided with the king and resented an inquiry which was a direct attack both on the crown and on their own management of the forfeitures. Methuen, the Irish chancellor, wrote to Vernon, the secretary of state: 'our new commissioners are come and I find, what I believed, that they will carry the execution of their commission very high and endeavour in their reports not only to make the grants more considerable in value, thereby to engage the house to proceed in that matter, but also to insert in their report such things, not directly within the direction of the clause, as may furnish ample matter for reflection on the king's ministers who have served him both in England and Ireland'[1]. Palmer, the deputy clerk of the council, complained: 'I am attacked every way, these commissioners of forfeitures reporting strange things that the grants are to be re-assumed without regard to purchasers. It will be a barbarous case and will undo half the Protestants here, amongst the rest myself; but we hope other things from an English parliament and, though we expect to have three years' value laid upon them, part surely will be on the grantee and part on the purchaser.'[2]

Palmer's personal anxiety related to his purchase of 679 acres in Meath, the estate of Dominick Barnwell, which had been granted to Sydney[3]. His letter brings out what was to be an important factor in determining the attitude of Irish Protestants to the Act of Resumption. Some of the grantees, notably the earls of Albemarle, Athlone and Romney (Keppel, Ginkel and Sydney) had sold their grants to Irish purchasers, in many cases at bargain prices.[4] The purchasers, who included

[1] *Cal. S.P. dom., 1699-1700*, pp. 223-4.
[2] Annesley MSS, xxvii. 22.
[3] Ibid., xxvii. 41.
[4] *Commrs' report*, pp. 24-5.

a number of the leading Protestant gentry, were naturally hostile to any attack on their vested interests. They agitated vigorously against the Act of Resumption and were influential enough to get it substantially modified in their favour.

The commissioners spent June and July 1699 in Dublin, taking evidence and attempting to investigate the voluminous and confused records of the forfeitures administration. Most of August and September was taken up with a tour which went as far afield as Waterford, Cork and Galway. At one time or another all the members except Drogheda took part in this tour, in which sworn evidence was taken from a large number of witnesses, who included forfeiting proprietors, articlemen and recipients of pardon, as well as leading Protestant gentry.[1]

When the commissioners returned to Dublin in the autumn their time was principally occupied with the violent controversies associated with the drafting of their report. The leader of the dissenting minority was Drogheda. Although he had been a vigorous critic of the government in the Irish parliament of 1697–8, he did not forget that in the preceding year he had been a lord justice and therefore in close association with the crown. When he learned that he had been appointed to the inquiry commission he protested that the news came to him as a 'mighty surprise', and wrote to Vernon: 'I assure you I never did so much as hear any such matter was in agitation. If I had, I would have used all means to have prevented myself from being one.' He found himself in an unpleasant dilemma; he did not wish to disoblige the king, and yet was afraid of the consequences if he refused to accept the parliament's commission. He asked Vernon to explain matters to William and communicate the latter's wishes.[2] It was of considerable advantage to the court party that the commission should include a member with Drogheda's outlook, and it may be presumed that he was encouraged to accept the appointment. Bishop King observed that Drogheda had refused to come in at first but had since agreed. 'It looks low for a man lately in the government to act in such a commission.'[3]

A lively description of the dissensions which took place between the commissioners was subsequently given to the commons when five of the commissioners and Hooper, their secretary, were called to the bar of the house and cross-examined.[4] The controversy centred on whether the report should include the grant of the private estate to Elizabeth Villiers,

[1] Annesley MSS, xxvii contains the depositions recorded by the commissioners.
[2] *Cal. S.P. dom., 1699-1700*, pp. 163-4.
[3] King to Southwell, 15 June 1699 (N.L.I., MS 2055).
[4] *History and proceedings of the house of commons*, iii. 109-22. The account there given forms the basis of this and the following three paragraphs.

THE COMMISSION OF INQUIRY, 1699

by now Lady Orkney. Drogheda is said to have declared that it would be flying in the king's face to report the grant. Trenchard rejoined that one might as well say that the whole commission was flying in the king's face. There was much argument whether Trenchard had said that the report would signify nothing if it did not include the grant, and whether he had called it a villainous grant. Trenchard's own version was that he might have said it was an extravagant grant, an unreasonable grant, an unconscionable grant; 'but that I used the word villainous I positively deny; it is a word I don't use in my ordinary conversation, a word that never comes out of the mouth of a gentleman, and is false'.[1]

The argument against mentioning the grant was that the commission was appointed by the act to inquire into estates forfeited since 13 February 1689, when William and Mary officially began their reign. Even if James was held to have forfeited his estate by abdication such forfeiture would have taken place before the date prescribed. This was countered with the argument that by coming to Ireland on 15 March 1689 James had committed treason against William and Mary, an argument which overlooked the fact that no attainder proceedings had been taken against James. Eventually it was decided by the majority that the grant should be brought into the report on the not very convincing ground that some of Lady Orkney's lessees were forfeiting persons.

At one stage the commission was equally divided, Trenchard, Annesley and Langford pressing for the inclusion of the grant, Drogheda, Brewster and Levinge opposing it. The casting vote was that of Hamilton of Tullymore, a county Down landowner of whig antecedents who had taken a leading part in the attempt to impeach Porter and Coningsby in 1693.[2] Hamilton decided that, although Lord Orkney was his relative and friend, it was too late in the day to consider omitting the grant from the report. For five months the commissioners had given the impression that they were 'peremptory for reporting the estate', and two of the dissenters, Brewster and Levinge, had taken part in the examination of witnesses about the valuation of the grant. Hamilton is said to have declared: 'we have made so great a noise about this estate by examining so many people to the value and sending for the rentrolls of it that it is now the public discourse that it will be reported and I know the world must needs say we are bribed and corrupted if we do it not'.[3]

Trenchard was ill and conducted the controversy from his bed. The

[1] Ibid., p. 121.
[2] Hamilton was brother-in-law of Mordaunt, third earl of Peterborough. There are references to his acting as confidential courier for Shrewsbury and Capel (*H.M.C.*, *Buccleuch MSS*, ii. 117). His son became Lord Clanbrassil.
[3] *History and proceedings of the house of commons*, iii. 120.

dissenting commissioners came to his room and offered to sign the report as it stood, if the references to the private estate were omitted. The majority group insisted on its inclusion. When the report was laid before Drogheda for signature he wrote on it that he and his fellow-dissenters agreed to it with the exception of eight or nine paragraphs, and in particular of the paragraph which referred to the private estate. This endorsement was signed by himself, Brewster and Levinge.[1] The majority objected that it was improper for three of the commissioners to protest against the rest. They accordingly tore out the sheet which contained the minority's endorsement, and submitted the report with four signatures only.[2] The three dissenters sent a letter to the English chancellor, explaining the circumstances of their refusal to sign the report and protesting against the conduct of the majority.[3]

Drogheda kept Vernon in close touch with these proceedings and asked him to let the king know he had endeavoured to serve him to the best of his power.[4] He had gone through a very unpleasant experience: 'I would rather dig for my living than endure for six months longer that which I have for the six months past'[5]. Drogheda had the gratification of hearing that William was not dissatisfied with what he had done. He decided that it would be safer to stay in Ireland, as he did not know what men of 'turbulent and restless spirits' might do if he came over to London.[6] His caution was justified by the fate of Levinge, whom the commons committed to the tower on the ground that he had spread baseless and scandalous reports about the four majority commissioners. He was alleged to have repeated to Methuen, the Irish chancellor, the conversation which was said to have taken place among the commissioners to the effect that the private estate was 'a villainous grant and would reflect more than any other'.[7]

Bishop King commented on the dispute with his customary sense and worldly wisdom: 'I think when all is done the scheme was foolishly contrived, for what had the dissenting commissioners ado to write letters or take notice of a report they would not sign? It had been time enough for them to have appeared when called for and then given their reasons with seeming unwillingness. Their party in the house should have contrived to have them called to give an account of their not signing and,

[1] *Cal. S.P. dom., 1699-1700*, p. 305.
[2] *Commons' jn.*, xii. 66.
[3] *H.L. MSS*, n.s., iv. 14-15.
[4] *Cal. S.P. dom., 1699-1700*, p. 275.
[5] Ibid., p. 306.
[6] Ibid., p. 326.
[7] *Commons' jn.*, xiii. 124-5.

if they could not have carried it that it should be so, they had no business to move any further, for to be sure they could carry nothing. I heard three of their reasons. First, the private estate was not forfeited, but merged in the crown and so not within their commission, which they ought not to stretch beyond the letter, being *in re odiosa*. Secondly, that the estates were over-valued, and the ground of the valuation was not sufficient to venture their credit on before the parliament. Thirdly, that the reflections [i.e. of bribery and corruption] were grounded on affidavits, which are no sufficient bottom on which to represent a man of estate and figure ill to the house of commons; for there is no man but must be made black enough by affadavits. These seem to be not altogether unreasonable, but to bring in private talk and conversation that pass in heat of discourse or freedom of time is a breach on humane society and abominable.'[1]

King may here be suspected of a certain amount of diplomacy. He was anxious to enlist Annesley's support in securing for the church the 'impropriate tithes' which had belonged to forfeiting persons. He succeeded in his object and the established church derived considerable benefit from the resumption proceedings.

On 15 December 1699 Annesley presented to the English commons the full record of the commission's investigations. This consisted of nine books of statistical matter together with a report which, Annesley explained, was 'an index to all the rest of the books'. All seven commissioners had signed the first eight books. The ninth book—the Book of the Private Estate—and the report itself were signed by the four majority commissioners. Annesley referred to the difference of opinion which had divided the commission, apologized for the belated submission of the report, and expressed the hope that if anything were said to the prejudice of the commissioners they would be given a hearing which, he was certain, would enable them to satisfy the house. He then withdrew and the report, the memorial of the dissenting minority, a letter which the minority had sent to the speaker, and the contents of the torn sheet were all read out. The house did not take long to make up its mind. A resolution was passed *nem. con.* on the same day that a bill should be brought in to apply to the use of the public all the forfeited estates and interests in Ireland and all grants which had been made since 13 February 1689 (the official beginning of William and Mary's reign).[2]

In April 1700, after the resumption bill had gone to the lords, the

---

[1] King to Annesley, 18 Feb. 1700 (T.C.D., MS N. 3. 2a, pp. 127-8).
[2] *Commons' jn.*, xiii. 65-6. The report is discussed in Appendix A (pp. 174-6, below).

commons ordered the report of the four majority commissioners to be printed together with the commons' address of 1693 (in which William had been asked not to make any grant of the Irish forfeitures until parliament had had an opportunity of discussing the subject) and 'his majesty's gracious reply'.[1] The report attracted wide attention and appeared in several editions, some published in London and some in Dublin. It has been used as the principal source for all accounts of the Williamite confiscation and the statistics which it contains have been reproduced by many historians, with some very misleading results. At the same time the report has been subjected to much criticism, and the consensus of opinion is that its authors were guilty of a considerable degree of prejudice and exaggeration. The principal criticisms which have been brought against the report are, firstly, that it was improper to have referred to the private estate, which was not within the commissioners' terms of reference, and, secondly, that the commissioners grossly overestimated the value both of the forfeitures proper and of the private estate.

The question of the private estate was the chief subject of controversy both among the commissioners themselves and in the subsequent commons debate. The majority commissioners frankly admitted that the private estate did not strictly fall within their terms of reference. The final paragraph of the report introduces the subject in the following words: 'we shall now conclude by laying before your honours another grant of a considerable value, which we are apprehensive does not fall within the letter of our inquiry. But since the benefit of some forfeited leases or holdings are therein granted we chose rather to lay the whole grant before you than be thought deficient in executing any part of our duty or what might be expected from us.'[2] This argument was not very convincing and Drogheda had lost no time in rebutting it. 'Some of the commissioners say that they have a power to return the value of that grant, Mrs. Villiers having granted to her all forfeited leases on that estate. But that does not empower them to make any return of the whole.'[3]

Oddly enough, contemporary historians make little comment on the question. Burnet, with episcopal discretion, does not refer to the grant at all. Others simply repeat the figures given in the report. Possibly the subject was thought dangerous for a commentator. Macaulay discussed the topic with his customary eloquence. He admitted that it was 'an

---

[1] *Commons' jn.*, xiii. 318-19.
[2] *Commissioners' report*, p. 28.
[3] Drogheda to Vernon, 25 Oct. 1699 (*Cal. S.P. dom., 1699-1700*, p. 275).

unfortunate grant, which could not be brought to light without much mischief and much scandal'. But his censure was chiefly directed against the majority commissioners for 'usurping functions which did not belong to them for the purpose of insulting the sovereign and exasperating the nation'. His argument was based on the supposition that the private estate was part of the 'old hereditary domain of the crown', and that the commissioners had as little to do with it as with 'the seignorage on tin in the duchy of Cornwall or with the church patronage in the duchy of Lancaster'.[1] He evidently did not realize that the estate was a personal grant made to James under the Act of Settlement. The same argument has been used by Turberville: 'it should be noticed that the reference to the countess of Orkney's estate was a piece of gross effrontery, as her lands were part of the crown property'.[2] As we have already seen, William's title to the estate was by no means clear.

It would probably be fair to say that the grant was not within the strict letter, but was within the spirit, of the mandate given to the inquiry commissioners. The private estate, no less than the forfeitures proper, became available for grant as a result of the successful termination of the Irish war; it must have seemed pedantic to exclude it from consideration on the ground that James had not forfeited it by attainder. William, with reluctance, had agreed to a bill being brought before the Irish parliament for the confirmation of the grant to Elizabeth Villiers.[3] Although the bill was in fact not introduced, this was an admission that the grant was not of ordinary crown property. It had been the subject of much criticism, in which Drogheda himself had taken a leading part. In area it was next to the grants made to Woodstock and Albemarle; in value it was the largest grant of all.

There is no doubt that the commissioners considerably overestimated the value both of the forfeited estates proper and of the private estate. Their valuations were to be put to the test when the estates subsequently came under the trustees. After adjustment has been made for the estates excepted in the Act of Resumption and for those taken out of the trust by subsequent acts, the figures for rents, and still more for sales, contained in the trustees' records fall far below the estimates made by the inquiry commissioners. This may partly have been due to other factors, such as the restrictions imposed on the Irish wool trade. Political uncertainty about the security of title obtainable for the forfeited estates of Jacobites, and the concerted hostility of Irish Protestants to the resump-

[1] Macaulay, *History of England*, iii. 716.
[2] Turberville, *The house of lords in the reign of William III*, p. 203.
[3] *H.M.C., Buccleuch MSS*, ii. 187.

tion proceedings must have also depressed the rents and sale-prices of the forfeited estates. But when all these considerations are allowed for it seems certain that the commissioners' estimate erred on the side of optimism. For instance, their calculations were based on the full value of certain estates in which the forfeiting proprietor had only a life interest. The estate of Dudley Bagenal of Dunleckny was one of these, although the commissioners themselves had noted that the property was settled on the son after his father's death. In several cases estates recorded as freehold property turned out to be leasehold. The encumbrances were also considerably greater than the commissioners had allowed for. Comparison of the commissioners' estimates with the amounts realized by the trustees is complicated by the fact that some estates were excluded from the Act of Resumption; on the other hand there were some additional forfeitures, such as the estate of John Grace of Courtstown, over which the trustees succeeded in establishing a claim. The comparative figures may be summarized as follows:[1]

	Estimated by commissioners £	Realized by trustees £
Forfeited estates	1,281,173	505,541
Private estate	266,619	218,960[2]
Total	1,547,792	724,501[3]

The commissioners were sensible that their valuation was open to criticism. In their report they observed that the forfeited estates were computed according to present values, 'were they now to be set without any regard to beneficial leases made before the forfeitures'. They argued, however, that much of the land classed as unprofitable in the surveys had become profitable, 'and many of them as good as any lands in the kingdom'. Such lands, they thought, would go far to make up the deficiency caused by the low rates of existing leases. The balance was to be made up by taking into account the value of woods and of lands liable to forfeiture but not recorded. In referring to the private estate

[1] The commissioners' figures were given in Irish currency, while those of the trustees were in sterling. For purposes of comparison the commissioners' figures have been converted to sterling. The Irish pound in 1699 was worth 16s. 8d. sterling (Report of public accounts commissioners, 11 Mar. 1704, N.L.I., MS 1541). In Irish currency the proceeds of the forfeitures proper (as distinct from the private estate) were estimated at £1,537,407.

[2] The figure for the sale proceeds of the private estate is derived from the book of sales of the private estate (Annesley MSS, xxxii *ad finem*).

[3] The figure is taken from the trustees' final report (*H.L. MSS*, n.s., v. 246).

they observed that almost all the old leases would have terminated by 1701.[1]

Their expectations were by no means realized, and there is much force in Burnet's comment: 'they did readily believe everything that was offered to them that tended to inflame the report, as they suppressed all that was laid before them that contradicted their design of representing the value of the grants as very high, and of showing how undeserving those were who had obtained them; there was so much truth in the main of this that no complaint of their proceedings could be hearkened to; and indeed all the methods that were taken to disgrace the report had quite the contrary effect; they represented the confiscated estates to be such that out of the sale of them a million and a half might be raised; so this specious proposition for discharging so great a part of the public debt took with the house; the hatred into which the favourites were fallen, among whom and their creatures the grants were chiefly distributed, made the motion go the quicker. All the opposition that was made in the whole progress of the matter was looked on as courting the men in favour.'[2]

It is remarkable that Burnet, as a supporter of William, should have so frankly admitted the indefensibility of the grants. He was clearly right in emphasizing the political importance of the high valuation placed on the forfeited estates. The report gave the impression that a million and a half pounds could be realized by the sale of the forfeitures proper, apart from the private estate. As previous estimates had been of the order of a million pounds, the result of the commissioners' investigations was highly satisfactory to the majority party in the commons and greatly strengthened the demand for the resumption of the royal grants. If the commons had been informed that the net proceeds of the forfeitures proper would amount to little more than £500,000, the case for resumption would have appeared a great deal weaker.

[1] *Commrs' report*, pp. 22 and 28.
[2] Burnet, *History of his own time*, iv. 426,

10

THE ACT OF RESUMPTION, 1700

The bill for the resumption of the forfeitures raised a first-class constitutional issue. It made a direct attack on William's policy, and challenged both his conception of the royal prerogative and his personal choice of the principal grantees. The attack was made by a majority in the commons and resisted by the ministry with the support of a majority in the lords. The king was known to be actively engaged in opposition to the measure.

On the second reading a motion was proposed that the commons should consider in committee a clause reserving to the king a proportion of the forfeitures. Vernon observed that the king was 'strangely bent upon having a clause for reserving one-third to his own disposal, though everybody that would make any judgment of the house told him what would be the consequences of it'. Vernon himself proposed the motion and was supported by Coningsby and others, but they were 'pretty well rapped over the fingers'.[1] Harley later recorded that William offered to dismiss Somers in return for £200,000 worth of the Irish forfeitures. 'This was offered and pressed very much, but I would never enter into that negotiation or give any encouragement to it.'[2]

The clause was negatived without a division, and the house resolved that the grants of forfeited and other estates in Ireland had been 'the occasion of contracting great debts upon the nation and bringing heavy taxes upon the people', and that the passing of the grants was 'highly reflecting on the king's honour'. An address embodying these resolutions was presented to the king.[3] The commons did not relish his reply that he was not only led by inclination but thought himself obliged in

[1] Vernon to Shrewsbury, 18 Jan. 1700 (*Letters illustrative of the reign of William III*, ii. 411-12).

[2] Harley, Autobiographical fragment, 25 Sept. 1707 (*H.M.C.*, *rep. 15*, app. iv. 452).

[3] *Commons' jn.*, xiii. 130.

justice to reward those who had served him well, and particularly in the reduction of Ireland, out of the estates forfeited to him by the rebellion there.[1]

Once again the device of tacking was employed to force the measure through the lords; with this object the bill was coupled with a bill for the taxation of land in England.[2] The lords sent the bill back with certain amendments, including a provision that the disposal of the lands should be effected by royal letters patent. The amendments were summarily rejected by the commons on the ground that the lords had no right to alter a money bill.[3] The lords at first refused to yield. They admitted that resumption was necessary on account of the large debt due to the army and other creditors. They could not, however, consent to the lands being disposed of by the commons, as it was the undoubted right of the crown to be the 'disposer of all bounties'.[4]

It is of interest that the lords should have admitted the principle of resumption and confined their challenge to comparatively minor points. This must largely have been due to Davenant's *Discourse upon grants and resumptions*, which had made a well-timed appearance in October 1699, just before the inquiry commissioners presented their report. It was an able statement, fortified with many historical precedents, which asserted the traditional right of the English people to resume grants made to royal favourites, particularly when the favourites were foreigners. Its theme was immediately evident in the title, 'A discourse upon grants and resumptions, showing how our ancestors have proceeded with such ministers as have procured to themselves grants of the crown revenue, and that the forfeited estates ought to be applied towards the payment of the public debts'. The grants made to Piers Gaveston by Edward II were cited as a parallel to those made by William to Bentinck and Keppel. Contemporary commentators made little attempt to defend William's grants, and those who opposed the resumption bill concentrated their attention on the exaggerations of the inquiry commissioners and on secondary features of the bill. Even Burnet, who was always a staunch Williamite, conceded that some of the grants had 'not been made on good and reasonable considerations, so that they could hardly be excused, much less justified'.[5]

A constitutional crisis was narrowly avoided. The situation was saved by the more prudent of William's supporters in the lords, who realized

[1] Ibid., xiii. 228.
[2] Ibid., xiii. 164.
[3] Ibid., xiii. 318.
[4] Ibid., xiii. 320.
[5] Burnet, *History of his own time*, iv. 430.

the dangers of a position in which king and lords were combined in opposition to a money bill sent up by the commons. Burnet gives an interesting account of his own attitude: 'many in the house of lords that in all other things were very firm to the king were for passing this bill notwithstanding the king's earnestness against it, since they apprehended the ill consequences that were like to follow if it were lost. I was one of these and the king was much displeased with me for it. I said I would venture his displeasure rather than please him in what I feared would be the ruin of his government.'[1] Finally Lord Jersey, who was Elizabeth Villiers's brother, is said to have prevailed upon William to tell his friends in the lords to give up their opposition to the bill.[2] William accordingly sent a private message by Albemarle, as a result of which the lords passed the bill without amendment.[3]

A graphic account of the crisis was given by Lord Dartmouth in his commentary on Burnet's history. 'While the bill was in suspense the whole city of London was in an uproar. Westminster was so thronged that it was with great difficulty anybody got into either house. I heard the king was come to the Cockpit and had sent for the crown with a resolution to dissolve us immediately, which I communicated to the earl of Shaftesbury who ran full speed with it to the house of commons, upon which they adjourned in great haste. Next morning the earls of Jersey and Albemarle told me that the king was convinced of the danger in rejecting the bill; but their present difficulty was that they could not prevail with their people either to join us or keep away.'[4] The problem of liquidating the opposition was finally solved: 'the archbishop backing out his brethren and the other lords dropping out by degrees was full as comical a scene as that the night before had been tragical'[5].

Evelyn noted in his diary that the dispute had turned out 'to the great triumph of the commons and country party but high regret of the court and those to whom the king had given large grants in Ireland'.[6] Burnet observed that the king 'became sullen upon all this and upon the many incivilities that are apt to fall in upon debates of this nature'.[7] The proceedings were in the highest degree mortifying to William, who did not trouble to conceal the fact. He wrote to Lord Galway, one of the deprived grantees: 'you may judge what vexation all their extraordinary

[1] Burnet, *History of his own time*, iv. 429.
[2] Ibid., iv. 428.
[3] *Private and original correspondence of . . . Shrewsbury*, p. 609.
[4] Burnet, *History of his own time*, iv. 428.
[5] Ralph, *History of England*, ii. 853.
[6] Evelyn, *Diary*, iii. 151.
[7] Burnet, *History of his own time*, iv. 431.

proceedings gave me and, I assure you, your being deprived of what I gave you with such pleasure was not the least of my griefs ... There have been so many intrigues this last session that without having been on the spot and well-informed of everything it cannot be conceived.'[1] William was, however, sufficiently master of his feelings to receive the newly appointed trustees and to wish them a good voyage to Ireland.[2]

The contest which took place over the resumption bill provided material for the first of Swift's political writings. *A discourse of the contests and dissensions between the nobles and the commons in Athens and Rome, with the consequences this had upon both those states* appeared in 1701. It is an elaborate attempt to show that the classical pattern of government consisted in a due balance of power between king, lords and commons: 'some reflections upon the late public proceedings among us and that variety of factions, into which we are still so intricately engaged, gave occasion to this discourse'[3]. Swift, who was at this time still a whig, concluded that the commons had overreached themselves and that the majority had been 'authors of a new and wonderful thing in England, which is for a house of commons to lose the universal favour of the members they represent'. He referred to 'the aversion of the people against the late proceedings of the commons' and to a general feeling that William had been hardly used.[4] Such sentiments seem to have been more prevalent among Irish Protestants than in England.

The preamble of the Act of Resumption referred to the Irish Jacobites as rebels and traitors, who 'by the blessing of God and the very great expense of your majesty's English subjects' had been reduced to their due obedience to the crown of England; it declared that it was highly reasonable to apply the estates of such rebels and traitors to the relief of the English taxpayer. The act vested in trustees the estates of all those convicted or attainted of high treason between 13 February 1689, when William and Mary began their reign, and the last day of Trinity term 1701, thus leaving a specified period for the trial of the still unconvicted Jacobites to whom the inquiry commissioners had referred in their report. The time-limit was fixed with the benevolent object that the Jacobites might 'be in some reasonable time quieted from the terror and apprehension of prosecution and that industry may be encouraged in Ireland'.[5] As we have already seen, the commissioners' expectations of further convictions and forfeitures were to be disappointed.

---

[1] William to Galway, 11 May 1700 (Tindal, *History of England*, iii. 401-2).
[2] Luttrell, *Brief historical relation*, iv. 640.
[3] Swift, *Prose works*, i. 262.
[4] Ibid., i. 269.
[5] 11 and 12 Will. III, c. 2, ss. 1, 10.

H   113

To the estates of those actually convicted were added those of all persons found by inquisition to have died or been killed in rebellion since 13 February 1689. The outlawry of the dead was a controversial matter which had frequently been debated. The lords made it one of their objections to the resumption bill, and expressed the view that they could not 'apprehend that by any law of this land or by any rule of reason or justice any person ought to be outlawed after death, since it is condemning a man unheard'.[1] The principle, however, had already received legal sanction in the Irish act of 1697, which provided that Catholics who within two years were found by inquisition to have died in rebellion should be deemed convicted and attainted of high treason.[2] A number of the estates actually forfeited belonged to those who had died 'in rebellion'. The act also specifically vested in the trustees all the estates and interests in Ireland of which James was seized at the time of his accession. This disposed of the contention that the private estate formed no part of the forfeitures. All grants both of the forfeitures and of James's estate were declared null and void.[3]

Provision was made to preserve the rights of persons whose interest in forfeited land was prior to 13 February 1689. Such persons were to enter claims before 10 August 1700; the trustees were to hear and decide the claims by March 1701.[4] These claims, which took up much of the trustees' time, included settlements made for the benefit of wives and children. An appreciable number of such claims were allowed and the Kenmare and several other estates were in this way saved from outright forfeiture. The mere fact that an estate was entailed was to be no bar, if there was not a specific deed of settlement in favour of the claimant; such estates were declared to be vested in the trustees to be absolutely sold and disposed of.[5]

It was specifically provided that nothing in the act should prejudice the interest of any person who had been adjudged as entitled to the articles of Limerick or Galway: 'for composing the minds' of all those concerned every such adjudication was confirmed.[6]

The Act of Resumption did not contain any provision particularly directed against those Catholics who were still in possession of their estates. It did, however, result in a fresh scrutiny of Irish land by the trustees, who were given wide powers of investigation and whose own

[1] *Commons' jn.*, xiii. 320.
[2] 9 Will. III, c. 5, s. 2.
[3] 11 and 12 Will. III, c. 2, s. 2.
[4] Ibid., ss 4, 11.
[5] Ibid., s. 1.
[6] Ibid., s. 5.

reputation largely depended on the financial results of their administration. As they interpreted the act to cover all land to which any outlawed person had a claim at any time since 1689, they were able to forfeit a certain number of additional estates. Thus John Grace of Courtstown, who was adjudged within the articles of Limerick and remained in possession of the family estate until 1701, was deprived of it on the ground that his elder brother Oliver, who was outlawed, had survived their father's death by nine days. Although Oliver was in France and never took possession of the estate, his title for those nine days was regarded as sufficient warrant for the trustees to take over the property.[1] Even when claims were successful, those concerned were put to considerable trouble and expense in prosecuting them before the trustees, who in many instances took several hearings over a single claim.

The amounts realized by the trustees were to be appropriated to 'officers' arrears, debts for transport service and clothing, debts and interest on tallies, orders, tickets and exchange bills and no other use whatever', except for payments made to the inquiry commissioners and for the trustees' own expenses; £1,000 each was granted to the four majority commissioners and to Drogheda for the great services performed by them. With a pointed variation of expression Brewster and Levinge were awarded £500 each in consideration of their expenses.[2] The commons appear to have thought it prudent not to exasperate the lords unnecessarily by cutting Drogheda's remuneration.

A limited number of William's grants were maintained. They included those made to Leslie, Baker and Roche as rewards for exploits in the Irish war, and also the grants made to Prendergast and de la Rue 'for timely discovery of a wicked and traitorous conspiracy to assassinate his majesty's sacred person'.[3] The grant given to Sir Charles Porter's children was saved by a small majority.[4] Surprisingly enough, saving clauses were passed in favour of the dependants of some leading Jacobites. The beneficiaries included the wives and children of Lord Kenmare and Dudley Bagenal and the daughters of the first Lord Kenmare. Provision was made to secure a jointure to Lady Slane 'by virtue of marriage articles which could not be executed by settlement as Lord Slane was a minor'.[5]

The act contained several clauses in favour of the established church, whose interests were closely watched during the progress of the bill by

[1] Grace, *Memoirs of the family of Grace*, p. 44.
[2] 11 and 12 Will. III, c. 2, ss 41-2.
[3] Ibid., ss 55-6.
[4] Ibid., s. 58; *Commons' jn.*, xiii. 293.
[5] 11 and 12 Will. III, c. 2, ss 53-4, 60.

two of the Irish bishops.[1] The trustees were to convey all forfeited rectories and tithes to the bishop's nominees for the rebuilding and repairing of churches and for the augmentation of small livings.[2] A very considerable number of 'impropriations'—church property which had passed into lay hands—had belonged to forfeiting persons and were now to be disposed of under the Act of Resumption. Their restoration to the church was an object for which Bishop King had been working. His legal advisers, Langford and Annesley, seem to have helped in getting this provision included in the bill. In a letter to King, Langford wrote: 'Annesley and I will do whatever lies in our power to get the forfeited impropriations restored to the church again. If my lord of Canterbury and other bishops were writ to about this matter it might contribute very much to obtaining it.'[3]

Less success attended another cause in which King was interested, that of Derry. In August 1689, just after the raising of the siege, William had written to the governors of Derry, assuring the officers, soldiers and inhabitants that he would take a fitting opportunity to recompense their sufferings and services.[4] But nothing was done except to make an individual grant to governor Baker's son. The citizens accordingly petitioned parliament for redress, representing that half the houses in Derry were destroyed during the siege and that their losses amounted to £30,000.[5] King was a strong supporter of their case and represented it to Southwell. 'If merit be considered or hearty goodwill well rewarded, the volunteers that defended this town and Inniskilling deserve their pay as well as any of the established troops.'[6] The first of the amendments offered to the resumption bill provided that payment should be made to the inhabitants of Derry. But the commons were not in a conciliatory mood and rejected this amendment as well as a number of other amendments in favour of individual claimants.[7]

Among the rejected amendments was a clause saving the articles of Waterford, Bophin, Sligo and Drogheda, which had surrendered on terms in the course of the war.[8] There is considerable obscurity about the conditions on which Waterford capitulated. Story's version is that, on 22 July 1690, William called on Waterford to surrender, offering

[1] E. Burridge to King, 23 Mar. 1700 (T.C.D., King MSS).
[2] 11 and 12 Will. III, c. 2, s. 47.
[3] Langford to King, 16 Nov. 1699 (T.C.D., King MSS).
[4] *A short view of the faithful services performed by his majesty's forces who defended the city of Londonderry.*
[5] *The Derry complaint.*
[6] King to Southwell, 14 Nov. 1699 (T.C.D., MS N. 3. 2a, p. 90).
[7] *Commons' jn.*, xiii. 291.
[8] Ibid., p. 292.

the same terms as he had given to Drogheda, namely a safe-conduct for
the garrison to the nearest town held by the Irish. The Waterford garrison found these conditions unacceptable and 'proposed some of their
own, which were that they might enjoy their estates, the liberty of their
religion and safe convoy to the next garrison'. William refused and
brought forward his heavy cannon, whereupon the garrison surrendered
on the Drogheda terms.[1] According to the official version, given in the
London Gazette, the terms which William offered to Waterford were
that the garrison should march out quietly and that the citizens should
enjoy their houses, goods and trade. In reply to this offer the garrison
made 'several extravagant demands, which would have been answered
with a sudden attack but that his majesty had compassion on the
Protestant families'. Finally, the garrison accepted the Drogheda terms
with the additional privilege of keeping their arms; some few officers
remained behind and asked for protection.[2] In March 1692 Thomas
Wyse, John Porter and other Catholic inhabitants of Waterford sent a
petition to William, representing that under the articles granted to the
town they were not to be deprived of their property, which included
their estates and businesses; they had not had the benefit of the articles
as their lands and businesses had been taken from them. They asked
that the Waterford articles should be confirmed under the great seal of
England.[3] The petition was referred to the lord lieutenant and a year
later, in March 1693, a warrant was issued which directed that the third
article of Waterford should be confirmed; the lord lieutenant was informed that the property referred to in that article included both real
and personal estate.[4] The lord lieutenant replied that it had been understood that the articles of Waterford did not apply to real estate, and
that several estates belonging to Waterford citizens had been seized. He
quoted Cox as saying that the king had refused to include real estate in
the terms given to Waterford.[5] There is no trace of the order finally
passed, but in the records compiled by the inquiry commissioners in
1699, the estates restored under articles include those of Thomas Wyse
and John Porter with the note that the restorations were under the
articles of Waterford. Neither Wyse nor Porter appears in the outlawry
lists and their estates appear to have been restored to them after informal seizure. They do not seem to have suffered as a result of the
refusal of parliament to provide for the Waterford articles in the resump-

[1] Story, *True and impartial history*, p. 109.
[2] *London Gazette*, 28-31 July 1690.
[3] *Cal. S.P. dom., 1691-2*, p. 180.
[4] Ibid., *1693*, pp. 62 and 81.
[5] Ibid., p. 157.

tion bill. Wyse was mayor of Waterford in 1690; he was the direct ancestor of Sir Thomas Wyse.

Pardons had already been granted to Lord Athenry, Colonel John Kelly of Skryne and Henry Crofton, the only claimants under the articles of Bophin and Sligo. They were therefore unaffected by parliament's refusal to include those articles in the bill. The case of the Drogheda articles is obscure. In 1697 the lords justices reported that the third article of Drogheda provided that the Catholic inhabitants of the town should not be molested in their property, and that they had not so far been deprived of their real estate, although several of them had been outlawed.[1] The inquiry commissioners' records do not show any estates restored under the articles of Drogheda, presumably because the estates in question had not been seized.

The thirteen trustees were chosen by ballot, a process which kept the commons up till six in the morning.[2] Annesley once more headed the poll. All the four majority commissioners figured in the list, which also included James Hooper, who had been secretary of the inquiry commission.[3] Hooper was a barrister of the Middle Temple who had been a manager of the land bank, the tory (and unsuccessful) reply to the Bank of England.[4]

The most distinguished of those appointed was Sir Cyril Wyche, a former president of the Royal Society, who had been secretary to three Irish lords lieutenant, had been an Irish lord justice in 1694–5, and had then been ambassador at Constantinople. He married a niece of Evelyn, who referred to him as a noble and learned gentleman.[5] He functioned in practice as chairman of the trustees. From what we have of his correspondence his colleagues appear to have regarded him with great affection and respect. The trustees were a much more harmonious team than the inquiry commissioners had been.[6] Another member of the Royal Society among the trustees was Sir Henry Sheres. He was distinguished for his work on the Tangier mole, which he both built and

---

[1] *Cal. S. P. dom., 1697*, p. 244.

[2] Luttrell, *Brief historical relation*, iv. 628.

[3] *Commons' jn.*, xiii. 307. The thirteen trustees were: Francis Annesley, John Baggs, John Cary, William Fellowes, James Hamilton (died soon after appointment), Thomas Harrison, James Hooper, John Isham, Henry Langford, Thomas Rawlinson, Sir Henry Sheres, John Trenchard and Sir Cyril Wyche.

[4] *Settlement of the land bank*.

[5] Evelyn, *Diary*, iii. 146.

[6] P.R.O.I. acquired a collection of Wyche's correspondence and official papers in 1930 (*P.R.I. rep. D.K. 57*, p. 7). An agreeable picture of the trustees' daily life is given in the letters sent by John Isham to his brother Sir Justinian, a tory member of the English commons (Isham MSS).

demolished. Pepys found him 'a good ingenious man, but do talk a little too much of his travels'.[1] He was suspected of Jacobite sympathies and was twice under arrest, in 1690 and again in 1696. His most recent assignment had been in connection with Dover harbour, on which he reported to the commons in February 1700, while the resumption bill was still before the house.[2] As an experienced engineer he was put in charge of the survey of a number of the forfeited estates. The only other trustee of any distinction was John Cary, a Bristol merchant who had written a number of essays on different aspects of trade. He had also written a reply to Molyneux's *Case of Ireland's being bound*.

The trust is of interest as a constitutional experiment. It was in effect a parliamentary agency, appointed for the exercise of executive and judicial functions which had hitherto been restricted to persons appointed by the crown. For the purpose of hearing claims the trustees were to be a court of record; they might commit to prison persons who refused to appear before them, and they were empowered to fine officers who did not obey their instructions. They were to manage the estates, collect rents and conduct sales.[3] The commons clearly regarded the trustees as their agents and periodically called on them to submit reports and send representatives to be examined in person on their proceedings. The commons entertained a large number of petitions in respect of the forfeitures and obtained reports on them from the trustees. Many of these petitions were granted by private acts of parliament, the passing of which formed a great part of the business of 1702. The lords appear to have been anxious to show that the trustees were not merely a commons' agency. Representatives of the trustees were more than once summoned to appear before the lords. The appointment of trustees by parliament proved a sterile line of development. Cabinet government was to be a less cumbrous device for securing parliamentary control over executive action.

Each trustee was to be paid £1,500 a year.[4] He was required to take an oath that he would not directly or indirectly take any fee or reward, except as provided by the act, or purchase any of the forfeited estates.[5] The trustees appear to have conducted themselves with reasonable honesty. The only complaint which seems to have been made against them related to the expenses allowed to those trustees who attended

---

[1] Pepys, *Diary*, p. 557.
[2] *Commons' jn.*, xiii. 201.
[3] 11 and 12 Will. III. c. 2, ss. 7, 15, 22, 27.
[4] Ibid., s. 43.
[5] Ibib., s. 7.

sessions of the English parliament.[1] Methuen observed that the trustees were 'entertained extremely great by those who have pretensions before them',[2] but the vigilance of their opponents was unable to produce any serious charge of corruption. After the trust was wound up the commons resolved that the trustees had in all respects discharged their duty with great integrity and fidelity. [3]

[1] Report of public accounts committee, 11 Mar. 1704 (N.L.I., MS 1541).
[2] Methuen to Vernon, 2 Jan. 1701 (*Cal. S.P. dom., 1700-2*, p. 189).
[3] *Commons' jn.*, xiv. 387.

11

THE FORFEITURE TRUSTEES
IN ACTION

The trustees began their task in June 1700. The Act of Resumption prescribed that they should hear all claims to the forfeited estates by 25 March 1701, and complete the sale of the lands by 23 March 1702. In the event the hearing of the claims took considerably longer than was expected, and supplementary legislation had to be passed to extend both these periods. As a result the trust continued to operate for a little over three years. The date finally fixed for the completion of the sales was 24 June 1703, after which the trustees were within forty days to hand over their records to the Irish revenue commissioners.

In the Annesley manuscripts we have first-hand evidence of the day-to-day work of the trustees. There are eleven volumes of minutes of various kinds, which between them cover most of the period during which the trust was in operation. These are supplemented by a number of reports on petitions and claims. There are very elaborate financial records, which include complete rent-rolls and lists of sales. The journal of accounts for the three years runs to 824 pages.[1]

The chief impression created is of the enormous labour involved in administering and selling the forfeited estates, and of the assiduity with which the trustees appear to have conducted their business. All the trustees present in Dublin seem to have attended the meetings, which were held almost daily and began at eight in the morning. In addition, particular functions were alloted to individual trustees as their special responsibility. At the outset directions were given to two of them, Baggs and Fellowes, to draw up a scheme of fees. Annesley and Trenchard were directed to draw up a scheme for taking charge of the estates

---

[1] See descriptive catalogue (*Anal. Hib.*, xvi. 359-64).

and compiling rent-rolls. Cary was to look after discoveries and, as a businessman, to deal with printing and stationery. Sir Henry Sheres, as an engineer, took charge of the survey.[1] A large staff of receivers and collectors for the various counties was appointed in addition to the administrative staff at Chichester House, which was the headquarters of the trust. The trustees made it their business to keep the establishment up to the mark. Thus a minute records that the trustees have observed a want of diligence in several clerks, and order each clerk to get a weekly certificate of his 'worthy performance' from the head of his office and lay it before the board each Saturday morning.[2] Annesley complained to King of the burden which the trust had laid upon him. 'I own ingeniously to your lordship that the last three years of my life have made me fifteen years older than I should otherwise have been.'[3]

There was at first much friction between the trustees and the Dublin government. The latter naturally resented the arrival of an independent set of administrators deriving their powers from an act of parliament which was regarded as an insult to the crown and an unwarranted interference with the rights of property. To begin with, the trustees seem to have adopted a high-handed attitude and to have shown a considerable want of tact. Wyche, an elder statesman who had not been associated with the controversies of the 1699 inquiry, did not come over until the other trustees had been at work for over a month. In his absence a somewhat pugnacious tone seems to have been set by Annesley and Trenchard. One of the first disputes concerned the right of the revenue commissioners to collect quit-rents from the forfeited estates. The style of the trustees' correspondence was decidedly truculent, but eventually the dispute was compromised by Methuen, the chancellor. Methuen himself came into conflict with the trustees, who objected to legal proceedings being taken to 'traverse' inquisitions by which individuals had been found to have died in rebellion: '. . . they came and insisted and argued the point before a great audience, and I gave openly the reasons why I thought the trustees were in the wrong to expect any cessation or stop of the justice and law of Ireland in this matter, and why I neither could nor would comply with them. I am pretty confident that the trustees were so desirous of an occasion to make an attack that they took hold of a very wrong one and gave me a great advantage, as I hear some of the wisest of them do in secret acknowledge.'[4] A sensation was caused

---

[1] Annesley MSS, ii. 8, 10 and 72.
[2] Ibid., iv. 2.
[3] Annesley to King, 12 Sept. 1702 (T.C.D., King MSS).
[4] Methuen to Vernon, 22 June, 7 and 10 July 1700 (*Cal. S.P. dom., 1700-2*, pp. 70-1 and 84-6).

when the trustees committed the under-sheriff of Dublin to custody for contempt of their authority. The under-sheriff applied to the king's bench, which ordered his release. Undeterred the trustees immediately rearrested him, and Methuen again felt called upon to intervene.[1] Finally the under-sheriff apologized to the trustees, who then ordered his discharge.[2]

The trustees made strenuous, and fruitless, efforts to obtain convictions against various persons who had so far escaped outlawry. The inquiry report had referred to the possibility of further forfeitures, and the trustees seem to have been anxious to justify the forecast before the expiry of the period prescribed in the Act of Resumption for treason proceedings. Their hopes were fed by informers, of whom the most notorious was Patrick Hurley. Hurley was an extraordinary adventurer, who had travelled Europe under the style of count of Mountcallan. He held various posts in Ireland under the Jacobite regime, and then went to France, where he was accused of embezzling the funds of Colonel Gordon O'Neill's regiment. Returning to Ireland he soon got into further trouble. When the trustees assumed office he was in custody on a charge of having staged a sham robbery, for which he had put in a claim for £1,500 compensation. He at once wrote to the trustees, offering to prove that Sir Donough O'Brien had taken part in 'the late rebellion'. He charged Sir Donough with having commanded a troop of horse in James's service since February 1689, with having been a sheriff under James and with having sent messages to France after the war suggesting schemes for the invasion of Ireland. Sir Donough, who was a Protestant, had remained in county Clare throughout the war. He had accepted the office of sheriff from James and had raised a troop of twenty men, but his explanation was that his Protestant neighbours had importuned him to do so for the suppression of rapparees. Various correspondents kept him in touch with Hurley's activities. One reported that Hurley was boasting that the trustees had promised him £15,000 if Sir Donough's estate were forfeited. Another wrote that Hurley had brought two witnesses over from France who had laid information against Sir Donough before one of the Dublin judges. The attorney-general advised that Sir Donough should come up to Dublin and justify himself to the government. The lords justices had no liking for these proceedings; Hurley was an unsavoury character, and Sir Donough 'a man of very considerable fortune, interest and figure'. They consulted the privy council, which considered that the law should take its course. Sir Donough came up to Dublin to stand his trial, but the case seems

[1] Same to same, 23 Nov. 1700 (*Cal. S.P. dom., 1700-2*, p. 151).
[2] Annesley MSS, ii. 194.

to have faded out—no doubt because the proceedings were protracted until the end of Trinity term 1701, after which there were to be no more treason proceedings arising from the war. Meanwhile Hurley was tried and convicted for perjury and for conspiring to defraud the Catholics of Clare of the sum which he had claimed as compensation for the alleged robbery.[1]

The trustees pressed for prosecution in a number of other cases, but met with very little response. The lords justices told them that as the object of such prosecutions was not to punish traitors but to produce additional forfeitures the trustees had better issue instructions themselves and pay the cost of the prosecutions.[2] A certain number of cases were brought to trial, which seem to have met with a uniform lack of success. In their first report to parliament the trustees admitted that no value could be put on additional forfeitures. 'Thirty-two persons active in the late rebellion and now resident in France, that were possessed of estates in this kingdom, were lately indicted in the city of Dublin upon the statute of foreign treason, and a grand jury of as equal and indifferent men as could be found were empanelled, and the evidence against most of them, as appeared by the examinations laid before us, was clear and positive; yet they were all acquitted.'[3] Dislike of the trustees seems to have created sympathy for the accused, even among members of the Dublin government.

The disfavour with which the trustees were regarded by Irish Protestants was largely due to the financial consequences which the Act of Resumption had for those Protestants who had bought or leased land from William's grantees. The Protestants had represented their case while the resumption bill was before parliament, and had drawn attention to the considerable sums laid out by 'judges, great men in the law and others encouraged by their example' in buying lands from the grantees. They were confident that the English parliament 'will not resume forfeitures when men of English blood and religion are to suffer so much by it; they will not suffer an inquisition to go into that country which will set every man at variance with his neighbour and turn many thousands of Protestant families out of their habitations'.[4]

---

[1] *The trial and conviction of Patrick Hurley.* The case against Sir Donough O'Brien is summarised in the lords justices' letter to Vernon, 7 Dec. 1700 (*Cal. S.P. dom., 1700-2*, p. 159). There are a number of letters on the subject in Lord Inchiquin's possession (N.L.I., Report on Inchiquin papers).

[2] Methuen to Vernon, 4 Aug. 1700 (*Cal. S.P. dom., 1700-2*, pp. 102-3).

[3] *H.L. MSS*, n.s., iv. 208.

[4] *The case of the forfeitures in Ireland fairly stated, with the reasons that induced the Protestants there to purchase them.*

This appeal met with a qualified response. A clause was included in the bill providing that 'whereas some may have unwarily purchased from or under several grantees or otherwise, which practice ought not to be countenanced, yet that they may have some relief any consideration unpaid is released and all securities for payment discharged'. In addition, £21,000 was allotted as compensation to be divided proportionately among purchasers who should prove before 10 August 1700 that they had made actual payments to the grantees. Another clause enjoined the grantees to repay the money they had received and declared that the purchasers might take legal action to recover the amount.[1]

When the claims were lodged it was found that about a hundred purchasers had between them paid nearly £60,000 to Albemarle, Athlone, Romney and some other grantees. The purchasers included many of the leading Protestants, among them Lord Chief Justice Pyne, Baron Donnellan and Alan Broderick, the solicitor-general. The largest purchaser was William Conolly, later speaker of the Irish commons. Other well-known figures included Bartholomew Van Homrigh, Vanessa's father, and Dr. Thomas Molyneux, brother of the more distinguished William. As a group they were known as the Protestant purchasers, although they actually included two Catholics, Walter Delamare and Mark Baggot.[2]

The Protestant purchasers regarded £21,000 as very poor compensation for an investment of £60,000; they do not seem to have thought much of their chances of recovering the balance from the grantees. In any case they did not wish to lose the lands which they had secured at advantageous prices and on which they claimed that they had already spent considerable sums for improvements. Accordingly they began an agitation, in which the leading part was taken by Conolly. A circular letter signed by Conolly and forty-two others, including Lords Abercorn, Inchiquin and Meath, was sent to the nobility and gentry of each county, asking them to submit petitions to the king against the Act of Resumption. Enclosed with each letter was a form of address to the king from his 'loyal and faithful subjects the Protestants of Ireland, lying under such oppressions by means of the late Act of Resumption and of the execution thereof' that they apprehended the ruin of all the Protestants of Ireland. The burden of their complaint was that the Catholics were the only beneficiaries of the act, and that the purchases and improvements made by the Protestants were lost. The addresses were to be signed and returned to Conolly or to his colleague, Marmaduke Coghill.[3]

[1] 11 and 12 Will. III, c. 2, ss. 31, 32, 34.
[2] *Commons' jn.*, xiii. 393-5.
[3] B.M., Eg. MS 917, f. 179.

THE FORFEITURE TRUSTEES IN ACTION

The national remonstrance, as it was called, seems to have received limited support. The general run of Protestants had no wish to fall foul of the English commons, who were certain to resent an appeal to the king against an act which had notoriously been passed by parliament in defiance of court opposition. The dean of Derry wrote to his bishop that the grand jury of both city and county had refused to support the address.[1] Southwell expressed relief that King and his fellow-bishops had taken no part in the address, which was likely to meet with a hostile reception in England.[2] A contemporary pamphlet set out in parallel columns the address actually presented and a burlesque upon it. The latter took the form of a representation to the commons, in which it was asserted that the chief claim of those who had bought from the grantees at three or four years' purchase was that they were Protestants and had acted 'agreeable to the known and established practice of purchasers in the kingdom, which is to regard the bargain more than the title'.[3]

The most effective criticism of the address was made in a pamphlet, of which the argument is apparent in the title—*A letter from a soldier to the commons of England occasioned by an address now carrying on by the Protestants in Ireland in order to take away the fund appropriated for the payment of the arrears of the army.* This pamphlet has a curious paragraph entitled 'Account of Prince Conolly': 'he is one whom fortune in a frolicsome mood has raised from the lowest of the people to make him equal in estate with the peers of the realm. When his majesty obtained his glorious victory at the Boyne, this man could not reckon so many pounds of his own as he does thousands now. His yearly expenses have from that time exceeded his visible acquisitions; his manner of living was so profuse that he got followers and was called Prince Conolly— The discreet and upright gazed at this glittering meteor and admired from what undiscovered mine he had raised so much riches. But now the mystic knot is untied; the commissioners for inquiry into the forfeitures opened the scene and the trustees set him in a true light.'

Conolly's rise from obscurity has always been a puzzle. It cannot be ascribed only to his trafficking in the forfeited estates, although he certainly made a great deal of money out of them. He was sufficiently prominent by 1689 to be included in the Jacobite Act of Attainder. We next hear of him in 1691, when he is referred to as agent for the mayor, commonalty and citizens of Londonderry in connection with a lease of

[1] Dean Bolton to King, 25 Jan. 1702 (T.C.D., King MSS).
[2] Southwell to King, 12 Feb. 1702 (ibid.).
[3] *The several addresses of some Irish folks to the king and the house of commons.*

126

THE FORFEITURE TRUSTEES IN ACTION

Lord Antrim's forfeited estate.[1] In 1692 he was a member of the Irish commons for Donegal borough. In that year he also appears as agent for the farming of Sir Patrick Trant's forfeited estate; he complained that as a result of prejudice he was forced to bid unnecessarily high for it.[2] The report of the inquiry commissioners refers to him as having gone into partnership with Thomas Broderick; between them they 'took vast quantities of lands and in great measure governed the cants (few daring to bid against them); they acted in partnership from 1695 and let afterwards to under-tenants at greater rents'.[3] Conolly also became agent to Albemarle and admitted taking money for himself from purchasers of Albemarle's grants.[4] On his own account he bought between eight and nine thousand acres from Albemarle, for which he claimed to have paid £3,000. It was thus greatly to his interest to get the Act of Resumption modified in favour of the Protestant purchasers. He was also on bad terms with the trustees who had made strenuous, but unsuccessful, efforts to prove that he had abetted a fraudulent claim.[5]

When William received the addresses he passed most of them on to the commons, who were highly indignant and sent for Lord Abercorn as one of the most conspicuous supporters of the remonstrance. Abercorn assured the house that he would be very ready to give an account of any paper he had signed if his signature were pointed out to him. As the king had astutely withheld the copy which Abercorn had signed, the commons could only dismiss him and proceed to a general censure of the addresses and their signatories: 'what stuck very much in their stomachs was that the addresses were made to the king and not to themselves'[6].

Nevertheless the agitation was not without results. A further act was passed which allowed the purchasers to buy the lands from the trustees at thirteen times the annual rent and, in addition to their share of the £21,000 previously allotted, gave them credit for one-third of what they had paid to the grantees. This in effect credited them with two-thirds of their outlay, but in several cases their original bargains had been so favourable that they still had very considerable sums to pay to the trustees.[7]

The claims of those Protestants who had taken leases from the gran-

---

[1] *Cal. S.P. dom., 1690-1*, p. 497.
[2] P.R.O.I., Wyche papers, petition book, p. 26.
[3] *Commrs' report*, p. 26.
[4] Annesley MSS, iv. 28; xxiii. 134.
[5] Ibid., iv. 23-59.
[6] Bishop of Clogher to King, 17 Feb. 1702 (T.C.D., King MSS).
[7] 1 Anne, c. 26.

127

tees were met by an act which allowed them compensation for expenditure incurred on 'real and lasting improvements'.[1] The lessees of the private estate were also allowed compensation for the fines which they had paid to Lady Orkney for the renewal of their leases.[2] This legislation, which was passed in the spring of 1702, put an end to the open campaign of the Irish Protestants against the Act of Resumption. Their hostility continued, and some months later the trustees complained that the notion was 'industriously spread about' in Ireland that the adjudications of the trustees and the titles of land sold by them were subject to re-examination by the Irish courts.[3]

On several occasions representatives of the trustees were required to appear before the English parliament and render an account of their proceedings. They were also asked to report on numerous petitions submitted by persons who were aggrieved by the Act of Resumption or by the proceedings of the trustees. Following on the trustees' reports no less than forty private acts were passed for the relief of such petitioners.[4] Most of the acts contained a provision that the lands concerned should be sold only to Protestants and restricted the right of Catholics to inherit them. Almost all the private acts provided that impropriate tithes should not be restored with the rest of the property, but be vested in the bishop for church purposes. This provision represented a substantial gain to the established church at the expense of the former owners. Seventeen of the acts contained clauses in favour of Catholics.

Some of these were in favour of persons adjudged within the articles of Limerick who had been deprived of their lands on the ground that the title had vested in a forfeiting person at some period since February 1689. A case of this kind was that of Nugent of Donore. At the beginning of the war the entailed estate of Donore was held by James Nugent, who died in 1690, and was outlawed after his death, when the property was already in the possession of his brother Thomas. Both Thomas and Thomas's son, Edward, were adjudged within the articles of Limerick and successively held the estate until 1700, when the trustees seized it on the ground that James had been outlawed. Edward represented to the commons that, had it not been for the Act of Resumption, he would have had a good title to the estate by virtue of the articles of Limerick, and that the trustees' interpretation of the act amounted to a breach of the articles. The private act passed in his favour restored the estate, but

[1] 1 Anne, c. 58 (private act).
[2] 1 Anne, c. 66 (private act).
[3] *Commons' jn.*, xiv. 64.
[4] The English statute book gives the bare titles of the acts. The full text is given in the Annesley MSS, xxii.

contained the usual proviso restricting its inheritance by a Catholic. A clause provided that nothing in the act should be construed to compel Edward Nugent himself to take the oaths or subscribe the declaration, or to hinder him from enjoying the land by reason of not doing so. He himself might remain a Catholic landlord, but his heir (who was not born until after the act was passed) was required to conform or lose the estate.[1] The convert rolls show that the heir duly conformed in 1734.

A similar case was that of Eustace of Yeomanstown. When the war ended this family consisted of three brothers, Maurice, Thomas and James. Maurice was in France, but was one of four officers 'beyond the seas' who were permitted by the fourth article of Limerick to have the benefit of the articles if they returned to Ireland within eight months. Maurice Eustace took advantage of the provision, recovered his estate and remained in possession of it until 1697, when he died without issue. Thomas, the second brother, who was outlawed and not included in the articles, died in 1692. James, the youngest brother, who was included in the articles, succeeded to the estate and remained in possession until 1700, when the trustees seized it on the ground that an interest in the entailed estate had been vested in the outlawed Thomas. An act was passed, which restored the estate to James on the usual conditions.[2]

Henry Luttrell represented that the king's title to Luttrellstown had ceased on Simon's death in 1698. Henry himself had been included in the articles of Limerick and, apart from Ginkel's promise to him and William's grant of the estate, became entitled to it when Simon died issueless. Under the provisions of the Act of Resumption, William's grant was set aside and the trustees asserted their right to the estate; Henry was advised that he must make out a claim under a deed of settlement. He lodged a claim, but rather than 'subject the same to any nice or strict construction' which the trustees might place upon the wording of the act he asked parliament to legislate in his favour. He referred to his great sufferings in the Irish army, incurred because he 'never was thought a friend or promoter of the French interest but of the English interest'. He also stated that he had prevailed on 8,000 of the Irish not to go to France after the surrender of Limerick, and that he himself had since attended William on every campaign in Flanders at his own expense.[3] A private act was passed in his favour, which contained the usual clauses restricting inheritance by a Catholic and excluding the

---

[1] Annesley MSS, xx. 107; xxii. 197. The act is 1 Anne, c. 52.
[2] Annesley MSS, xx. 199 and xxii. 98. The act is 1 Anne, c. 57.
[3] Annesley MSS, xx. 47. Another copy of the petition is in Bodl. Rawl. MS, A. 253 (*Anal. Hib.*, i. 79).

impropriate tithes.[1] Henry Luttrell remained a Catholic, but his heir conformed to the established church.

Lawrence Fitzgerald of Cloninge, county Kildare, had submitted on the terms of the proclamation of 7 July 1691, but had nevertheless forfeited his estate. John Mapas of Rochestown was outlawed at the age of ten for high treason supposed to have been committed when he was seven. A private act was passed permitting both these outlawries to be reversed. In these particular cases there was no bar against inheritance by Catholics.[2] The same act contained a provision in favour of Thomas Plunkett of Portmarnock. His elder brother William had died in March 1691, in his twentieth year. William had with reluctance become a member of the militia under the Jacobite regime, and on that account had been indicted of high treason in the autumn of 1690. After his death the case came up and he was outlawed for non-appearance. The estate was accordingly seized and granted away. Thomas, the younger brother, who had escaped outlawry, compounded with the grantee and obtained possession of the property, which he retained until the arrival of the trustees.[3] The clause in Thomas's favour contained the usual restriction on inheritance by a Catholic. The restriction, however, appears not to have been enforced, as in 1778 the name of Thomas Plunkett of Portmarnock occurs in a list of Catholic noblemen and gentlemen to whom the Catholic Committee resolved to send letters.[4]

Lords Cahir, Carlingford and Kingston, who had been pardoned and whose outlawries had been reversed in the Dublin court, were subsequently discovered to have also been outlawed in the palatinate court of Tipperary. That court had made no return of its outlawries to the inquiry commissioners in 1699, and neither they nor the outlawed persons seem to have known of the proceedings. When the trustees discovered them they laid claim to the estates. An act was passed which permitted the reversals of these Tipperary outlawries, but at the same time excluded the impropriations and restricted inheritance by Catholics.[5] The latter provision was apparently not enforced in Cahir's case. The ninth Lord Cahir, who was born in 1711, was one of the great Catholic land owners in the latter part of the eighteenth century. The third earl of Carlingford died in 1704 and was succeeded by his nephew, who was already of age and was therefore not debarred by his religion from holding the estate. The earldom, but not the Taafe viscountcy, became ex

[1] Annesley MSS, xxii. 140. The act is 1 Anne, c. 26.
[2] Annesley MSS, xxii. 186. Act is 1 Anne, c. 74.
[3] Annesley MSS, xx. 93.
[4] *Archiv. Hib.*, ix. 33.
[5] Annesley MSS, xxii. 131. The act is 1 Anne, c. 38.

tinct when he died issueless in 1738. The estate then became the subject of dispute between the sixth Viscount Taafe, who was a Catholic, and a Protestant relative. The land was ordered to be sold and the proceeds divided between the claimants, one-third going to Taafe.[1] John King, who later became the third Lord Kingston, had incurred the opprobrium of the Protestant community by marrying a Catholic wife and turning Catholic himself. He took the Jacobite side in the war and sat in the 1689 parliament. After the war he asked for pardon, to which exception was taken on the ground that his two sons were in France, being educated as Catholics. It was suggested that the pardon should be made conditional on his sons being brought to England and educated as Protestants. 'Otherwise it may prove of ill consequence to the public and be strengthening to the popish interest, which by this means will have a man of quality to lead them and, if he recovers his brother's estate, will be very formidable in Connacht, where they are generally Irish Papists.'[2] Kingston decided to comply, and the pardon was granted after it was ascertained that the elder son had arrived in England and had been placed in a suitably Protestant environment.[3] Kingston himself conformed and took his seat in the Irish lords, but the authorities long continued to exercise themselves over the beliefs of his family. Twenty years later Archbishop King was moved to remonstrate in the following terms: 'I ought not to conceal from your lordship that it is much observed that your family is altogether Papists, and that you live as much after the old Irish manner as the merest Irishman in the kingdom'[4].

The first of these private acts was that passed in favour of Tyrconnell's widow, the former Frances Jennings, sister of the duchess of Marlborough. She had been outlawed and was thus debarred from claiming her jointure from Tyrconnell's forfeited estate. In 1693 a warrant had been issued to stop proceedings against her, but the Irish lords justices protested that she had been so remarkable in acting against their majesties and the Protestant interest that everyone's eye was watching her case. They assured Queen Mary that Lady Tyrconnell had acted not with the duty of a wife to her husband, but with the malice of an open enemy, provoking her husband on all occasions against the Protestants of Ireland.[5] Their representation proved effective, and a further warrant

---

[1] The disposal of the Taafe estate was regulated by 15 Geo. II, c. 49. See *D.N.B.*, article on Nicholas, sixth Viscount Taafe. He was of age when 1 Anne, c. 38 was passed.
[2] Capel to Shrewsbury, 24 Sept. 1694 (*Cal. S.P. dom., 1694-5*, p. 344).
[3] *Cal. S.P. dom., 1694-5*, p. 410.
[4] King to Kingston, 9 June 1722 (T.C.D., MS N. 3. 7, p. 128).
[5] *Cal. S.P. dom., 1693*, pp. 357-8.

was issued directing them to proceed with the indictment.[1] With Anne's accession and the predominance of the Marlborough interest, Lady Tyrconnell was in a strong position. The act passed in her favour eluded the vigilance of the Irish bishops, who lobbied indefatigably for the exclusion of tithes from all estates restored by private acts. 'My lady Tyrconnell's bill was hurried with such unusual expedition through both houses, both whigs and tories striving who could favour it most, that we could not overtake it with our saving in either house; this it is to be the sister of a favourite; indeed I do not know any bill this session that has passed so very quietly and unanimously.'[2]

Acts were also passed in favour of several of the minor grantees who had been deprived by the Act of Resumption. Among these was William Spenser, the poet's grandson, who had been granted the estate forfeited by his Catholic cousin, Hugolin. William Spenser had become a Protestant and had assisted the Williamite cause by acting as a guide to Ginkel.[3] Provision was also made to restore a custodiam to the widow and children of Manus O'Brien, who had given the Williamite army information (on which it did not act quickly enough) of Sarsfield's plan to attack the guns at Ballyneety.[4]

Robert Edgeworth, Maria's great-uncle, succeeded in obtaining an act which put him in possession of the estate of his father-in-law, Sir Edward Tyrrell. Tyrrell died in 1690, shortly after being taken prisoner at Cork; in the following year he was outlawed and his estate seized. Robert Edgeworth, who seems to have been something of an adventurer, married Tyrrell's daughter and heiress and persuaded her to turn Protestant. Thereafter he devoted his energies to the attempt to recover her estate. He met with no success, and represented to parliament that he had been continually thwarted by Rochfort, the Irish attorney-general, and his friend Baron Donnellan, both of whom were anxious to secure it for themselves. This consideration seems to have recommended him to the trustees, who reported that Edgeworth had rendered considerable service in the reduction of Ireland and that he and his wife had a large family of small children and were objects of compassion. An act was passed directing the trustees to convey the estate, which was valued at £1,500 per annum, to Robert Edgeworth and Catherine his wife.[5]

In the majority of cases the reports of the trustees were favourable to

[1] *Cal. S.P. dom., 1693,* p. 388.
[2] Bishop of Clogher to bishop of Ossory, 2 Apr. 1702 (T.C.D., King MSS). The act is 1 Anne, c. 1; the text is in Annesley MSS, xxii. 55.
[3] Annesley MSS, xx. 183; xxii. 153. The act is 1 Anne, c. 63.
[4] Annesley MSS, xx. 88; xxii. 223. The act is 1 Anne, c. 62.
[5] Annesley MSS, xx. 80; xxii. 79. The act is 1 Anne, c. 49.

petitioners. The private acts reduced to an appreciable extent the area vested in the trustees. This provided them with a welcome opportunity of explaining away the difference between the financial results forecast in the inquiry commissioners' report and those actually realized by the sale of the forfeited estates.

The restrictions which these private acts placed on the purchase and inheritance of lands by Catholics were modelled on those which had been imposed by an English act of 1700 in respect of lands in England and Wales.[1] The restriction on purchase foreshadowed the first of the popery acts, passed by the Irish parliament in 1703. In 1708 the English parliament complained that the restrictions had been evaded, and that a great part of the estates taken out of the trust by private acts had been purchased by or on behalf of Catholics. Advantage was therefore taken of the need to pass a supplemental act for the Clanricarde estate to provide that Protestants might make discoveries of lands which had thus come into the possession of Catholics.[2]

The survey of the forfeited estates formed an important part of the trustees' proceedings. Nearly all the lands vested in the trust had been involved in the Cromwellian confiscation and were recorded in the Books of Survey and Distribution, together with the areas assigned to them on the basis of the Down survey. These areas were in all cases used in the forfeiture proceedings until after the passing of the Act of Resumption in 1700. The areas specified in William's grants correspond with those recorded in the Survey and Distribution books and the statistics in the inquiry commissioners' report are on the same basis.

There was, however, a general opinion that the official records underestimated the areas, set out in the restoration settlement, and in particular that much of the land shown as unprofitable was not correctly classified. Thus the committee which reported on the forfeitures to the English commons in 1694, said that the forfeited area was calculated on the survey returns, 'when in truth each parcel of land contains considerably more than what it is surveyed at, besides all the unprofitable land thrown in'.[3] The inquiry commissioners in 1699 commented: 'from our observations much of the lands called unprofitable in the surveys (excluding those in Kerry which we account as nothing) are now profitable, and many as good as any in the kingdom'[4]. In 1701, after the trustees' surveys had begun, Annesley observed that land which had been un-

[1] 11 and 12 Will. III, c. 4.
[2] 7 Anne, c. 29.
[3] *Commons' jn.*, xi. 57.
[4] *Commrs' report*, p. 22.

profitable when the Down survey was made was now 'the most valuable part of the kingdom', and that the area of the forfeited lands according to the trustees' survey would greatly exceed that 'returned in the ancient survey'.[1] Annesley made the same point to the English commons in 1702, saying that 'the acres on survey are considerably more than the old proprietors knew them to be or are returned in the Civil, Down, or Strafford surveys'.[2]

The scheme for the general survey of the lands vested in the trust was drawn up by Sir Henry Sheres, together with instructions to the surveyors. Robert Clements was appointed director-general of the survey; under him were four directors and a number of surveyors. Later the staff was increased by the appointment of a 'chief protractor' with seven protractors under him.[3] A great part of the forfeited lands was surveyed by the trustees. The maps thus made were collected into twenty-three volumes which remained in the Irish records until their destruction in 1922.[4] A certain number of tracings of the trustees' surveys have been preserved.[5] The Quit Rent Office set of the Books of Survey and Distribution also records the trustees' figures for the area of the lands sold by them, and these can thus be compared with the Down survey figures. They sometimes correspond, but there are a significant number of cases in which different results were obtained by the two sets of surveyors in measuring the same piece of land, the higher and more accurate figure usually being that of the trustees' survey.

In some cases the difference is due to the trustees' survey treating land as profitable which had previously been classed as unprofitable. This procedure was the subject of loud complaint from those affected. 'The management of their surveyors shows in what sense their unprofitable acres are very good land. There is a gentleman in town who tells us that when they were surveying the land which he held they took in a bog of which he never made one shilling, that contained ten times as many acres as his land did. Land, it seems, that is good for nothing is very good land to increase their number of acres; but I fear that land whereon nothing but fairies tread will raise only fairy money.'[6]

A fresh survey was clearly desirable. Apart from the inaccuracy of

[1] Annesley to Simon Harcourt, 25 Aug. 1701 (N.L.I., Ormonde MSS, clvii. 153).
[2] *Commons' jn.*, xiii. 764.
[3] Annesley MSS, ii. 72 and v. f. 72.
[4] *Ir. rec. comm. rep., 1816-20*, pp. 334-52.
[5] Some of these are in the British Museum; others, transferred from the Quit Rent Office, are in the Public Record Office of Ireland, which has also a set of the 6 in. O.S. maps with the outlines of the Down and trustees' surveys superimposed.
[6] *Jus regium*, p. 51.

the Down and Strafford surveys, the restoration settlement resulted in a great many subdivisions of former holdings. There also seem to have been a number of disputes over encroachments and the removal of land-marks.[1] The surveys thus provided a fresh basis on which the trustees' sales and conveyances could go forward. For all lands which were included in the survey the trustees used the areas so obtained. Difficulties thus arise in making an exact comparison between the total area sold by the trustees and the area restored under the articles or otherwise. On the whole, however, the difference between the two sets of figures is not more than 5 per cent, although for some individual estates it is considerably higher. The discrepancy gives the impression that a somewhat greater proportion of Jacobite land was sold by the trustees than was actually the case, but the difference is too small to affect the general assessment of the Williamite confiscation.

[1] Annesley MSS, iii. 54; iv. 119.

12

THE HEARING OF CLAIMS

O ne of the most urgent and complicated of the tasks of the
trustees was the hearing of claims. The Act of Resumption
prescribed that any person who claimed to have had an interest
in a forfeited estate before 13 February 1689 (the date of William and
Mary's accession) must enter his claim by 10 August 1700. The trustees
sat until midnight that day 'to give the claimants fair play'; some claims
were lodged at the last moment. The hearing of claims was to be completed by 25 March 1701, a limit which it was subsequently found necessary to extend.[1]

Altogether 3,140 claims were submitted, of which 1,861 were allowed
in whole or in part.[2] The number of successful claims is less significant
than this statement suggests. The claims varied widely in character.
Lessors, lessees, widows claiming their dowers and daughters their portions are all represented among the claimants. More than half the claims
allowed were made by Protestants who had financial interests of various
kinds in the forfeited estates. Only in a minority of cases were estates
claimed by the next heir of a forfeiting person under a marriage contract or deed of settlement. The mere fact that an estate was entailed
was not sufficient to establish a claim.[3] A number of the claims preferred
by heirs were successful, but there were some conspicuous cases in
which such claims failed and the estates were sold outright. Thus John
Grace failed to make out his claim to the Courtstown estate. His wit-

---

[1] 11 and 12 Will. III, c. 2, ss. 11, 12; John Isham to Sir Justinian Isham, 13 Aug.
1700 (Isham MSS).

[2] *A list of the claims as they are entered with the trustees at Chichester House*, 1701,
of which several sets have been preserved. The P.R.O.I. copy contains annotations,
made by W. Monck Mason from records subsequently destroyed, which show the
decision on each claim. Annesley MSS, viii-xii and xiv, contain records of many of
the hearings.

[3] 11 and 12 Will. III, c. 2, s. 1.

nesses had deposed that there was a deed of settlement drawn up in Dublin under the personal direction of Clancarty as trustee. This was contradicted by the evidence of Clancarty's sister, nephew and coachman, who stated that Clancarty was in London on the relevant date.[1]

The extent to which successful claims enabled the families of former owners to recover their estates was much more limited than has been suggested.[2] Comparison of the decisions with the entries in the Books of Survey and Distribution indicates that some forty freehold estates, with a total area of about 70,000 profitable acres, were restored by the trustees to the families which previously owned them. In twelve cases, involving an area of some 28,000 acres, the claimants themselves had been adjudged within the articles of Limerick or Galway but were obliged to claim because forfeiting persons had had a title to the lands at some time after 1688. Apart from the immediate restorations, there were fifteen cases in which the claim was allowed after the death of the forfeiting proprietor, whose life-interest was thereupon sold by the trustees. The estates of which the life-interest only was sold amounted to some 95,000 acres, the greater part of which was represented by the Kenmare estate. Although the families which thus preserved their estates were not numerous, they included some well-known names. Lords Gormanston and Trimleston were among those who recovered their lands immediately; their titles remained under attainder and were accorded to them only by courtesy. Sir Nicholas Browne's son, Valentine, and Dudley Bagenal's son, Walter, were among the heirs who established claims to reversions on the death of their forfeiting fathers.

Anthony Preston, 'called Lord Viscount Gormanston', and his wife were allowed a claim on the Gormanston estate by deeds of 1684.[3] The seventh viscount died in Limerick in March 1691 and was outlawed in Meath a month after his death. The next heir was his nephew Jenico, who was adjudged within the articles of Limerick and started proceedings for the recovery of the estate from Richard Coote, to whom it had been leased by the crown. Coote had been granted the manor of Gormanston under the Cromwellian settlement, but had been robbed of his prize when a decree of innocency was given to the seventh viscount. He had made determined efforts to resist this second attempt to dislodge him, and obstructed the execution of the decree passed by the court in Gormanston's favour. The Gormanston family records contain com-

---

[1] *Commons' jn.*, xiii. 865.

[2] By W. H. Hardinge (*R.I.A.Trans.*, antiquities, xxiv. 279). Hardinge's conclusions have been severely criticised by Butler, *Confiscation*, pp. 229-30.

[3] Claim 786. The trustees' decree, dated 27 Aug. 1701, has been preserved, see N.L.I., Report on Gormanston papers.

plaints by Jenico of the beating of bailiffs and of other obstruction offered by Coote. They also contain an account of the disbursements which Jenico had to make in the course of the proceedings, including an item of £12. 6s. 11d. for two dinners given to juries at the Crown in Fishamble Street.[1] As a counterblast to the legal proceedings Coote asked the Irish commons to include in a current bill of 1695 a clause enabling him to keep the Gormanston estate. His petition was rejected.[2]

Jenico died in 1697 and was succeeded by his brother Anthony, who had also been adjudged within the articles of Limerick. He, too, had to deal with Coote, who took the case to the English lords. The lords upheld the decree of the Irish court and ordered that the estate should be given to Lord Gormanston.[3] Under the provisions of the Act of Resumption Anthony had to put in a claim for the estate, although it had already been restored to him. It would otherwise have been forfeited on the ground that it had since February 1689 been for some time in the possession of the seventh viscount, a forfeiting person. The trustees seem to have made no difficulty about allowing the claim. Two other claims to the same lands and under the same deed were allowed to Nicholas and Robert Preston, who seem to have been younger brothers and to have lodged claims as a precautionary measure.[4]

The claim of John Barnwell, 'called Lord Trimleston', was allowed to a remainder in tail of the estate forfeited by Mathias, the tenth Lord Trimleston. The claim was proved by deeds of 1686, made in connection with marriage articles.[5] Mathias was in Limerick at the time of the capitulation, and was one of the hostages given by the Irish in the mutual interchange which took place during the negotiations.[6] He had been outlawed in Dublin during the summer of 1691, and did not take advantage of the articles but went off to France. In 1692 he was killed fighting in Low Germany. The estate was granted to Sydney, but by 1695 it had been recovered by John, Mathias's brother and heir.[7]

John, who appears to have been sent to France for his education and who was only twelve at the end of the war, was indicted but not actually outlawed. In 1697 he appears as indicted of foreign treason in a list of persons who 'stand indicted of treason and have surrendered themselves on the exigent or first process and are bound by recognizances to appear

[1] N.L.I., Report on Gormanston papers.
[2] *Commons' jn. Ire.*, ii. 143 (13 Dec. 1695).
[3] Luttrell, *Brief historical relation*, iv. 361.
[4] Claims 953 and 1870.
[5] Claim 1331.
[6] *H.M.C. rep. 10*, app. v. 166.
[7] *Cal. treas. bks*, x. 987.

in the court of king's bench'.[1] In 1699, it was proposed to press for his conviction and outlawry on the report of an informer named Geary. Lord Galway wrote to Vernon that he had not been in favour of the decision to proceed further against Trimleston, but that he had been reluctant to disagree with Bolton, the other lord justice, who had pressed for prosecution. 'I shall be sorry if poor Lord Trimleston loses his property through my acquiescence. Supposing he was an ensign in King James's guards, as Geary declares, I do not think his guilt is so great that he should lose his property on that account; for he was a mere child, for whom his relatives had procured this commission to give him wherewithal to live at the college.'[2] No further action seems to have been taken until the trustees came over. The informer, Geary, then approached them with a list of witnesses to prove that 'John Barnwell, commonly called Lord Trimleston, was concerned in the late rebellion'. The trustees sent the depositions to the attorney-general, intimating that they thought it proper to proceed with the prosecution. The lords justices passed orders accordingly, but nothing seems to have resulted.[3]

Among the successful claimants was Thomas Dongan, second earl of Limerick, who established a claim to the estate of his brother William. In Charles II's reign Thomas Dongan had been in command of the Irish regiment in the service of France. Charles offered him a pension of £500 a year to leave the French service, and appointed him to be, first, deputy governor of Tangier, and then governor of New York. He held the latter appointment until about 1687, and seems to have been successful in pacifying the Iroquois and in developing the town of New York. He remained in America until 1691, when he returned to England to find that his brother had been outlawed and had gone to France with James.[4] Hearing that his brother's estate was to be granted to Ginkel, Dongan asked Queen Mary to give him time to make out a claim to the reversion in the event of his brother's dying without leaving a son. He was given six weeks to make out his claim, and Ginkel's grant was held up for that time.[5] He failed to produce his proofs within the allotted time and the estate was accordingly given to Ginkel, who sold it to a number of 'Protestant purchasers'. Dongan then decided to go back to America. At the end of 1693 he was granted 'a vessel called the Margaret, a prize

---

[1] *Cal. S.P. dom., 1697*, pp. 499-501.

[2] Ibid., *1699-1700*, p. 168.

[3] Annesley MSS, ii. 15 and 21; *Cal. S.P. dom., 1700-2*, p. 148.

[4] For an account of Dongan see Browne, 'Thomas Dongan, soldier and statesman, Irish Catholic governor of New York 1683-8' (*Studies*, xxiii. 489-501). The author says that Dongan failed to recover the estate.

[5] *Cal. treas. papers, 1557-1696*, p. 191.

of 160 tons burthen', on the ground that he had spent the greater part of his estate on defending New York against the French and that he had been 'defeated of his brother's estate in Ireland'. He had asked for the ship as he was determined to go and live on a small estate he had in America.[1]

William, earl of Limerick, died in 1698; his only son had been killed at the Boyne. Thomas, as the heir, returned to Europe to see what could be done to revive his claim. The Act of Resumption contained a provision that, in view of the great services rendered to England by Thomas Dongan and of the sums due to him for arrears of pension and the expenses of fighting against the French and Indians of Canada, he should be given £8,000 out of the proceeds of his brother's estate, unless he preferred to claim the estate.[2] Dongan elected to claim the estate, but was tardy in making his claim. He appeared before the trustees on 15 August 1701, a year after the last date prescribed, and asked them to accept a claim. The trustees pointed out that they had no power to do so.[3] Dongan then submitted a petition to the English commons, asking for an extension of the time allowed for entering his claim. He represented that he had known of a settlement made by his brother but that the deed had been mislaid during the war. Despairing of being able to find it he had got a clause included in the Act of Resumption giving him £8,000 instead. The deed was found in December 1700, but by then the statutory period for lodging claims was over.[4]

This petition was strongly opposed by Henry Westenra and others, who had paid Ginkel over £8,000 for his grant of Lord Limerick's estate. They objected to Dongan being allowed to claim 'on pretence of some never before heard of deed'. In any case they considered themselves entitled to a share of the money they had paid to Ginkel. The trustees reported that there was no reason to doubt the bona fides of Dongan's claim and that he had always 'preserved the character of a man of honour'. They thought, however, that Westenra and the other purchasers were entitled to receive a third of their money.[5] A private act was passed allowing Dongan to claim. By this time the share re-coverable by the Protestant purchasers had gone up to two-thirds. It was therefore provided that Dongan should pay them this proportion. He was also deprived of the impropriate rectories and tithes which formed part of the estate.[6]

[1] *Cal. treas. papers, 1557-1696*, p. 332.
[2] 11 and 12 Will. III, c. 2, s. 53.
[3] Annesley MSS, iv. 305.
[4] Ibid., xx. 116.
[5] Ibid., xx. 164.
[6] Ibid., xxii. 5. The act is 1 Anne, c. 40.

The claim was allowed, but his failure to find the missing deeds in time had cost Thomas Dongan dear. He complained bitterly to the lord lieutenant of the heavy expense of paying the Protestant purchasers, of the loss of his tithes and glebelands worth £6–700 a year, and of the severity of the trustees who had kept the rents they had received from the estate and had left him to pay the interest charges which had accrued during the period of their management. In 1704 he petitioned the queen for a monetary grant to make up for his American expenditure and the arrears of his pension and also to help him to clear his Irish estate, which was much encumbered on account of his brother's attainder. A minute was recorded on the petition that the lord treasurer was to speak to Ormond on the case, but it does not appear that anything substantial resulted.[1] Castletown was still part of the Dongan estate at this time. Dongan sold it to William Conolly in 1709.[2]

A successful claim was made by Thomas Fitzgerald, knight of Glin. His father had been killed in 1689 during the siege of Derry at the battle of Windmill Hill. An inquisition was held on his estate in 1696, at which it was found that by a deed of settlement he was only tenant for life.[3] His widow was therefore left in undisturbed possession of the estate, which was accordingly not included in the return made by the inquiry commissioners in 1699. The trustees continued this arrangement and subsequently allowed the son's claim.

A case about which we have information from various sources and which illustrates the difficulties faced by claimants was that of Mark Baggot of Mountarran, county Carlow. Mark was adjudged within the articles of Limerick; his father John was adjudged not to be within the articles. At the inquisition held on the forfeited estate the Baggots produced a deed which settled the property on Mark after his father's death. The jury refused to accept the deed and held that the estate was vested outright in the father. It was then granted to Albemarle.[4] Mark proceeded to negotiate for the purchase of the estate, which extended to more than 3,000 acres. Albemarle's agents seem to have been satisfied of the validity of the deed of settlement, and the lands were disposed of to Mark for the modest sum of £300. With the passing of the Act of Resumption the estate became vested in the trustees, and Mark accordingly lodged his claim before them. Before it came up for hearing his

---

[1] *Cal. S.P. dom., 1703-4*, pp. 162-3; *Cal. treas. bks*, xix. 35.
[2] Registry of deeds, Dublin, no. 646.
[3] Harris, Collectanea, x. 277.
[4] *Cal. treas. bks*, xi. 438.

father had died; the admission of the claim would thus mean the immediate restoration of the property to Mark.

The case was strongly contested. Evidently considerable local feeling against Mark Baggot had been worked up among the Carlow Protestants, as appears from a representation made to Ormond by the high sheriff, grand jury and other Protestant gentry. The duke was requested to 'obstruct and discountenance Mark Baggot, a violent Papist, son of John Baggot late of Mountarran in this county, from returning to reside or have his abode among us; the said Mark having been titular high sheriff of this county in 1689 and acted as such with that insufferable pride, rigour and insolence towards the Protestants here as will never be forgotten. Wherefore, as his neighbourhood will be unwelcome to all, so will it bring a terror and heartburning to the poorer sort especially, for whose sake as well as our own we make this our humble request to your grace.'[1] The objections seem to have centred on Mountarran, which was not part of the freehold property granted to Albemarle, but was held on long lease by the Baggots from Ormond. When John Baggot was outlawed and his estate forfeited, Ormond, quite irregularly, gave a fresh lease of Mountarran to Richard Wolsely, the son of Brigadier William Wolsely who had played a prominent part in the war. Richard Wolsely was determined not to give the house up to Mark Baggot, and this seems to have been the primary cause of opposition to the latter's claim.

Mark Baggot had an ally in Bishop King, with whom he had struck up a friendship based on a common interest in mathematics and portable barometers. A considerable number of Baggot's letters are to be found in King's correspondence. Several of them deal with his claim, and the correspondence makes it clear that King recommended Baggot to the favourable consideration of the trustees. In one of his letters Baggot laid his case before King in the following terms: 'the gentleman who lives in my house in the country to which I hope to be restored by the trustees, being fond beyond measure of the improvements made by my father and expecting no compliance from me in letting him continue tenant, uses all his interest and power to hinder and delay the allowance of my claim. Among other artifices he has been very industrious, not immediately by himself but by his friends, to give an ill character of me to some of the trustees, but particularly to Sir Henry Sheres, as if I had been a cruel and ill-natured violent person in the late juncture; which by good fortune understanding, I took the freedom of making use of your lordship's name to Sir Henry and told him your lordship knew me be-

[1]H.M.C., Ormonde MSS, n.s., viii. 39.

fore, in and since the late troubles and could give some account of my actions and behaviour in that time. Sir Henry expressed great honour and esteem for your lordship, and told me that your lordship's account alone would satisfy him, and that he would be glad to find that I had not deserved the character he had of me. Which occasions my begging the favour of a line from your lordship with one enclosed to Sir Henry Sheres, as soon as your lordship conveniently can, for the objection made on the clause in my deed is not yet over. It is to be argued next week and your lordship's letter before it comes on would be very seasonable.'[1]

When the claim came up for hearing it was first suggested that the settlement had not been made for valuable consideration, but Baggot was able to show that it formed part of a marriage contract under which his wife brought him an estate of £150 a year.[2] It was next contended that there was a 'razure' in the deed which made it void, but the court held that the razure had been made before the deed was executed.[3] Finally, it was argued that the settlement was voluntary and revocable, and a wealth of legal precedents was adduced to show that this ought to be a bar to the claim. Against this Baggot was able to show that the deed was revocable only with the consent of his wife's trustees. The court took a week to consider the point and then gave judgement in favour of the claimant, both for the freehold estate and for the lease of Mountarran.[4]

As a result of the decision Baggot got possession of the freehold estate, but his return to Mountarran was still resisted by Wolsely. Baggot offered to allow Wolsely to remain until the end of the tenancy year and to buy his stock. The trustees thereupon ordered that Wolsely should on that date give possession to Baggot, failing which Baggot would be put in possession by a sheriff's order.[5] The next move was made by Cox, who by then was lord chief justice as well as one of Ormond's trustees. Cox represented that Ormond would be obliged to repay to Wolsely £1,100, the premium for his lease of Mountarran. The duke, who was heavily embarrassed, was quite unable to pay this sum. Baggot told the duke that he would pay the amount himself if, in place of his existing lease for three lives, he were granted a fresh lease on the same terms as had been given to Wolsely, a lease for lives renewable for ever.[6] More than a year later Wolsely was still in possession and Cox

---

[1] Baggot to King, 30 Jan. 1701 (T.C.D., King MSS).
[2] Annesley MSS, x. 165.
[3] Ibid., x. 224-8.
[4] Ibid., xi. 392-5 and xii. 53.
[5] Ibid., iv. 152.
[6] Baggot to King, 24 May 1701 (T.C.D., King MSS).

told the trustees that the duke had received no rent from him for two years.[1] Baggot seems never to have recovered possession of Mountarran. In a 1705 list of Catholics entitled to carry arms he is shown as late of Mountarran.[2]

A complicated and contested act of claims related to the Sarsfield estate.[3] William Sarsfield, Patrick's elder brother, married Mary, the daughter of Charles II and Lucy Walter. In consideration of the marriage the king put William in immediate possession of his ancestral estate of Lucan, in which a Cromwellian, Sir Theophilus Jones, had a life-interest. Jones was reprised with 'concealed lands' elsewhere to compensate him for being dispossessed of Lucan. William and Mary Sarsfield had a son, Charles, and a daughter, Charlotte. William died in 1675. By his will the estate was left, first to his son Charles, and failing him to his brother Patrick. Charlotte was to get only a portion of £1,000 and an annuity of £50. When the boy Charles died in 1683, Patrick proved the will in the prerogative court of Armagh and took possession of the estate. William Sarsfield's widow had by this time remarried, her second husband being an English civil servant named Fanshaw. She and her husband alleged that the will was a forgery and started legal proceedings against Patrick. The proceedings had made little headway by 1689, when Fanshaw was included in the attainder act passed by the Irish parliament. He, not unnaturally, attributed his attainder to Patrick's influence.[4]

After the Boyne the estate was seized by the Williamite commissioners of forfeitures as Patrick's property. A number of representations were made to William's government on behalf of Charlotte Sarsfield, and in 1696 a warrant was issued directing that she should be put in possession of the manor of Lucan. The warrant recited that Patrick had taken advantage of her infancy and of her absence in England to get possession of the estate, and that he had wrongfully detained it until he was expelled by the king's arms.[5] When Charlotte appeared to be securely in possession of the property she received, and accepted, an offer of marriage from Agmondisham Vesey, son of the archbishop of Tuam. The Act of Resumption came as a rude shock to Vesey. The trustees seized the estate, and Vesey's only remedy was to lodge claims on behalf of himself and his daughters; Charlotte herself had meanwhile died.

[1] Annesley MSS, v. 167.
[2] *H.M.C., Ormonde MSS*, ii. 475.
[3] For a report on the documents relating to the Sarsfield estate see *P.R.I. rep. D.K. 56*, pp. 342-96.
[4] *Cal. treas. papers, 1697-1702*, p. 563.
[5] *Cal. S.P. dom., 1696*, p. 156.

The case before the trustees turned on the validity of William Sars-field's will. The original was not forthcoming. Patrick was said to have taken it out of the prerogative court and to have handed it to his sisters, who brought it with them to France. A copy was obtained from the prerogative office and exhibited to the trustees together with Patrick's receipt for the original. One of the witnesses to the will also appeared and testified to the accuracy of the copy. The trustees held that the estate had been left to Patrick by the terms of William's will, and that it had not descended to the claimants. The claims were therefore dis-allowed.[1] From the record there seems no reason to suppose that the will was a forgery or that the trustees' decision was wrong. It naturally displeased the Veseys. The archbishop, writing to his son, expressed his indignation at the trustees' judgment 'in affirmance of a will unproved'. In the same letter he observed: 'your children that can just speak are taught to say they love the trustees because they must love their ene-mies.'[2] A contemporary dialogue makes Trenchard, thinly disguised as Truncheon, remark that the trustees intend to divest Vesey and his children of their estate 'on a pretence of a will which does not appear and which we have great reason to believe was a forgery from the begin-ning'.[3] Vesey contrived to get a private act passed in England by which he obtained possession of the estate on payment of three times the rent at which the trustees had let it in 1702.[4]

A claim which was later to have important repercussions was that lodged by Maurice Annesley in respect of the estate of Christopher Sherlock. Maurice was a cousin of Francis Annesley; by a natural piece of patronage the trustees had appointed him receiver for county Kildare. The estate forfeited by Christopher Sherlock was charged with portions for his sisters Hester and Mary and with legacies to his younger brothers. Maurice Annesley's story was that the widowed mother of these children appealed to him to lease the estate from the forfeiture commissioners, and also persuaded him to act as guardian of the minors. He alleged that he had spent considerable sums for the maintenance and education of the children and had also provided the daughters with their portions. The claim allowed by the trustees for these disbursements came to more than the value of the estate, possession of which was accordingly handed over to Annesley; the reversion only was sold by the trustees. The legal proceedings which were subsequently brought by Hester Sherlock

[1] Claims 1316-17; Annesley MSS, iii. 17; xiv. 68-71.

[2] Archbishop of Tuam to Agmondisham Vesey, 18 Sept. 1702 (P.R.O.I., Sarsfield-Vesey collection).

[3] *Secret history of the trust.*

[4] Annesley MSS, xxii. 99. The act is 1 Anne, c. 57.

against Annesley led to a clash between the Irish and English lords, which had important constitutional consequences. Hester Sherlock, losing her case in the exchequer court, took it to the Irish lords, who upheld her claim. Annesley then applied to the English lords, who denied the appellate jurisdiction of the Irish lords and ordered that the estate should be handed over to Annesley.[1] After a battle royal the issue was for the time being decided by the Declaratory Act of 1719, which remained an Irish grievance until the time of Grattan's parliament.

It is not easy to determine the equity or inequity of the trustees' decisions. The Protestant pamphlets of the time took the line that the claims of Protestants were unfairly disallowed and those of Catholics undeservedly admitted. Apart from the improbability of any great favouritism having been shown towards Catholics, the record indicates that most of the Protestant claims for mortgages or leases were admitted, and that more than half the claims for the recovery of estates under deeds of settlement were unsuccessful. It was natural that unsuccessful claimants should charge the trustees with prejudice and unfairness. They were not directly charged with corruption, and the vigilant hostility of the Irish Protestants would certainly have detected any cases of laxity.

A charge was levied against Maurice Annesley of having taken a hundred guineas to secure Francis Annesley's support for a claim lodged by Lewis Moore of Balyna. Moore's affidavit denying the allegation was taken at the Kildare assizes and sold as a penny broadsheet. Colonel Charles Moore of Balyna, the son of Rory O'More, had been outlawed in the summer of 1691 and had then been killed at Aughrim. His cousin Lewis, an ancestor of the More-O'Ferrall family, was not outlawed and successfully claimed under a deed of settlement.[2] Maurice Annesley's relations with Thomas Dongan were also equivocal. From a subsequent lawsuit it appears that in return for a promise to recommend Dongan's case in England Annesley obtained a lease of land on very favourable terms. The deed, in Annesley's 'own handwriting and very artfully drawn', recited that Dongan made the lease in consideration of 'special affection to the said Annesley for many services done'.[3]

Sir Henry Sheres attributed the Protestant criticism to the 'new and unknown practice' introduced by the trustees, who did not consider the distinction of Protestant and Papist to be any part of the question, with the result that a 'Protestant knave was sure not to succeed against an

---

[1] *The case of Maurice Annesley*; *Parliamentary cases, 1715-20*, nos. 136-7.
[2] Claim 151; *Secret history of the trust*; *Mr Moore of Ballyna's deposition*.
[3] *The case of Thomas, earl of Limerick . . . versus Maurice Annesley, respondent.*

injured Papist'.[1] King observed that many Catholics had succeeded in establishing claims before the trustees which would not have been allowed by a jury. 'Yet in the method in which the matter was put I do not see how it could have been avoided. The relief they had was by deeds, supposed forged, and swearing, and it was observable that where these would help they seldom failed to carry their claims; but some were so unlucky that there was no room for these in their cases, as when fines and records were against them. Also when it came to a nice point of law, as several times happened, I do not find they had any favour; and I doubt the most innocent and righteous claims were often defeated and the unjust allowed.'[2] King's verdict is probably as near the truth as we are likely to get.

[1] B.M., Eg. MS 917, f. 169.
[2] King to Southwell, 28 Mar. 1702 (B.M., Eg. MS 917, f. 183).

13

THE SELLING OF THE FORFEITED
ESTATES, 1702-3

The Act of Resumption provided that the trustees should begin to sell the forfeited lands at any time after 10 November 1700 and complete the sales by 25 March 1702. The selling was to be by cant, or auction, of which notice was to be given fourteen days in advance. The purchase money might be paid in the form of debentures (paper which had been issued in lieu of payment to army officers, clothiers and owners of transport ships), malt tickets (tickets for a million pound lottery issued in 1697 and secured by a duty on malt) or exchequer bills. All of these were to be accepted 'as freely as if they were sterling'. The trustees were, however, authorized to demand enough cash to meet their own outgoings. All receipts over and above the trustees' expenses were to be appropriated to officers' arrears, to debts due for transport and clothing, or to meeting the principal and interest on debentures, malt tickets and the other forms of paper which sustained the precarious fabric of Williamite finance.[1] The trustees were unable to keep to the time-table. Claims took much longer to decide than had been expected, and the passing of supplementary legislation to appease the Irish Protestants caused further delay.

The act for the relief of the Protestant purchasers of the forfeited estates in Ireland, passed in the spring of 1702, gave to those who had purchased lands from Albemarle, Athlone, Romney and other grantees the privilege of buying in their purchases at thirteen times the annual rent, provided that they did so by 25 March 1703. They were also allowed an abatement of one-third of the original purchase price in addition to the £21,000 previously allotted for their relief.[2] Most of the purchasers

[1] 11 and 12 Will. III, c. 2, ss. 22, 40, 41.
[2] 1 Anne, c. 26.

148

took advantage of the act, and the trustees were thereby enabled to begin their sales. Altogether they disposed of about 80,000 profitable acres to fifty 'Protestant purchasers'. This area included the greater part of the estates of Lords Clare and Slane in addition to a number of smaller properties.

The auctions of the remaining lands vested in the trust began in October 1702, but great difficulty was experienced in obtaining satisfactory bids.[1] In December 1702 two of the trustees presented the English commons with a memorial dilating on the difficulties of selling the forfeited lands. Their chief complaint was of the current belief that the adjudications of the trustees and the titles conveyed by them would be subject to re-examination by the Irish courts. Prospective bidders were also put off by the apprehension that each lot might be held liable for the whole quit-rent with which the original estate was charged. For those who bought lots from Clancarty's enormous estate such an interpretation might be disastrous.[2] In January 1703 the same trustees presented a second memorial to the commons, stating that since the sales began in the previous October less than £40,000 worth of land had been sold; there was little competition, there being 'few or no second bidders'. The trustees thought that there was not enough purchasing power in Ireland and said that few of the English debenture holders had put in an appearance; apparently they preferred interest in England to land in Ireland. The commons' immediate response to the last suggestion was a resolution to provide for the stoppage of interest on debentures.[3] Protests were soon forthcoming from the debenture holders. The army officers maintained that without interest the debentures could not be disposed of at 'any tolerable discount', and that they themselves could not 'with such broken sums as were coming to them' buy lands in Ireland where they had no connections or friends. The shipowners complained that they had not received principal or interest on their debentures for over nine years. The clothiers protested that without interest their debentures would not be saleable for more than half their nominal value.[4]

The protests were effective and the act for advancing the sale of the forfeited estates, passed in February 1703, contained no clause for the stoppage of interest. The act gave power to the trustees to apportion the liability for quit-rent. It also provided for the payment of the purchase money in instalments, one-third before 24 June 1703, one-third

[1] *A book of postings and sales.*
[2] *Commons' jn.*, xiv. 64.
[3] Ibid., xiv. 113.
[4] Ibid., xiv. 172.

by 25 December 1703 and the remainder by 24 June 1704.[1] A subsequent act gave a further extension of six months 'by reason of the present scarcity of money in Ireland'.[2]

Most of the remaining property was offered for sale between March and May 1703, but in spite of the recent concessions there was little improvement in the rate of disposal. Few properties were sold for more than the reserve price and the greater part of the land remained undisposed of. James's private estate attracted a good many bidders, mostly country gentlemen who owned other land in the neighbourhood. Three-quarters of the private estate was sold to some 170 purchasers. On the other hand, only one-quarter of Clancarty's estate and none of Sir Patrick Trant's could be disposed of by auction. These estates consisted of large, continuous blocks of territory. They must have seemed a less attractive proposition for the individual purchaser than the private estate, which consisted of comparatively small lots scattered among the holdings of established Protestant gentry.

In April 1703 King, by now archbishop of Dublin, wrote to Annesley: 'I hear from several hands that the forfeitures go off at great rates and the addressers [i.e. the promoters of the remonstrance against the Act of Resumption] the great buyers, which will stop their mouths for ever; for how can they allege it an ill title on which they venture so much.'[3] Conolly was one of the principal purchasers; Marmaduke Coghill and some other promoters of the remonstrance were also purchasers, but on a comparatively small scale. But King, who was in England at the time, had been given rather too optimistic an account of the auctions. By the end of May 1703 the greater part of the lands put up to auction were still undisposed of.

It was unfortunate for the trustees that the sale of the forfeited estates should have taken place at a time when the economic position of Irish Protestants was severely affected by the restrictions imposed in 1698 and 1699 on the export of woollen goods. King, writing in 1702, commented that Irish land values had fallen as fast as they had previously risen. He attributed the decline to the 'Woollen Bill', the lowering of the Irish rate of exchange, the stoppage of foreign trade and the proceedings of the trustees.[4] Dislike of the resumption proceedings, lack of confidence in the trustees' ability to convey a good title, and the hope of picking up bargains at the close of the auctions were also factors which

[1] 1 Anne, st. 2, c. 18.
[2] 2 and 3 Anne, c. 19.
[3] King to Annesley, 6 Apr. 1703 (T.C.D., MS N. 3, 2b, p. 188). For the remonstrance see pp. 125-7 above.
[4] King to Southwell, 28 Mar. 1702 (B.M., Eg. MS 917, f. 183).

must have been responsible for the poor demand for forfeited lands. The possibility of a Jacobite restoration and the consequent revival of claims by forfeiting proprietors provided additional reasons for caution.

The trustees, faced with the necessity of winding up their proceedings by 24 June 1703, adopted the expedient of transferring the unsold lands to an English company. Such a solution had already been the subject of considerable discussion. The Act of Resumption contained a provision that the forfeited estates might be purchased by a corporation, notwithstanding the Statute of Mortmain.[1] This policy was strongly advocated in a pamphlet which appeared in 1701, *An argument proving that it is more to the interest of the government and nation of England that the forfeited estates in Ireland be purchased by an incorporated company than by single purchasers*. Some interesting points were made, and the pamphlet illustrates the English dislike of the colonial nationalism which had developed in Ireland under Molyneux's influence. The writer apprehended that individual purchasers would, 'by becoming proprietors and inhabitants of Ireland, be immediately engaged on the side of Ireland's national interest as separate or opposed to that of England'. On the other hand, a company with its headquarters in England could be counted on as an unfailing upholder of the English government. The argument was supported by the example of the Londonderry scheme, 'the only means under God whereby Ireland was preserved from being completely swallowed up by the late rebellion before other help could be ready'. Anxiety was also expressed that, if the lands were offered for individual purchase, they might be bought by Catholics. The Act of Resumption contained no provision to bar Catholics from buying. In April 1701 Sheres, in a letter to Wyche, observed that he and Annesley thought that Catholics would outbid Protestants for the forfeited estates, and especially so in Connacht to enable them to keep their hold in that province.[2] It was not until 1702 that Catholics were debarred from buying the forfeited estates.[3]

When it became clear that much of the land put up to auction would remain unsold, it was decided to bring in a company to take over the balance. The chosen instrument was the 'governor and company for making hollow sword-blades in England'. The company seems to have been taken over by London merchants, who chose this particular corporation because its charter allowed it to purchase land freely. It had been incorporated in 1691 to establish the manufacture in Cumberland

[1] 11 and 12 Will. III, c. 2, s. 23.
[2] P.R.O.I., Wyche papers, 2nd series, 137.
[3] 1 Anne, c. 26, s. 14.

of swords for the use of the army in the French war. The right of purchasing land had been included in its charter with the object of enabling it to build mills on the banks of rivers and to provide accommodation for a large number of swordmakers imported from Germany. The company had not prospered and the sword cutlers were quite ready to dispose of their charter to the London merchants.[1]

The Hollow Blades company bought almost half of the land of which the outright title was conveyed by the trustees. Their purchases amounted to more than 250,000 profitable acres, spread over twenty-two counties. They included the greater part of the estates of Lord Clancarty and Galmoy and the whole estate of Sir Patrick Trant, in addition to many lesser properties. The net amount paid by the company for their purchases was £208,867. The majority of the lands thus acquired were included in an omnibus transaction by which property valued at some £170,000 was knocked down to the company for £97,000 on 23 June 1703, the day before the trust came to an end.

In spite of the favourable rates at which the company's lands had been acquired the venture did not prosper. Opinion in Ireland seems to have been antagonistic to it. In October 1703 the company represented to the Irish parliament that it proposed to lend money at 6 per cent on the security of Irish land, provided that it could be indemnified from the Statute of Mortmain. It asked for legislation to enable it to take conveyances of lands in Ireland (i.e. lands other than those which it had bought from the trustees under the Act of Resumption, which specifically excluded the Statute of Mortmain). No action was taken on this petition, apart from laying it on the table.[2] It has been suggested that the Irish parliament, knowing that the company had purchased the forfeited lands at very low rates, was unwilling that it should extend its purchases lest it should become too powerful an influence in Ireland.[3] The company then applied to the government in England asking for permission to lend money on the security of the forfeited estates to persons who had not completed the payment of the purchase money. It had been advised that the Mortmain provision of the Act of Resumption applied only to the conveyances which the company had itself obtained from the trustees. This petition also seems to have met with no success.[4]

A series of suits was instituted against the company in respect of

[1] Tindal, *History of England*, iii. 607-8.
[2] *Commons' jn. Ire.*, ii. 331 (9 Oct. 1703).
[3] Anderson *Historical and chronological deduction of the origin of commerce*, ii. 192.
[4] State Papers, dom., 14 Feb. 1704, quoted by Scott, *Joint-stock companies*, iii. 438.

several of the forfeited estates which it had purchased. In 1708 it represented to the English commons that a number of suits had already started and that others were threatened which would affect a great part of the company's property. It had been induced to purchase the forfeited estates in the belief that the trustees' conveyances would give 'sufficient, absolute and indisputable title'. The company was barred from making any other defence as it had not got the old title deeds, 'such being generally secreted or kept from the said trustees and the purchasers under them by the forfeiting persons or their agents'.[1] An act was passed in the company's favour which fixed a time-limit of two years for the institution of further suits. The act recited that the title of the company derived from the trustees had been called in question and that several judgments had been given against the company in Ireland, one of which had been upheld in the queen's bench court in England and also in the house of lords.[2]

Notwithstanding the protection given by this act, the company decided to sell out. A notice was inserted in the *London Gazette* that the company's Irish estates were to be sold for one-third cash and two-thirds by such payments as might best suit the purchasers.[3] From the registered deeds which record the disposal of the company's estates it does not appear that they were seriously affected by lawsuits. Portions of the property were disposed of to various Irish purchasers. These included Dr Richard Steevens, who bought over 2,000 acres in King's County which later became part of the endowment of Steevens' Hospital, Dublin.[4] The bulk of the property was sold for £133,333. 6s. 8d. to to Francis Edwards, a London merchant and a member of the Hollow Blades company.[5] Edwards left his property to an unmarried daughter who gradually disposed of it. In 1729 Miss Edwards was drawing £7,000 a year in rents, but the estate was greatly reduced by sales in the course of the next fifteen years.[6]

After the winding up of its Irish land enterprise the Hollow Blades company passed into the control of the directors of the South Sea company and went in for speculative banking. It was thus involved in

---

[1] 'The case of the governor and company for making hollow sword-blades', quoted by Relton, *Account of fire insurance companies*, pp. 126-9.
[2] 6 Anne, c. 61.
[3] *London Gazette*, 24-28 Feb., 1709.
[4] Regd. deed 716, 15 June 1709; Kirkpatrick, *History of Steevens' Hospital*, p. 17.
[5] Regd. deeds 5,355 and 8,230, 8 July 1714 and 7 July 1716. The agreement to sell was made in 1711. The deeds were held up on account of litigation between Edwards and the company.
[6] Prior, *List of absentees*. p. 3.

the bursting of the South Sea Bubble and went into liquidation in 1720.[1] The association of the Hollow Blades with Ireland was too brief for this experiment in company ownership to have had any real significance. It cannot be compared to the story of the Londonderry scheme. There is no reason to regret the rapid disintegration of the enormous estates acquired by a mushroom concern which seems to have had no other object than the financial exploitation of the situation created by the Act of Resumption and the sale of the forfeited estates.

The deeds of sale passed by the trustees were preserved in the Dublin Rolls Office. They were destroyed in 1922, but an abstract, published in 1825 by the Irish records commission, gives particulars in each case of the purchaser, the townlands and area purchased, the price and the forfeiting proprietor.[2] The abstract summarizes the conveyances passed in favour of about five hundred persons, but many of these conveyances relate to mortgages, tithes, leases, life-interests, etc. Analysis of the abstract shows that 360 persons made outright purchases of 568,000 profitable acres, the estates of 179 forfeiting proprietors, including James's private estate.

The great majority of the purchasers represented families already established in Ireland before 1688. They included a number of persons prominent in Irish public life, who thus acquired a corporate interest in the maintenance of the Williamite settlement, although their individual purchases were not very large. Some seventy of the purchasers were members of the Irish commons in one or both of the parliaments which immediately preceded and followed the trustees' tenure of Chichester House. There were four peers, including Lord Abercorn who bought in for £700 the heavily encumbered estates of his uncle Claud.

The list of purchasers included two archbishops, two bishops and a number of lesser clergy of the established church. One of the last-named category was Benjamin Pratt, fellow and later provost of Trinity College, Dublin, who bought part of James's estate in Meath. Most of the clerical purchases represented private investments. King, however, who had by this time become archbishop of Dublin, bought on behalf of the see, but at his own expense, the lands of Seatown, which had originally belonged to the archbishops of Dublin but had passed into the possession of a family called Russell. The then archbishop had got a grant of the land at the Restoration, but Bartholomew Russell, who had obtained a decree of innocency, succeeded in recovering possession

[1] Scott, *Joint-stock companies*, iii. 440.
[2] *Ir. rec. comm. rep., 1821-5*, pp. 348-96. For a summary of the sales see Appendix B, pp. 177-92, below.

when the case was heard 'before popish judges' in 1687. Russell was later outlawed and the land was granted by William to the archbishop. When this grant was annulled by the Act of Resumption the archbishop entered a claim before the trustees. The claim was not allowed and a petition to the English commons was equally unsuccessful.[1] King subsequently got a refund of his money as a result of an act passed by the English parliament.[2]

Several of the purchasers were members of families prominent in the Irish life of the eighteenth century. Brigadier Henry Conyngham, who bought Slane Castle, was the father of the first Lord Conyngham. The title then passed to Henry Conyngham's grandson who was also grandson of Francis Burton who had bought a large part of Lord Clare's estate. The family was thus doubly endowed with Williamite forfeitures. James Agar of Kilkenny, who bought much of Galmoy's estate, was the grandfather of Archbishop Agar. Other notable purchasers were Francis Bernard, Sir Matthew Deane and Percy Freke, ancestors respectively of Lords Bandon, Muskerry and Carbery.

Apart from the Hollow Blades very few of the purchasers came from England. The most important of those who did was John Asgill, who bought 15,000 acres outright as well as a life-interest in the Kenmare and Bagenal estates. Asgill soon got into difficulties over the payment of the various family allowances with which the Kenmare estate was charged. He was obliged to hand over the Hospital estate in county Limerick to Melchior Levallin, the brother-in-law of Lady Kenmare. Other creditors took proceedings against him and he was eventually declared a bankrupt.[3] Another English purchaser was Sir William Scawen, a London merchant who bought the Galway portion of the private estate with the debentures which he had received as payment for clothing Colonel Churchill's regiment.[4]

It is evident that the forfeited estates had little attraction for English buyers. Investors were doubtless discouraged by the adventurers' experience of the restoration settlement and by fear of a second Stuart restoration. The Williamite confiscation did not result in a fresh wave of settlers; it consolidated the position of the settlers already established.

[1] Annesley MSS, xx. 90.
[2] 4 and 5 Anne, c. 13.
[3] *Parliamentary cases, 1730-5*, nos. 59, 139.
[4] Annesley MS xliii has particulars of the cancelled debentures.

Apart from the short-lived enterprise of the Hollow Blades the general effect of the trustees' sales was to break up a number of great estates and to distribute them among a comparatively large number of individuals. This was particularly the case with the private estate, which was divided among 170 purchasers. There were twenty-seven buyers of Tyrconnell's estate, and sixteen of Slane's.

The trustees made their final report to parliament on 29 November 1703. They were chiefly concerned to account for the great difference between the estimates of 1699 and the realizations of 1703.[1] They made the most of the exemptions contained in the Act of Resumption, the act for the relief of Protestant purchasers, and the private acts passed for the benefit of individuals. The commons ordered that the trustees' report and statement of accounts, together with the report made by the inquiry commissioners in 1699 and its accompaniments, should be referred to the public accounts commissioners; the latter were to report 'how they find the fact and what observations arise from the said books and reports'.[2] The public accounts commissioners presented their report to the commons on 11 March 1704.[3] It included a detailed, but somewhat disingenuous, comparison of the inquiry commissioners' estimates with the amounts actually realized by the trustees. The method of comparison was designed to side-track the criticism that the forfeited estates were heavily encumbered and that their net value was much less than the inquiry commissioners had estimated. The English commons received this account with satisfaction and resolved that the trustees had in all respects discharged their duty with great integrity and fidelity to the satisfaction of the house and the advantage of the public.[4]

The Irish commons vented their general dissatisfaction by expelling Annesley on the ground that the inquiry report of 1699 had contained unwarranted reflections on the Protestants of Ireland.[5] They did not venture on open criticism of the English parliament or of the Act of Resumption. As Edward Southwell put it: '. . . everybody spoke with the greatest deference to England, declaring that they did not hereby intend to reflect on what had passed, though the act had been very severe; but they could not but do themselves right on one of their own country and body when they had been so traduced'. Southwell himself voted against Annesley's expulsion, which he regretted 'as he is a

---

[1] *The report of the trustees for the forfeited estates of Ireland*, 1704. The comparative figures are given on p. 108, above.
[2] *Commons' jn.*, xiv. 253.
[3] N.L.I., MS 1541.
[4] *Commons' jn.*, xiv. 387.
[5] *Commons' jn. Ire.*, ii. 321 (28 Sept. 1703).

gentleman of very fair character who has often been useful to this country [i.e. Ireland] and because such heats do not easily stop where they are intended'.[1]

Some years later the Irish commons returned to the subject with more courage and presented an address in which they complained of the 'heavy pressures' under which they groaned 'owing to the insincere and oppressive actings of the late trustees'. After touching on the 'unnecessary and unwarrantable severities by the trustees used towards the Protestants of this kingdom when at the same time the Papists found favour from them', they concentrated on the particular charge that the trustees had returned large amounts as due for collection which had either been paid or were never due. In certain cases tenants shown in arrears were in possession of receipts. Maurice Annesley, one of the trustees' 'receivers and favourites', had collected £461 for which he had given receipts, and yet the amount was returned by the trustees as in arrear. In other cases persons were returned as owing rent for lands of which they never were tenants. The trustees had returned £112,569 as due for payment, and over three hundred informations or suits had been brought in an attempt to collect the amount. The result had been that the amount recovered was hardly enough to pay for the proceedings. The queen was requested to have the case laid before the British parliament; the lord lieutenant was asked to deprive Maurice Annesley of his commission of the peace.[2] No reply appears to have been given to this address.

[1] Edward Southwell to Godolphin, 25 Sept. and 2 Oct. 1703; same to Nottingham, 3 Oct. 1703 (*Cal. S.P. dom., 1703-4*, pp. 131-2, 140-1, 143).
[2] *Commons' jn. Ire.*, ii. 533 (14 Aug. 1707).

14

THE AFTERMATH

The winding up of the trust in 1703 marked the concluding stage of the Williamite confiscation. During its protracted course the proprietorship of a considerable part of Ireland had been subjected to a bewildering series of changes. The succession of custodiams, grants, restorations and sales of grants, which characterized the period from 1690 to 1699, was followed in 1700 by the drastic expropriation of private interests imposed by the Act of Resumption. The trustees' administration entailed a further period of uncertainty; during the lengthy process of claims and private legislation the eventual ownership of much land remained in doubt. These changes must have caused considerable harm to the economy of the country. In particular, we have many references to the wholesale cutting of timber by occupiers anxious to extract the maximum of profit from what might prove to be the temporary tenure of the lands assigned to them.

With the conclusion of the trustees' proceedings stability was at last reached. For the next three-quarters of a century the penal code was to be the predominant influence in Irish life. During that period the proportion of land in Catholic ownership was steadily reduced, but the process was one of attrition and not of violent change. It was partly due to the actual operation of the popery laws, and in particular to the system by which Catholics could part with land but, except by subterfuge, could make no new acquisitions. But the principal factor which reduced the Catholic holding was the conforming of landowners to the established church.

The Protestant community, which had viewed the resumption proceedings with extreme disfavour, was now chiefly concerned to maintain the resulting settlement, and to resist any compromise with dispossessed Jacobites. Addresses were presented by the Irish commons to successive sovereigns representing the fatal consequences of reversing the outlawries of any of those attainted for the rebellions of 1641 and 1688.[1] The first of these addresses was provoked by the pardon given by Anne to Lord Slane as a reward for his military services. The reaction of the Irish Protestants was thus described by King: 'the reversal of my lord Slane's outlawry makes a mighty noise through this kingdom; for aught I can remember the destroying of our woollen manufactory did not cause so universal a consternation'.[2] The alarm diminished when it became known that the pardon did not imply the restoration of Slane's forfeited estate. Similar panic was caused by the attempt of Clancarty's son to procure the reversal of his father's outlawry. Archbishop Boulter supported the case of those who had purchased the forfeited Clancarty estate. He observed that 'as probably two-thirds of the estates of Protestants here were popish forfeitures originally the uneasiness is universal, since they think if the attainder of any family be reversed now another family may at another time obtain the same favour, and another at another season; so that no possessor of such forfeited estate can tell how long he or his may continue in the quiet enjoyment of what they have bought under English acts of parliament'.[3] Boulter's recommendation prevailed and Clancarty's outlawry remained unreversed. The Irish commons also noted with disapproval the attempts of former owners to bring suits for the recovery of lands 'forfeited by the horrid rebellion of 1688'. They resolved that any attempt to disturb the Protestant purchasers would be 'of dangerous consequence to his majesty's person and government, the succession in his royal house and highly prejudicial to the Protestant interest in this kingdom'.[4] Replies were given to the commons' addresses that the king would effectively discourage applications for the reversal of outlawries in any case that might affect the interest of Protestants.[5] No estates were restored by pardon after 1703, nor does it appear that any substantial loss was caused to Protestant purchasers as a result of lawsuits brought by representatives of the former proprietors.

Widely differing estimates have been made of the area left in Catholic ownership at the close of the Williamite settlement. Butler concluded that on the most generous estimate this area could not have exceeded 500,000 profitable Irish acres. This conclusion followed from his assumption that the area covered by the inquiry commissioners' report

[1] *Commons' jn. Ire.*, ii. 609-10 (20 June 1709); iii. 169 (7 Dec. 1717); iii. 451 (5 Mar. 1727); iii. 553 (19 Mar. 1728); iv. 195 (17 Dec. 1735).
[2] King to Swift, 12 Mar. 1709 (Ball, *Correspondence of Jonathan Swift*, i. 140-1).
[3] Boulter to bishop of London and duke of Newcastle, 9 Feb. 1736 (*Letters by Hugh Boulter*, ii. 119-20).
[4] *Commons' jn. Ire.*, iv. 333 (18 Feb. 1740).
[5] Ibid., iii. 563 (29 Apr. 1728); iv. 205 (24 Feb. 1736).

represented all, or nearly all, the land owned by Catholics at the outbreak of the war. Butler's figure represents one-fifteenth of the total profitable area as the Catholic share. There is, however, some confusion in his account. In one passage he allows for a proportional addition of unprofitable land; in another passage he makes no such allowance and concludes that 'when the court of claims set up by the Resumption Act had done its work it is doubtful whether as much as one-twentieth of the soil of Ireland remained in the hands of Catholics'.[1] The German historian, M. J. Bonn, estimated that the Williamite settlement left rather more than one-sixth of Ireland in Catholic ownership.[2] Edmund Curtis put the figure somewhat lower, reckoning that by 1700 Catholics had the freehold of about one-eighth of the country.[3] Analysis of the Books of Survey and Distribution, read with the accompaniments to the inquiry commissioners' report and the records of the trustees, indicates that the Catholic share of the profitable land had declined from 22 per cent in 1688 to 14 per cent in 1703. The latter figure lies between the estimates of Bonn and Curtis and is considerably higher than Butler's. Almost half the area which remained in Catholic ownership in 1703 was held by persons adjudged within the articles of Limerick or Galway; the effect of the articles was much greater than appears from the figures given in the inquiry commissioners' report. Pardons and successful claims accounted for a further fifth. The balance was held by persons whose trials were dropped or ended in acquittal or against whom no proceedings were taken.[4]

The reduction of the Catholic share from 14 per cent in 1703 to the 5 per cent which was Arthur Young's estimate in 1776,[5] was largely due to the conforming of landowners to the established church. The convert rolls contain the names of a great many representatives of those Catholic families which had by various means succeeded in retaining their property after 1688. The conforming of numerous Blakes, Frenches and Lynches effectively reduced the Catholic predominance in Connacht. The Protestant interest in that province was strongly reinforced when Browne of Westport conformed in 1729 and Martin of Ballynahinch in 1737.[6] By the end of the penal period the ranks of landed Catholics were

[1] Butler, *Confiscation*, pp. 232, 237. Beckett, *Hist. of Ireland*, p. 104, puts the Catholic share at one-fifteenth of the total; he apparently follows Butler.
[2] Bonn, *Die englische Kolonisation*, ii. 158.
[3] Curtis, *Ire.*, p. 276.
[4] See Appendix C, pp. 193-4, below.
[5] Young, *A tour in Ireland*, ii, part 2, p. 44.
[6] The rolls have been almost entirely destroyed. P.R.O.I. has transcripts, made by John Lodge in the eighteenth century, and also a calendar of the rolls.

sadly depleted. Even so, the Catholic petition of 1777 was headed by the signatures of six peers—Dillon and Gormanston, whose ancestors were within the articles of Limerick; Fingall and Cahir, whose ancestors had been pardoned; Kenmare (a Jacobite creation) and Trimleston, who held their estates as a result of claims allowed by the trustees. Other signatories included Sir Patrick Bellew, Robert Butler of Ballyraggett and Thomas Kavanagh of Borris, all of whose estates were held under the articles of Limerick.[1]

The Williamite settlement was a compromise. The resistance offered by the Irish for fifteen months after the Boyne and William's anxiety to get rid of the distracting Irish war were responsible for the comparatively favourable terms given by the articles of Limerick and Galway. Those articles were in practice kept in so far as they related to the forfeiture of estates. Claimants were freely admitted to the benefit of the articles, and those admitted either recovered their estates or were secured from the threat of further forfeitures. The policy adopted at Limerick was extended to include the pardon of a limited number of individuals who could not claim the benefit of the articles. With the conclusion of the war William's government showed no anxiety to take further proceedings against Catholics who remained in Ireland, and had not already been outlawed. This official apathy met with the strong disapproval of Irish Protestants. The omission of the celebrated 'protection clause' from the ratification of the Limerick articles was an attempt on William's part to appease the more violent Protestants, who had consistently pressed for the complete dispossession of Catholics. The omission of the clause was not, however, followed by a fresh wave of forfeitures. The principal victims of the Williamite confiscation were firstly, those Catholics of the pale who were so ill-advised as to submit immediately after the Boyne; secondly, those who were killed or taken prisoner or were in France when Limerick capitulated; thirdly, those who like Sarsfield and Galmoy preferred fighting in France to staying at home under a Williamite administration.

The comparative mildness of William's forfeiture policy was to a great extent offset by the penal laws, and in particular those of 1704 and 1709 which imposed serious disabilities on the Catholic holders of landed property. Under the crushing pressure of the penal laws the owners of a great part of the lands secured to Catholics by articles or otherwise conformed to the established church. Although continuity of ownership was thus maintained, the conformists were quickly assimilated and formed an almost indistinguishable part of the Protestant ascend-

[1] Curry, *An historical and critical review*, ii. 293.

ancy. During the greater part of the eighteenth century the minority who retained both their faith and their lands were subjected to constant anxiety and remained completely isolated from Irish public life.

The Williamite confiscation reinforced the territorial predominance which Protestants had enjoyed since the Cromwellian settlement and which had been maintained, although in a diminished form, after the restoration. But the area forfeited by Catholics between 1688 and 1703 was proportionately much less than that which they had lost as a result of the combined effect of the Cromwellian and restoration settlements. In 1688 Catholics had little more than one-third of the land which they had held in 1641. In 1703 they still had nearly two-thirds of the land which they had held in 1688. More than half the land which thus escaped forfeiture passed out of Catholic ownership in the next three-quarters of a century. The acts of 1778 and 1782, which respectively allowed Catholics to take 999 years' leases and to purchase freeholds, marked the turn of the tide. The Catholic recovery resulting from this legislation was very gradual, but became more marked with the passing of the Encumbered Estates Act of 1849. The real revolution in land ownership came with the successive land acts and, in particular, with the Wyndham act of 1903. Since 1922 further redistribution has continued on a considerable scale in both parts of Ireland. The first half of the twentieth century destroyed the whole pattern of land ownership created by the successive confiscations of the seventeenth century. It may be reckoned that in the latter half of the eighteenth century some five thousand Protestant landlords owned nearly the whole of Ireland. By the middle of the twentieth century they had been replaced by more than 300,000 farmers, mainly Catholic, but in the north including many Protestants—nearly all of them buying their holdings from the land commissioners by instalments. The prolonged dominance of the Protestant oligarchy had ended. Ireland had become a country of peasant proprietors.

BIBLIOGRAPHY

T he Williamite confiscation has received little attention from historians. General histories of the period refer to it either briefly or not at all; such accounts as they contain are for the most part limited to a summary of somewhat puzzling statistics. The few writers who have specialized in the subject of Irish confiscations have not succeeded in establishing the facts and figures of the Williamite period on a firm foundation.

The standard version of the confiscation is based on the figures of the report of the inquiry commission of 1699, the misleading character of which is discussed in Appendix A.[1] An attempt to use record material for the history of the confiscation was made in 1864 by W. H. Hardinge, keeper of the Irish landed estates record office. Unfortunately the attempt was not scientific; Hardinge's figures for William's grants and for claims allowed under the Act of Resumption are quite unreliable. They have been quoted by several later writers as if they were authoritative.[2] M. J. Bonn assigned to the Williamite confiscation only six of the seven hundred pages of his *Die englische Kolonisation in Irland* (1906). His treatment of the subject shows industry but no great critical sense. In addition to the inquiry commissioners' report he made use of the statute book, contemporary pamphlets and Hardinge's figures; but he made little attempt to reconcile the discrepancies contained in his material.[3] In spite of its title R. H. Murray's *Revolutionary Ireland and its settlement* (1911) contains remarkably little about the Williamite confiscation. Such account as Murray gives is confused and in many

---

[1] See pp. 174-6, below. The figures are quoted by Froude, *Ire.*, i. 245, Murray, *Revolutionary Ireland and its settlement*, p. 242, and numerous other writers.

[2] *R.I.A. Trans.*, antiquities, xxiv. 265–318. Hardinge's figures are used by W. K. Sullivan, in O'Brien, *Ir. hist. 1691-1870*, pp. 10-15, Murray, op. cit., p. 329, and Curtis, *Ire.*, p. 276.

[3] Bonn, op. cit., ii. 153–8.

respects misconceived; most of his material is taken from such secondary sources as Froude and Bonn.

The only real attempt to solve the problems of the Williamite confiscation was made by W. F. T. Butler who, in his *Confiscation in Irish history* (1917), subjected the figures of the inquiry commissioners' report and those of Hardinge to a critical, but somewhat inconclusive, examination. His discussion of the report was handicapped by the fact that he was apparently not aware of its accompaniments, which would have given him the answers to many of his questions and have disposed of his assumption that the commissioners' figures accounted for virtually the total area held by Catholics. He showed that Hardinge's account of the proceedings of the court of claims was completely misconceived. Butler drew attention to the unsatisfactory character of all previous accounts of the Williamite confiscation and came to the conclusion that 'when one comes to examine the various printed accounts there is scarcely any set of transactions in our history as to which it is so difficult to arrive at the exact facts'. Butler drew his material from the inquiry commissioners' report, the relevant acts of parliament, and Hardinge's paper; but he did not examine the manuscript accompaniments to the commissioners' report.[1]

In the present book the attempt has been made (*a*) to establish the statistical outlines of the Williamite settlement, i.e. the numbers of persons and the areas of land affected by outlawries, pardons, grants, claims and sales, and (*b*) to fill out the narrative and describe the fortunes of various families as they were affected by these proceedings.

(*a*) The statistical material is mainly to be found in the following sources—none of which has previously been used in any published account of the Williamite settlement:[2]

1. The Quit Rent Office set of the Books of Survey and Distribution, which records holdings of land under the restoration settlement as well as sales by the trustees for the Williamite forfeitures.

2. The accompaniments to the report of the inquiry commission of 1699 (copy in T.C.D., MS N. 1. 3), which contain the names of all the persons outlawed and admitted to articles and pardons, together with particulars of the estates forfeited and restored, and a statement of William's grants.[3]

3. The Annesley manuscripts, which contain copies of proceedings

[1] Butler, *Confiscation*, pp. 219–30.

[2] The outlawry proceedings and the records of the forfeiture trustees were preserved in *P.R.O.I.* until 1922, when the record office was blow up. A list of those records is contained in Wood, *P.R.O.I. guide*, pp. 67 and 152–6.

[3] For a fuller account see Appendix A (pp. 174-6, below).

of the inquiry commissioners and the forfeiture trustees, taken by Francis Annesley and preserved at Castlewellan, county Down (microfilms in N.L.I.).[1]

4. The printed lists of the claims heard by the trustees.[2]

5. *The book of postings and sales of the forfeited estates*, 1703.

6. The abstract of the trustees' conveyances (*Ir. rec. com. rep., 1821–5*, pp. 348–96).

These sources have been used to establish figures for the changes in the ownership of land between 1688 and 1703 (Appendix C).[3]

(*b*) Sources for the narrative include the Annesley manuscripts, which in addition to statistical material contain correspondence of the inquiry commissioners and minutes of the trustees' proceedings. They also contain a number of private acts of parliament, the text of which is not otherwise available. Additional information has been collected from parliamentary records, from pamphlets and from scattered references in State Papers and contemporary correspondence. Particular use has been made of Bishop (later Archbishop) King's correspondence in Trinity College, Dublin. His comments on the proceedings connected with the articles of Limerick and the resumption of the forfeited estates are of interest. He was also personally concerned with certain specific issues, on which his correspondence provides useful evidence.

Synopsis

A. SOURCES

I. Manuscript material

1. NATIONAL LIBRARY OF IRELAND, DUBLIN
2. PUBLIC RECORD OFFICE OF IRELAND, DUBLIN
3. ROYAL IRISH ACADEMY, DUBLIN
4. TRINITY COLLEGE, DUBLIN
5. BRITISH MUSEUM, LONDON
6. LAMPORT HALL, NORTHAMPTON

II. Printed material

1. RECORD PUBLICATIONS
2. RECORDS OF PARLIAMENT IN ENGLAND AND IRELAND

---

[1] See descriptive catalogue in *Anal. Hib.*, xvi. 359-64.

[2] A P.R.O.I. copy contains the trustees' decisions entered in manuscript by W. Monck Mason from records subsequently destroyed.

[3] See pp. 193-4, below.

3. PUBLICATIONS OF THE IRISH MANUSCRIPTS COMMISSION
4. PUBLICATIONS OF THE HISTORICAL MANUSCRIPTS COMMISSION
   (OF GREAT BRITAIN)
5. OTHER DOCUMENTARY MATERIAL
6. NEWSPAPERS
7. PAMPHLETS AND OTHER CONTEMPORARY WRITINGS

B. LATER WORKS
   I. GENERAL WORKS
   II. SPECIAL STUDIES

A. Sources

I. MANUSCRIPT MATERIAL

1. NATIONAL LIBRARY OF IRELAND, DUBLIN

Ainsworth reports on manuscripts in private custody:
   (i) Dillon papers;
   (ii) Verdon and Mahon papers;
   (iii) Donovan and Gormanston papers;
   (iv) O'Donovan papers;
   (v) Nugent and Everard papers;
   (vi) Palmer and Sligo papers;
   (vii) Inchiquin papers.
Harris, Walter, Collectanea de rebus Hibernicis, x (MS 10).
Letters of William King, 1690–1715 (MS 2055).
List of claims under articles of Limerick adjudged in 1694 (MS 174).
Manuscripts of the Annesley collection, Castlewellan, county Down
   (microfilms P 259–66 and 276).
Ormonde manuscripts, clvi and clvii.
Report from the commissioners for taking, examining and studying the
   public accounts, 1704 (MS 1541).
   The report is included in a collection of pamphlets which belonged to John
   Cary, one of the trustees.

2. PUBLIC RECORD OFFICE OF IRELAND, DUBLIN

Books of Survey and Distribution (Quit Rent Office set).
Copies of maps of the Down and trustees' surveys.
Dunboyne peerage papers.
Haydock papers.
Lodge, John, Transcripts of convert rolls.

BIBLIOGRAPHY

Phillipps manuscripts, Irish correspondence and king's letters, 1697–1782.
Sarsfield-Vesey collection.
Transcripts of chancery and exchequer inquisitions.
Wyche papers.

3. ROYAL IRISH ACADEMY, DUBLIN

Books of Survey and Distribution (Taylor set).
Documents on the reduction of Ireland, 1689–91 (MSS 24. G. 1–7).

4. TRINITY COLLEGE, DUBLIN

Copies of the books appended to the report of the parliamentary commission on forfeitures, 1699 (MS N. 1. 3).
  An account of these books is given in Appendix A (pp. 174-6, below).
Correspondence of George Clarke, secretary-at-war, 1690–2 (MSS K. 5. 1–13).
Correspondence of William King:
  (*a*) Letter books containing copies of letters written by King, 1696–1727 (MSS N. 3. 1–11).
  (*b*) Boxes of original letters to King (unnumbered).
Papers relating to affairs of state in Ireland, formerly belonging to Sir Robert Southwell and Edward Southwell (MS I. 6. 10).

5. BRITISH MUSEUM, LONDON

Correspondence and papers of George Clarke (Eg. MS 2618).
Correspondence and papers of Robert and Edward Southwell (Add. MSS 21,506 and 38,153; Eg. MS 917).
Letter from the lords justices of Ireland to William Blathwayt, 1699 (Add. MS 9716).
Names of the persons outlawed and indicted of high treason in Ireland sworn before Sir Richard Reynell, chief justice, 1691 (Harl. MS 7545).

6. LAMPORT HALL, NORTHAMPTON

Letters of John Isham to Sir Justinian Isham, Bart., 1700–3 (Isham MSS).

II. PRINTED MATERIAL

1. RECORD PUBLICATIONS

Calendar of state papers, domestic series, 1689–1704, 13 vols, 1895–1938.
Calendar of treasury books, viii–xxiii (1685–1709), 1923–52.
Calendar of treasury papers, 1557-1707, 3 vols, 1868–74.

BIBLIOGRAPHY

Inquisitionum in officio rotulorum cancellariae Hibernicae asservatorum reportorium, i (Lagenia) and ii (Ultonia), 1826–9.

Public Record Office of Ireland, Reports of the deputy keeper:

Seventeenth report, appendix i (Report on contents of attainder chest), 1885.

Fifty-sixth report, appendix iv A (Memorandum on Sarsfield-Vesey collection), 1931.

Fifty-seventh report, appendix iii C (Memorandum on Wyche papers), 1936.

Reports of the commissioners appointed by his majesty to execute the measures recommended in an address of the house of commons respecting the public records of Ireland; with supplements and appendixes, 3 vols, 1811–25.

2. RECORDS OF PARLIAMENT

Cobbett's parliamentary history of England, v, London, 1809.

Firth, C. H. and Rait, R. S., *Acts and ordinances of the interregnum, 1642–60*, 3 vols, London, 1911.

Grey, A., *Debates of the house of commons, 1667–94*, 10 vols, London, 1742.

The history and proceedings of the house of commons, iii, London, 1742.

House of lords manuscripts, new series, iv and v, 1908–10.

The journals of the house of commons.

The journals of the house of commons of the kingdom of Ireland, Dublin, 1796.

The journals of the house of lords.

The journals of the house of lords of Ireland, Dublin, 1779.

Parliamentary cases, 1715–35.

A compilation (in the library of Trinity College, Dublin) of printed statements of cases prepared in connection with appeals to the house of lords.

Statutes at large of England and of Great Britain, 10 vols, London, 1811.

Statutes at large passed in the parliaments held in Ireland, 13 vols, Dublin, 1786.

3. PUBLICATIONS OF THE IRISH MANUSCRIPTS COMMISSION

Analecta Hibernica

i (Report on Bodl. Rawl. MS A. 253), 1930;

xvi (Report on Annesley collection), 1946.

Books of Survey and Distribution, i, county of Roscommon, ed. R. C. Simington, 1949.

Négociations de M. le Comte d'Avaux en Irlande, 1689–90, 1934.

BIBLIOGRAPHY

4. PUBLICATIONS OF THE HISTORICAL MANUSCRIPTS COMMISSION

Fourth report, appendix (Ginkel corr., De Ros MSS), 1874.
Twelfth report, appendix, part vi (House of lords MSS, 1689–90), 1889.
Fourteenth report, appendix ii (Portland MSS), 1894.
Fifteenth report, appendix, part iv (Portland MSS), 1894.
Buccleuch MSS (Montagu House), ii (Shrewsbury corr.), 1903.
Downshire MSS, i, 1924.
Finch MSS, ii (Nottingham corr.), 1922.
Leyborne-Popham MSS (George Clarke's autobiography), 1899.
Ormonde MSS, ii, 1899.
Ormonde MSS, new series, viii, 1903.

5. OTHER DOCUMENTARY MATERIAL

Archivium Hibernicum, ix (Minute book of the Catholic committee, 1773–92), Maynooth, 1942.
Ball, F. E., *Correspondence of Jonathan Swift*, 6 vols, London, 1910–14.
A book of postings and sales of the forfeited and other estates and interests in Ireland, Dublin, 1703.
   A collection of the sale-notices issued by the trustees.
Boulter, H., *Letters written by Hugh Boulter, D.D., lord primate of Ireland*, 2 vols, Dublin, 1770.
Brady, W. M., *State papers concerning the Irish church in the time of Queen Elizabeth*, London, 1868.
Coxe, W., *Private and original correspondence of Charles Talbot, duke of Shrewsbury*, London, 1821.
Curtis, E. and McDowell, R. B., *Irish historical documents*, London, 1943.
A diary of the siege and surrender of Limerick, London, 1692.
   The official Williamite account, 'published by authority'.
A geographical description of the kingdom of Ireland, 2nd ed., London, 1720.
Gilbert, J. T., *A Jacobite narrative of the war in Ireland, 1689–91*, Dublin, 1892.
Jacob, G., *A new law-dictionary*, London, 1729.
James, G. P. R., *Letters illustrative of the reign of King William III*, 3 vols, London, 1841.
Japikse, N., *Correspondentie van Willem en van Hans Willem Bentinck, eersten Graf van Portland*, iii, Hague, 1937.
Lansdowne, *The Petty-Southwell correspondence, 1676–87*, London, 1928.

BIBLIOGRAPHY

A list of the claims as they are entered with the trustees at Chichester House, Dublin, 1701.
A collection of the notices issued by the trustees, giving particulars of claims.

A list of the names of such of the nobility, gentry and commonalty . . . who are all by an act of a pretended parliament . . . attainted of high treason, together with the true and authentic copies of several of the acts of the said pretended parliament, London, 1690.

A particular relation of the surrender of Galway, London, 1691.
The official Williamite account, 'published by authority'.

The report of the commissioners appointed by parliament to inquire into the Irish forfeitures, London, 1700.

The report of the trustees for the forfeited estates of Ireland, Dublin, 1704.

6. NEWSPAPERS

Dublin Intelligence, 1690–1703.
The London Gazette, 1690–1709.
Both of these are official publications.

7. PAMPHLETS AND OTHER CONTEMPORARY WRITINGS

An argument proving that it is more to the interest of the government and nation of England that the forfeited estates in Ireland be purchased by an incorporated company than by single purchasers, London, 1701.

Burnet, G., *History of his own time*, 6 vols, Oxford, 1823.

Cary, J., *A vindication of the parliament of England in answer to a book written by William Molyneux of Dublin, esquire*, London, 1698.

The case of the forfeitures in Ireland fairly stated, with the reasons that induced the Protestants there to purchase them, London, 1700.

The case of Maurice Annesley, esquire, in answer to the complaint of Mr Eustace Sherlock, 1705.

The case of Thomas, earl of Limerick, and William Sherlock, appellants, versus Maurice Annesley, respondent, (c. 1706).

[Cox, R.], *Aphorisms relating to the kingdom of Ireland*, 1689.

[Davenant, C.], *A discourse upon grants and resumptions*, 2nd ed., London, 1700.

A declaration for Ireland or no declaration, London, 1689.

The Derry complaint, Dublin, 1699.

Evelyn, J., *Diary*, ed. W. Bray, 4 vols, London, 1879.

The exorbitant grants of William III examined and questioned, London, 1703.

Harris, W., *The history of the life and reign of William-Henry, . . . king of England, Scotland, France and Ireland, etc.*, Dublin, 1749.

BIBLIOGRAPHY

The humble petition of John Power, esquire, commonly called Lord Power (*c.* 1706).

Jus regium, or the king's right to grant forfeitures, London, 1701.

[King, W.], *The state of the Protestants of Ireland under the late King James's government*, London, 1691.

Lawrence, R., *The interest of Ireland in its trade and wealth stated*, Dublin, 1682.

[Leslie, C.], *An answer to a book intituled The state of the Protestants in Ireland under the late King James's government*, London, 1692.

A letter from a soldier to the commons of England occasioned by an address now carrying on by the Protestants in Ireland in order to take away the fund appropriated to the arrears of the army, London, 1702.

Luttrell, N., *A brief historical relation of state affairs from September 1678 to April 1714*, 6 vols, Oxford, 1857.

Marsh, N., 'Diary' (*Irish Ecclesiastical Journal*, v), Dublin, 1848.

Molyneux, W., *The case of Ireland's being bound by acts of parliament in England stated*, London, 1698.

Mr Moore of Ballyna's deposition relating to the paragraph in the six-penny secret history of the trust, 1702.

Mullenaux, S., *A journal of the three months royal campaign of his majesty in Ireland*, London, 1690.

O'Kelly, C., *Macariae excidium, or the destruction of Cyprus*, ed. J. C. O'Callaghan, Dublin, 1850.

Pepys, S., *Diary*, ed. G. G. Smith, London, 1905.

Petty, W., *Economic writings*, ed. C. H. Hull, 2 vols, Cambridge, 1899.

[Prior, T.], *A list of the absentees of Ireland and the yearly value of their estates and incomes spent abroad*, 1729.

Ralph, J., *The history of England during the reigns of King William, Queen Anne and King George I*, 2 vols, London, 1744–6.

Reasons for his majesty's issuing a general pardon to the rebels of Ireland, London, 1689.

The secret history of the trust, with some reflections upon the letter from a soldier, in a familiar discourse between J. Truncheon, esquire, and Mr Inquisitive, London, 1702.

The settlement of the land bank, 1695.

The several addresses of some Irish folks to the king and the house of commons (1701).

A short view of the faithful service performed by his majesty's forces who defended the city of Londonderry, 1700.

State of the Papist and Protestant proprieties in the kingdom of Ireland, London, 1689.

BIBLIOGRAPHY

Story, G., *A continuation of the impartial history of the wars of Ireland*, London, 1693.

[Story, G.], *A true and impartial history of the most material occurrences in the kingdom of Ireland during the last two years*, London, 1691.

Swift, J., *The prose works of*, ed. T. Scott, i, ii, vi, London, 1897–1903.

Tindal, N., *The history of England*, 4 vols, London, 1788–9.

The trial and conviction of Patrick Hurley, late of Moughan, in the county of Clare, gent., Dublin, 1701.

Ware, J., *The history of the writers of Ireland*, revised by W. Harris, Dublin, 1764.

B. Later Works

I. GENERAL WORKS

Anderson, A., *An historical and chronological deduction of the origin of commerce*, 2 vols, London, 1774.

Beckett, J. C., *A short history of Ireland*, London, 1952.

Complete baronetage, ed. G. E. C(okayne), 6 vols, Exeter, 1900–9.

Curtis, E., *A history of Ireland*, 6th ed., London, 1950.

Dictionary of national biography, ed. L. Stephen and S. Lee, 66 vols, London, 1885–1901.

Feiling, K., *A history of the tory party, 1640–1714*, Oxford, 1924.

Froude, J. A., *The English in Ireland in the eighteenth century*, 3 vols, London, 1887.

Macaulay, T. B., *The history of England from the accession of James II*, 3 vols, London, 1906 (Everyman ed.).

Marx, K., *Capital*, 2 vols, London, 1930 (Everyman ed.).

Ranke, L. von, *A history of England principally in the seventeenth century*, 6 vols, Oxford, 1875.

Relton, F. B., *An account of the fire insurance companies, associations, projects and schemes established and projected in Great Britain and Ireland during the seventeenth and eighteenth centuries*, London, 1893.

Scott, W. R., *The constitution and finance of English and Scottish and Irish joint-stock companies to 1720*, 3 vols, Cambridge, 1912.

Sullivan, W. K., 'From the treaty of Limerick to the establishment of legislative independence, 1691–1782' in *Two centuries of Irish history, 1691–1870*, ed. R. B. O'Brien, 2nd ed., London, 1907.

Turberville, A. S., *The house of lords in the reign of William III*, Oxford, 1913.

Young, A., *A tour in Ireland*, 2 vols, Dublin, 1780.

BIBLIOGRAPHY

II. SPECIAL STUDIES

Bonn, M. J., *Die englische Kolonisation in Irland*, 2 vols, Stuttgart and Berlin, 1906.

Browne, P. W., 'Thomas Dongan, soldier and statesman, Irish Catholic governor of New York, 1683-8' in *Studies*, xxiii. 489–501 (1934).

Butler, W. F. T., *Confiscation in Irish history*, 2nd ed., Dublin and London, 1918.

Crofton, H. T., *Crofton memoirs*, York, 1911.

Curry, J., *An historical and critical review of the civil wars in Ireland . . . with the state of the Irish Catholics*, 2 vols, Dublin, 1786.

Dunraven, Caroline, countess of, *Memorials of Adare*, Oxford, 1865.

Edwards, R. D., *Church and state in Tudor Ireland*, London, 1935.

Goblet, Y. M., *La transformation de la géographie politique de l'Irlande au xviie siècle*, 2 vols, Paris, 1930.

Grace, S., *Memoirs of the family of Grace*, London, 1823.

Hardinge, W. H., 'A concluding memoir on manuscript mapped and other townland surveys in Ireland, from 1688 to 1864' in *R.I.A. Trans.*, antiquities, xxiv. 265–315 (1864).

Kirkpatrick, T. P. C., *The history of Doctor Steevens' hospital, Dublin, 1720–1920*, Dublin, 1924.

Murray, R. H., *Revolutionary Ireland and its settlement*, London, 1911.

Prendergast, J. P., *The Cromwellian settlement of Ireland*, London, 1865.

Simms, J. G., 'Land owned by Catholics in Ireland in 1688' in *I.H.S.*, vii. 180–90 (1951).

Simms, J. G., 'The original draft of the civil articles of Limerick' in *I.H.S.*, viii. 37–44 (1952).

Simms, J. G., 'Williamite peace tactics, 1690–1' in *I.H.S.*, viii. 303–23 (1953).

APPENDIX A

NOTE ON THE REPORT OF THE
INQUIRY COMMISSIONERS, 1690

The report, on which all previous accounts of the Williamite confiscation are based, contains a series of statistics giving the number of persons (*a*) outlawed, (*b*) comprised in adjudications under
the articles of Limerick and Galway, (*c*) specially pardoned—together
with the areas of land forfeited and restored. It has thus provided historians with a convenient set of figures, which apparently enabled a more
clear-cut and factual account to be given of the Williamite confiscation
than was possible for any previous Irish confiscation. Unfortunately, the
statistics of the report are misleading and have led to a number of
erroneous conclusions about the character and extent of the Williamite
confiscation. The figures may be summarized as follows:

A. *Individuals*
    Outlawed (*a*) in England   57
            (*b*) in Ireland   3,921   3,978[1]
    Adjudged under articles of Limerick
        and Galway   1,283
    Pardoned by royal favour   65

B. *Area*
(expressed in terms of profitable Irish acres)
    Forfeited and not restored   752,953
    Forfeited and restored
        (*a*) by articles   233,106
        (*b*) by royal favour   74,733

                                     1,060,792[2]

[1] Actually 3,921 is the total of the names in the outlawry lists for England and
Ireland taken together.
[2] *Commissioners' report*, pp. 9-13.

From these figures it has been inferred that 3,978 estates were for-
feated, of which 1,283 were restored under the articles of Limerick and
Galway and 65 by royal favour, which would leave a balance of 2,630
confiscated estates.[1] Butler drew attention to the difficulty of reconciling
these figures with the much lower figures available for the estates recovered by Catholics at the restoration.[2]

The difficulty can be resolved by reference to the full record of the
commissioners' investigations contained in nine books, to which the
report was designed to serve as an index.[3] The first book contains the
names of those outlawed, the second gives particulars of the forfeited
estates, the third and fourth give the names of those adjudged under the
articles of Limerick and Galway, and the fifth gives particulars of pardons and reversals of outlawry. The remaining books deal with grants,
encumbrances, debts and James's 'private estate'. The first, third, fourth
and fifth books contain lists of outlawries, adjudications, pardons and
reversals, supplied to the commissioners by the Irish courts. The commissioners incorporated the totals of these lists in their report without
making it clear that they had no relation to the number of estates recorded in the second book. The compilation of the second book—the
Book of Forfeitures—was the major contribution made by the commissioners themselves to their task of taking account of the Irish forfeitures. The book sets out on double pages the estates forfeited in the
several baronies of each county. The left-hand pages show estates forfeited and not restored; the right-hand pages show estates which were
forfeited but later restored to their owners either under the articles or
by royal favour. The names of all the forfeiting proprietors in each
barony are given, but individual estates are not clearly differentiated.
The most remarkable feature of the book is the small number of estates
recorded, only 457 in all. The left-hand pages give a total of 272 persons
whose estates, amounting to 752,953 acres, were forfeited and not
restored. The right-hand pages give a total of 161 persons whose estates,
amounting to 233,106 acres, were restored under the articles of Limerick
and Galway, and of 24 persons whose estates, amounting to 74,733
acres, were restored by royal favour.

[1] Ranke, *History of England*, v. 207; Froude, *Ire.*, i. 245; Butler, *Confiscation*,
p. 227; Curtis, *Ire.*, pp. 275-6.

[2] Butler, op. cit., p. 220.

[3] See p. 105, above. Sets of the nine books are in the house of lords (*H.L. MSS*,
n.s., iv. 17-30) and in T.C.D., MS N. 1. 3. The latter came from the collection of
James Weale, a well-known antiquary, who traced it to the library of William
Lowndes, secretary to the treasury in 1699. Weale acquired his copy in 1831 and
noted that he had compared it with the original which was presented to the house of
commons. The commons copy was subsequently destroyed in the fire of 1834.

APPENDIX A

The explanation for the difference between the number of those outlawed and the total number of estates recorded is that the great majority of those outlawed were not landed proprietors. The outlawry lists describe a number of individuals as yeomen or traders; many others belonged to families which had already been dispossessed of their lands. Of the 1,283 claims under the articles of Limerick and Galway, 1,267 succeeded; about half the successful claimants belonged to landed families. Only 161 estates were recorded as restored under the articles because the commissioners took account only of estates which had actually been seized by the Williamite authorities. Many of those admitted to the articles owned estates, particularly in Connacht, which had not been seized by the end of the war. The area recorded as restored under the articles was less than half the total area owned by 'articlemen'. The figure of 65 persons recorded as pardoned by royal favour is misleading. The fifth book—the Book of Pardons and Reversals—is in two sections, the first containing 28 pardons, the second containing 37 reversals by special warrant. Eleven names occur in both lists, thus reducing the total to 54. A number of these had no land, while others had not been outlawed but had obtained pardons as a precautionary measure. The total number of estates which were seized and then restored to the recipients of pardons was only 24.

The figures cited in the report are thus extremely misleading. But it does not seem likely that the commissioners deliberately tried to give a false impression. Their principal object was to show that it was well worth the while of the English parliament to appropriate the proceeds of the forfeited estates, and also that the extent of the forfeitures would have been greater still had it not been for the incompetence, partiality and corruption of the executive. It would not have helped their argument to suggest that the number of forfeited estates was greater than it actually was; they were primarily interested in the area and value of the estates and not in the number of their owners. After giving the number of persons outlawed the report stated that the second book contained particulars of the estates 'that the said persons, or any of them, were interested in'. The qualifying clause may be said to meet the point that most of the names in the first book—the Book of Outlawries—do not occur in the second book—the Book of Forfeitures.

APPENDIX B

SUMMARY OF TRUSTEES' SALES, 1702-3

The summary is based on the abstract of conveyances given in the *Irish records commissioners' reports, 1821–5*, pp. 348–96. The areas are expressed in profitable Irish acres. The figures relate to outright sales of land.

1. FORFEITED ESTATES SOLD

Name of forfeiting owner	County	Area
Abercorn, Claud, earl of	Tyrone	9,681
Archer, Henry	Kilkenny	140
Archer, Patrick	Meath	370
Arthur, Francis	Clare	174
Arthur, Nicholas	Clare	440
Baggot, John	Limerick	727
Bagenal, Dudley	Carlow	403
Balfe, Robert	Meath	121
Barnwell, Dominick	Meath	1,029
Barnwell, Matthew	Meath	526
Barrett, John	Cork	11,570
Barry, Edmond	Cork	1,681
Barry, John	Cork	481
Bellew, Thomas	Meath	189
Birford, Ignatius	Meath	1,250
Blanchfield, Edmund	Kilkenny	2,893
Boyton, Edward	Roscommon	282
Brereton, John	Queen's Co.	835
Brittas, Theobald, Lord	Limerick	1,142
Browne, Andrew	Mayo	120
Browne, James	Mayo	940
Bryan, Walter	Kilkenny	493
	Queen's Co.	398
Bolger, James	Kilkenny	85
Burke, Thomas	Galway	138
	Mayo	938
Burke, Ulick	Galway	35

Name of forfeiting owner	County	Area
Burke, Walter	Mayo	5,899
Burke, William	Galway	441
Byrne, Barnaby	Meath	703
Byrne, Charles	Carlow	150
Carthy, Daniel M'Fin	Kerry	1,965
Cowell, John	Wexford	326
	Wicklow	45
Chamberlain, Michael	Dublin	112
	Meath	278
Cheevers, Christopher	Louth	582
Cheevers, Edward (Lord Mountleinster)	Galway	1,415
Clancarty, Donogh, earl of	Cork	139,732
	Kerry	8,880
Clare, Daniel, Viscount	Clare	30,180
Clinton, Thomas	Louth	925
Coghlan, Terence	King's Co.	3,169
Comyn, John	Clare	137
Connell, Maurice	Dublin	207
Coppinger, Thomas	Cork	158
Coppinger, Walter	Cork	2,557
Creagh, William	Clare	113
Crump, Adam	Meath	364
Crump, Richard	Dublin	100
Dalton, Henry	Westmeath	400
Dalton, John	Westmeath	455
Daly, Teige	Galway	213
Darcy, Nicholas	Louth	1,054
	Meath	2,289
	Westmeath	3,628
Dempsey, James	Kildare	800
Dillon, Christopher	Roscommon	1,169
Dillon, Garrett	Roscommon	292
	Westmeath	326
Dillon, Gerald	Mayo	2,840
	Roscommon	825
	Westmeath	1,042
Dowdall, Henry	Meath	687
Dowdall, Sir Luke	Meath	1,157
Driscoll, Cornelius	Cork	332
Egan, Thomas	Kildare	231
Etchingham, John	Wexford	919
Eustace, Alexander	Kildare	618
Eustace, Lawrence	Kildare	361
Eustace, Sir Maurice	Dublin	261
	Kildare	2,442
Everard, Sir John	Tipperary	1,743
Everard, Patrick	Longford	52
	Roscommon	241

Name of forfeiting owner	*County*	*Area*
Evers, Christopher	Meath	269
Fagan, Richard	Dublin	1,429
	Meath	919
	Sligo	2,507
Farrell, Fergus	Longford	244
Farrell, Iriel	Galway	308
	Roscommon	97
Fitzgerald, Edward	Kilkenny	1,685
Fitzgerald, James	Limerick	900
Fitzgerald, Sir John	Limerick	2,068
Fitzmaurice, James	Kerry	1,300
Fitzpatrick, Dermot	Clare	254
Fleming, Thomas	Louth	176
Flynn, Feighry	Roscommon	3,440
Gallway, Arthur	Cork	56
Gallway, Edmond	Cork	723
Gallway, Edward	Cork	4,122
Gallway, Walter	Cork	1,418
	Waterford	282
Galmoy, Piers, Viscount	Kilkenny	11,356
	Wexford	4,931
Geoghegan, Charles	King's Co.	2,816
Geoghegan, Edward	Westmeath	780
Gilligan, James	Wexford	500
Goold, Ignatius	Cork	1,070
Goold, John	Kerry	210
Grace, John	Kilkenny	651
Grace, Richard	Clare	75
	Kilkenny	424
	King's Co.	1,185
Grace, Robert	Kilkenny	7,406
	King's Co.	216
Graham, Richard	Queen's Co.	137
Hackett, James	Dublin	487
	Meath	101
Hoare, Martin	Waterford	5,046
Hovendon, Robert	Armagh	818
Hussey, Thomas	Meath	447
James, The late King	Carlow	768
	Cork	11,479
	Dublin	4,531
	Down	558
	Galway	5,830
	Kildare	8,749
	Kilkenny	4,149
	King's Co.	1,001
	Limerick	14,486
	Londonderry	80

APPENDIX B

Name of forfeiting owner	*County*	*Area*
	Meath	12,083
	Roscommon	3,996
	Tipperary	10,051
	Waterford	15
	Westmeath	9,021
	Wexford	533
	Total 87,330	
Keating, William	Meath	330
Kelly, Lawrence	Galway	161
	Roscommon	157
Kigan, Murtagh	Westmeath	87
Lacy, Thomas	Roscommon	342
Lally, James	Galway	812
Larkan, John	Kilkenny	202
Lawless, Walter	Kilkenny	181
Leigh, Francis	Kildare	4,505
Leicester, Thomas	King's Co.	1,781
Lovelock, Dominick	Galway	102
Lyne, John	Kerry	652
Lowther, Edmund	Meath	64
MacCarthy, Charles of Ardnaclugg	Cork	848
MacCarthy, Charles of Carrignavar	Cork	366
MacCarthy, Charles of Toonadrooma	Cork	1,008
MacCarthy, Justin	Cork	4,109
MacCarthy, Teige	Cork	3,753
Magennis, Murtagh	Armagh	352
MacNamara, Donogh	Clare	140
Magee, Patrick	Cavan	132
Magrath, Redmond	Clare	172
Malony, Dan	Clare	176
Martin, Peter	Galway	2,805
Mathews, Patrick	Monaghan	120
Meagher, Thady	Tipperary	226
Moore, Ambrose	Kerry	254
Morris, Edmund	Queen's Co.	14
Mulledy, Sir Anthony	Meath	2,569
Mulledy, Redmond	Westmeath	4,341
Morrough, Andrew	Cork	501
Nagle, Pierce	Cork	1,570
Nagle, Sir Richard	Cork	3,557
Nangle, Robert	Westmeath	932
Nangle, Walter	Meath	668
Nihill, David	Clare	238
Nottingham, Peter	Dublin	1,020
	Meath	63
Nottingham, Robert	Dublin	9
Nugent, Christopher	Roscommon	1,549
	Westmeath	588

APPENDIX B

Name of forfeiting owner	County	Area
Nugent, Sir John	Meath	932
	Roscommon	1,980
	Westmeath	4,231
O'Brien, Donogh	Clare	40
O'Brien, Teige	Clare	88
O'Connor, Charles	Roscommon	175
O'Connor, Roger	Roscommon	326
O'Hara, John	Down	160
O'Keefe, Daniel	Cork	8,488
O'Neile, Henry	Mayo	3,688
O'Neile, Sir Neile	Antrim	7,134
O'Neile, Toole	Down	30
Peppard, Christopher	Louth	16
Plunkett, Edward	Meath	202
Plunkett, Thomas	Meath	473
Power, James	Clare	65
Reilly, Hugh	Cavan	140
Rice, Edward	Kerry	170
	Limerick	551
Ronan, Nicholas	Cork	222
Russell, Bartholomew	Dublin	524
Ryan, Charles	Kilkenny	968
Ryan, John	Clare	1,005
Ryan, Martin	Clare	50
Sarsfield, Dominick	Cork	2,497
Sarsfield, Patrick	Dublin	1,348
	Kildare	5,263
Sheile, Denis	Westmeath	96
Sherlock, Christopher	Kildare	846
Skiddy, Nicholas	Kerry	1,250
Skiddy, Thomas	Kerry	252
Slane, Christopher, Lord	Cavan	1,236
	Louth	1,123
	Meath	9,614
	Monaghan	104
	Roscommon	457
Strange, Abraham	Wexford	140
Sutton, John	Kildare	148
Sutton, Thomas	Dublin	171
Sweetman, Edward	Dublin	132
Talbot, George	Roscommon	1,025
Talbot, James	Dublin	140
	Galway	225
Talbot, William	Louth	234
Talbot, Sir William	Meath	139
	Wicklow	1,530
Trant, Sir Patrick	Dublin	116
	Kerry	18,091

APPENDIX B

Name of forfeiting owner	*County*	*Area*
	Kildare	1,448
	King's Co.	10,359
	Limerick	1,242
	Queen's Co.	12,022
Tuite, Walter	Westmeath	1,521
Tuite, William	Galway	648
Tully, Matthew	Galway	198
Tyrconnell, Richard, earl of	Dublin	1,992
	Kildare	3,781
	Louth	339
	Meath	3,605
Tyrrell, Peter	Westmeath	530
Wadden, John	Mayo	292
Walsh, Robert	Kilkenny	1,675
Warren, John	Carlow	200
White, Nicholas	Clare	66
	Wexford	90
White, Patrick	Wexford	30
Wray, Sir Drury	Limerick	83

2. ESTATES PURCHASED

Name of purchaser	*County*	*Area*
Abercorn, James, earl of	Tyrone	8,982
Adams, Randall	Westmeath	455
Adams, Randolph	Westmeath	194
Agar, James	Kilkenny	3,776
Allen, John	Dublin	229
Anderson, Arthur	Kilkenny	322
Anderson, James	Antrim	732
	Down	558
	Kildare	257
	Kilkenny	36
Annesley, Francis	Kildare	161
Armstrong, Charles	Kildare	225
Asgill, John	Cork	6,538
	Kildare	2,961
	King's Co.	1,269
	Louth	873
	Meath	2,058
	Tipperary	131
	Wexford	326
	Westmeath	856
Ashe, Thomas	Kildare	800
Ashurst, Sir William	Roscommon	298
Atkins, Robert	Cork	310
Baker, Thomas	Dublin	107

APPENDIX B

APPENDIX B

Name of purchaser	County	Area
	Louth	41
	Meath	966
Card, Samuel	Kildare	500
	Meath	111
	Westmeath	1,135
Carleton, Christopher	Dublin	468
Carleton, John	Tipperary	49
Carpenter, George	Kilkenny	1,068
Carter, Thomas	Dublin	12
	Limerick	5
	Meath	2,157
Chaigneau, Lewis	Dublin	213
Clayton, John	Dublin	167
Cockerell, William	Cork	976
Coghill, Marmaduke	Dublin	222
	Kilkenny	140
Colley, Henry	Kildare	52
Colthurst, Nicholas	Cork	1,375
Connor, Daniel	Cork	1,311
Connor, Thomas	Kerry	652
Conolly, William	Meath	998
	Roscommon	2,182
	Westmeath	4,819
	Wexford	629
Conyngham, Henry	Meath	1,838
Cooke, John	Tipperary	481
Cooke, Richard	Dublin	171
Cosgrave, Edward	Kerry	170
	Limerick	551
Cox, Sir Richard	Cork	381
	Kilkenny	453
Craige, Robert	Tipperary	1,067
Crawford, Thomas	Kilkenny	202
Crow, Edward	Galway	502
Cuppaidge, Faustin	Meath	54
Curtis, Robert	Kildare	1,593
	Louth	11
	Meath	172
Cusack, John	Clare	825
Dalyell, Thomas	Kildare	2,871
Damer, Jospeh	Tipperary	103
D'Arabine, Bartholomew	Westmeath	654
Daunt, Thomas	Cork	99
Davis, Henry	Dublin	473
	Kildare	669
Dawson, Ephraim	Westmeath	1,333
Dawson, James	Dublin	53
	Kildare	252

APPENDIX B

Name of purchaser	County	Area
	Limerick	809
	Tipperary	82
Deane, Joseph	Cork	222
Deane, Sir Matthew	Cork	1,080
	Limerick	76
Des Blosset, Solomon	Dublin	7
	Meath	551
Despard, William	Queen's Co.	398
Des Vignoles, Charles	Kildare	251
Dillon, Sir John	Meath	1,509
Dixon, Abraham	Cork	2,240
Domvile, Sir Thomas	Dublin	140
Dopping, Anthony	Westmeath	160
Dopping, Samuel	Meath	1,798
Drisdall, Griffith	Kilkenny	7
Drury, John	Meath	143
Dubay, Lewis	Kilkenny	139
Dunscomb, Willliam	Cork	240
Eccles, John	Dublin	63
Echlin, Robert	Dublin	955
	Kildare	97
Edge, Timothy	Dublin	81
Edgeworth, Robert	Westmeath	776
Elsmere, Josiah	Kildare	49
Erberry, Mathias	Cork	237
Evans, George	Cork	66
	Limerick	94
Eyre, John	Galway	213
Falkner, Daniel	Kildare	87
Farthing, Robert	Cork	1,074
Fitzmaurice, William	Limerick	2,068
Fitzpatrick, Richard	Kildare	303
	Queen's Co.	835
Forbes, Arthur	Meath	95
Ford, Edward	Dublin	573
	Meath	523
Forrest, Daniel	Dublin	73
Forster, John	Dublin	595
Fortescue, William	Monaghan	120
Francklyn, Joseph	Cork	310
Freke, Piercey	Cork	2,847
Garstin, John	Meath	37
Garstin, Norman	Monaghan	104
Gaynor, Mrs Vere	Westmeath	172
Geoghegan, Terence	Clare	172
	Westmeath	20
Gibbons, Samuel	Meath	282
Gibbons, William	Dublin	127

APPENDIX B

Name of purchaser	County	Area
Gore, Ralph	Kilkenny	21
Gore, William	Roscommon	175
Gorges, Richard	Meath	852
Gower, Henry	Tipperary	119
Graham, Edmund	Dublin	150
Graham, John	Louth	998
	Meath	1,652
Green, Abraham	Limerick	564
Gumbleton, Richard	Cork	828
Gunning, Bryan	Roscommon	457
Hall, William	Dublin	28
Hamilton, Gustavus	Roscommon	339
Hamilton, James	Meath	63
	Tyrone	389
Hamilton, William	Down	30
Hampson, Charles	Westmeath	11
Harman, Wentworth	Kildare	302
Harrison, William	Waterford	282
Hartstonge, John, bishop of Ossory	Kilkenny	174
Hatch, Nicholas	Meath	40
Hewetson, William	Kildare	231
Higgins, Bryan	Mayo	2,840
	Roscommon	825
	Westmeath	1,042
Hingston, James	Cork	353
Hoare, Edward	Cork	1,987
Hodder, John	Cork	132
Hodder, Thomas	Cork	594
Hollow Blades	Antrim	3,763
	Armagh	352
	Clare	219
	Cork	130,944
	Down	160
	Dublin	618
	Galway	1,777
	Kerry	32,202
	Kildare	3,318
	Kilkenny	17,922
	King's Co.	18,223
	Limerick	6,585
	Londonderry	80
	Louth	1,054
	Mayo	3,307
	Meath	1,725
	Queen's Co.	12,159
	Roscommon	63
	Sligo	2,133
	Tipperary	4,616

APPENDIX B

Name of purchaser	County	Area
	Waterford	5,046
	Westmeath	2,372
	Wexford	5,071
	Total 253,709	
Holmes, Peter	King's Co.	177
Holroid, Isaac	Meath	447
Howth, Lord	Dublin	4
Hughes, John	Kildare	549
	Westmeath	579
Hull, Dame Frances	Cork	125
Hunt, John	Limerick	178
Hutchinson, Hugh	Cork	1,418
Ingoldsby, Richard	Kildare	403
Irwin, Henry	Sligo	374
Ivers, John	Clare	395
Jackson, Daniel	Dublin	96
Jackson, Samuel	Dubiln	180
Jacob, Matthew	Tipperary	464
Johnson, Catherine	Carlow	144
Johnson, George	Armagh	818
Johnston, James	Longford	52
Johnston, Robert	Cavan	132
Jones, George	Westmeath	63
Jones, Lewis	Dublin	112
Jones, Richard	Meath	116
Judkin, Joseph	Tipperary	226
Keightley, Thomas	Kildare	1,357
Kellett, Richard	Tipperary	100
Kelly, Brian	Galway	161
Kelly, Joseph	Kilkenny	115
Kent, John	Kilkenny	98
Kiernan, James	Dublin	263
King, Robert	Tyrone	310
King, William, archbishop of Dublin	Dublin	524
Lambe, William	Meath	80
Langford, Sir Arthur	Antrim	982
	Meath	2,095
Langrish, John	Kilkenny	239
Lapp, John	Waterford	15
Leagh, John	Meath	30
	Westmeath	598
Leeds, Michael	Dublin	76
Levinge, Sir Richard	Louth	339
	Westmeath	1,610
Lewis, James	Galway	308
Lewis, Richard	Tipperary	253
Lloyd, Andrew	Kildare	110
	Meath	655

Name of purchaser	County	Area
Lloyd, Richard	Kildare	410
	Roscommon	772
Loftus, Henry	Wexford	30
Low, Samuel	Meath	27
Lowe, David	Tipperary	948
Lowther, George	Meath	323
Ludlow, Stephen	Cork	7,594
	Meath	468
Luther, Henry	Cork	192
	Tipperary	260
Maddock, Joseph	Kildare	436
Magan, Thomas	Westmeath	1,362
Mahon, Bartholomew	Roscommon	179
Mainwaring, William	Kiklenny	456
Mansell, Thomas	Limerick	144
Marriott, Joseph	Kildare	76
Marsh, Jeremiah	Kilkenny	105
Mason, Robert	Galway	138
Massy, Samuel	Roscommon	342
Mathews, Humphrey	Wicklow	45
Meade, Benjamin	Dublin	93
Meade, Sir John	Cork	3,674
	Tipperary	45
Meares, John	Westmeath	149
Meares, Lewis	Westmeath	454
Meredith, Arthur	Meath	1,070
Minchin, William	Tipperary	225
Mitchell, Joseph	Roscommon	3,343
Moland, Joseph	Kildare	335
Molyneux, Thomas	Dublin	236
	Meath	189
Montgomery, Alexander	Meath	364
	Roscommon	3,465
	Tipperary	537
Moore, Elinor	Cork	101
Moore, John	Cork	143
Moore, William	Mayo	3,688
Morris, Abraham	Cork	2,174
Morrison, John	Cork	68
Mountjoy, Lord	Dublin	4
Murphy, Patience	Cork	976
Napper, James	Meath	56
Neale, Benjamin	Wexford	90
Newenham, John	Cork	743
Newenham, Thomas	Cork	553
Newstead, Richard	Westmeath	891
Newton, John	Louth	539
O'Brien, Sir Donough	Clare	614

APPENDIX B

Name of purchaser	County	Area
Ogle, Henry	Louth	7
	Meath	494
Ormsby, John	Roscommon	817
Osborne, Henry	Meath	223
Pacey, John	Dublin	422
Pakenham, Robert	Meath	195
	Westmeath	3,781
Page, John	Meath	305
Paine, William	Meath	156
Palmer, William	Meath	697
Partington, Peter	Meath	270
Paul, Jeffery	Kildare	1,464
Pearson, Matthew	Kildare	211
Peppard, Jacob	Kildare	65
	Meath	89
Perry, John	Tipperary	637
Persse, Henry	Galway	593
Philipps, Chichester	Westmeath	580
Philipps, Richard	Cork	47
Piercey, Henry	Dublin	14
Piers, Honoria, Lady	Westmeath	30
Piers, William	Westmeath	249
Pike, John	Tipperary	84
Piper, Stephen	Meath	334
Pollard, Walter	Westmeath	35
Ponsonby, William	Kilkenny	281
Powell, Richard	Limerick	255
Pratt, Benjamin	Meath	439
Preston, John	Meath	85
Price, Nicholas	Wexford	288
Putland, Thomas	Cork	4,597
Pyne, Sir Richard	Cork	1,964
Pyper, John	Tipperary	57
Ram, Abel	Meath	96
Rathwell, John	Meath	169
Riggs, Edward	Cork	2,859
Riggs, Stephen	Dublin	505
Rigmaiden, Robert	Meath	233
Riley, Edward	Meath	585
Robinson, Sir William	Carlow	150
	Louth	407
Roch, Edmond	Cork	2,557
Rochfort, Robert	Dublin	421
	Meath	314
	Westmeath	922
Rogers, George	Cork	1,087
Rogers, Robert	Cork	345
Rogers, William	Dublin	60

APPENDIX B

Name of purchaser	County	Area
Rogerson, Sir John	Dublin	205
	Kildare	365
	Westmeath	173
Rolls, Samuel	Cork	122
Roth, Abraham	Kilkenny	550
Rotton, John	Dublin	104
Ryan, Morgan	Clare	122
St George, Henry	Roscommon	94
St George, Richard	Kilkenny	142
St John, Thomas	Clare	176
St Leger, John	Cork	251
Sandford, Henry	Roscommon	97
Scawen, Sir William	Galway	4,729
Schuldam, Edmund	Clare	88
Shaw, Robert	Galway	1,156
Shaw, William	Antrim	572
Sheares, Humphrey	Cork	1,245
Sheppard, Anthony	Westmeath	70
Sherigley, Folliott	Dublin	428
Sherlock, William	Kildare	812
Shields, Michael	Meath	179
Shinton, Richard	Meath	330
Singleton, Edward	Meath	2,672
Sisson, Thomas	Westmeath	271
Smith, Edward, bishop of Down and Connor	Dublin	338
Smith, Ralph	Westmeath	159
Smith, Robert	Westmeath	23
Smith, Thomas, bishop of Limerick	Limerick	867
Smith, William	Cork	280
Somerville, Thomas	Meath	1,066
Southwell, Sir Thomas	Limerick	29
Spread, John	Cork	223
Spread, William	Cork	132
Stafford, William	Meath	687
Steele, Lawrence	Kildare	607
Stephens, Walter	Carlow	166
Stepney, Thomas	Limerick	182
Sterne, Robert	Cork	692
Stewart, Robert	Wicklow	1,530
Stewart, William	Westmeath	639
Stratford, Edward	Tipperary	16
Swan, Edward	Dublin	20
Sweet, Stephen	Cork	2,515
	Clare	65
	Dublin	95
	Kilkenny	2,913
Tayler, William	Limerick	1,813
Taylor, Thomas	Meath	232

APPENDIX B

Name of purchaser	County	Area
Temple, Robert	Westmeath	727
Tigh, Richard	Carlow	79
Tilson, Thomas	King's Co.	277
Trench, Frederick	Galway	198
Trench, James	Cork	450
Trench, John	Galway	2,805
	Roscommon	97
Tuke, Samuel	Roscommon	830
	Westmeath	79
Twigg, Robert	Limerick	435
Vance, Patrick	Westmeath	134
Van Homrigh, Bartholomew	Cork	1,143
	Kildare	573
Vaughan, Hector	Clare	319
Vesey, Agmondisham	Dublin	1,348
	Kildare	5,263
Vesey, John, archbishop of Tuam	Mayo	1,839
Vincent, John	Limerick	330
Wade, Charles	Meath	825
Wade, John	Dublin	100
	Meath	2,326
Wakeham, Richard	Cork	99
Wakeham, Robert	Cork	476
Wakeham, William	Cork	42
Walker, James	Roscommon	326
Waller, Edward	Dublin	47
	Limerick	113
Waller, Robert	Meath	132
Wallis, Thomas	Cork	971
Ware, Thomas	Cork	615
Warren, Wallis	Cork	570
Way, Thomas	Kilkenny	99
Webb, William	Limerick	91
Weldon, Walter	Carlow	200
Wesley, Garrett	Kildare	125
	Meath	248
Westland, William	Meath	14
Westropp, Mountiford	Limerick	260
Westropp, Robert	Clare	238
Westropp, Thomas	Limerick	176
Whaley, Thomas	Meath	100
White, John	Limerick	1,034
	Tipperary	668
Whitwell, Nathaniel	Meath	95
Widdenham, Henry	Limerick	413
Wilkinson, William	Kilkenny	606
Wilson, Edward	Galway	310
Wilton, George	Cavan	140

APPENDIX B

Name of purchaser	County	Area
Wolsely, Richard	Carlow	403
Wood, John	Westmeath	93
Worth, Edward	Kilkenny	363
Wybarrow, Richard	Kildare	49
Young, James	Westmeath	65

3. TOTALS OF AREAS CONVEYED BY TRUSTEES

County	Area
Antrim	7,134
Armagh	1,170
Carlow	1,521
Cavan	1,508
Clare	33,413
Cork	202,289
Down	748
Dublin	12,671
Galway	13,331
Kerry	33,024
Kildare	29,192
Kilkenny	32,308
King's Co.	20,527
Limerick	21,199
Londonderry	80
Longford	296
Louth	4,449
Mayo	14,717
Meath	41,844
Monaghan	224
Queen's Co.	13,406
Roscommon	16,353
Sligo	2,507
Tipperary	12,020
Tyrone	9,681
Waterford	5,343
Westmeath	27,878
Wexford	7,469
Wicklow	1,575
Total	567,877

ABSTRACT OF THE WILLIAMITE SETTLEMENT

The following figures for areas refer to profitable land only and are given in Irish acres:

		acres *(000s)*	*per cent*
1. Area held by the Catholics of Ireland in 1688		1705	22
2. Area transferred from Catholic to Protestant ownership between 1688 and 1703			
(*a*) Sold by trustees	481		
(*b*) Left unsold by trustees	2		
(*c*) Grants excluded from Act of Resumption	31		
(*d*) Owned by families which had become Protestant by 1703 (including Clanricarde estate)	103	617	8
3. Area remaining in Catholic ownership in 1703			
(*a*) Under articles of Limerick and Galway	525		
(*b*) Under pardons	88		
(*c*) Allowed by trustees to successful claimants	137		
(*d*) Owned by persons acquitted or not proceeded against	338	1088	14

The analysis is based on the Books of Survey and Distribution and the forfeiture records. Petty's figure of 7,500,000 acres for the total profitable area has been taken as the basis for the calculation of percentages. King James's private estate has not been included in the statement. The area shown as allowed to successful claimants is exclusive of cases in which the claimant was also adjudged within articles or in receipt of pardon; it includes land, such as the Kenmare estate, in which the claim was allowed with effect from the death of the forfeiting holder.

The area recorded by the inquiry commission of 1699 as forfeited and not restored (752,953 acres) is approximately equivalent to the area transferred from Catholic ownership (617,000 acres) plus the area allowed to Catholic claimants by the trustees (137,000 acres). The commissioners' figure for estates forfeited but restored under articles (233,106 acres) is less than half the total area held by persons admitted to the articles. In the majority of such cases the estates had not been seized by the end of the war and were therefore not entered in the forfeiture records.

APPENDIX D

CATHOLIC HOLDINGS IN IRELAND IN 1641, 1688 AND 1703

The accompanying maps show the changes in the proportion of Irish land held by Catholics from 1641 to 1703. The figures on which the maps are based represent profitable and unprofitable land taken together; they are expressed in Irish acres measured according to the seventeenth-century surveys, and have been compiled from the Books of Survey and Distribution and the records of the Williamite forfeitures. The total for each of the three years is as follows:

Year	acres (000s)	per cent
1641	6,439	59
1688	2,356	22
1703	1,605	14

The percentage figures are based on the area of Ireland given in the Taylor Books of Survey and Distribution in the Royal Irish Academy—10,868,949 acres. The percentage for each county has been calculated with reference to the county areas given in *A geographical description of Ireland*, an early eighteenth-century work based on Petty's maps. The county has been taken as a unit; thus the whole of Antrim has been shaded, although the Catholic holding is mostly accounted for by Lord Antrim's estate, which covered much of the northern part of the county. Similarly, the great change which took place in county Cork between 1688 and 1703 was chiefly accounted for by the forfeiture of the Clancarty estate, the greater part of which was in the barony of Muskerry. King James's private estate has not been included in the 1688 figures.

195

PROPORTION OF LAND HELD BY CATHOLICS

%
50—100
25—49
15—24
10—14
5—9
0—4

1703   14%

1688   22%

1641   59%

INDEX

References to the lists of forfeiting owners and of purchasers in Appendix B (pp. 177–82 and 182–92) are not included.

Abbert (Galway), 37

Abercorn, Charles Hamilton, 5th earl of, 89

Abercorn, Claud Hamilton, 4th earl of, 89, 154

Abercorn, James Hamilton, 6th earl of, 125, 127, 154

Acts of parliament (England): *see* Attainder, Declaratory, Mortmain, Private acts, Protestant purchasers, Resumption, Trial of treason

Acts of parliament (Ireland): *see* Attainder, Explanation, Limerick (articles of), Outlawry, Repeal, Settlement, Slander

Acts of parliament (United Kingdom): *see* Encumbered estates, Land

Adare (Limerick), 40, 52

Agar, Charles, successively abp of Cashel and Dublin, 155

Agar, James, 155

Albemarle, Joost van Keppel, 1st earl of, grant of estates to, 20, 39, 70, 87–8, 97, 107, 111; estates sold to 'Protestant purchasers', 99, 101–2, 125, 141, 148; and resumption bill, 112

Anglesey, Arthur Annesley, 1st earl of (2nd creation), 99

Annakisky [Annakisha] (Cork), 54

Anne, Queen, 94, 132, 157, 159

Annesley, Francis (Ballyshannon, co. Kildare), 22

Annesley, Francis (Castlewellan, co. Down): protests against William's grants, 87; appointed to inquiry commission (1699), 98–100; and dispute over commission's report, 103; presents report to English commons, 105; appointed forfeiture trustee (1700), 118 and *n.*; his work as trustee, 121–2,

151; expelled from Irish commons (1703), 156–7; relations with Bishop King, 100, 105, 116; his manuscripts, 99, 121, 164–5

Annesley, Maurice, 145–6, 157

Annesley, William, 1st Baron, 99

Antrim, Alexander McDonnell, 3rd earl of, 19, 24, 31, 32, 127; and articles of Limerick, 46, 50, 63

Archer, John, 48

Ardfry (Galway), 71

Arlington, Henry Bennet, 1st earl of, 17

Armagh, Catholic abp of; *see* Maguire, Dominick

Armagh, Protestant abp of; *see* Boyle, Michael; Boulter, Hugh

Armagh, prerogative court of, 144, 145

Articles; *see* Bophin, Drogheda, Galway, Limerick, Sligo, Waterford

Asgill, John, 155

Athenry, Edward Bermingham, 13th Baron, 79, 118

Athlone, town of, 90

Athlone, Godard van Reede, baron de Ginkel, 1st earl of: his negotiations (1690–1), 26–9; at Galway (1691), 28, 66–71, 77–8; at Limerick (1691), 28–9, 56–9, 76, 85; grant of estates to, 85, 88–9; estates sold to 'Protestant purchasers', 101–2, 125, 139–41

Attainder, act of (Eng., 1657), 32; act of (Jacobite, 1689), 21–5, 30, 31, 126, 144; bills of (Eng., 1689–95), 24–5, 30, 31–3, 82–6; *see also* Outlawry

Aughrim, battle of, 28, 67, 70, 77, 146

Avaux, Jean-Antoine de Mesmes, comte d', 21, 66

Bagenal, Dudley, 33, 84, 108, 115, 137

Bagenal, Walter, 137

INDEX

Fitzgerald, Thomas, knight of Glin, 141

Fitzgerald family, 18, 46

Fitzpatrick family, 17

Fitzwilliam, Thomas, 4th Viscount, of Merrion, 46

Forfeitures, Book of (1699), 42, 175–6

Forster, Francis, 81

Fox family, 42

Foyle, river, 90

Freke, Percy, 155

French, Arthur, 68, 69

French, Nicholas, 37–8

French, Robert, 71

French family, 72

Froude, James Anthony, 31, 95, 164

Galmoy, Piers Butler, 3rd Viscount: his estates, 19, 152, 155; outlawry proceedings against, 33, 35; goes to France after surrender of Limerick (1691), 45, 161

Galtrim (Meath), 34

Galway, articles of (1691): their terms negotiated, 27–8, 66–7; dispute regarding interpretation of, 68–9; hearing of claims, 46–7, 71–2; and act of resumption, 114, 137; their effect on scale of confiscation, 15, 45, 72, 160, 176

Galway, county, lands held by Catholics in, 41, 66, 72; outlawry proceedings in, 39, 64; influence of O'Shaughnessys in, 91

Galway, town of, 27, 46, 102

Galway, 'tribes' of, 72

Galway, Henry de Massue de Ruvigny, Viscount, later earl of: on missing clause of Limerick articles, 61 and n., 62; on Galway articles, 68; on Trimleston's case, 139; grant of estate to, 86, 88–9; grant resumed, 112–13; see also Lords justices

Galway, John, 74

Galway, Walter, 41

Gaveston, Piers, 111

Geary, [—], an informer, 139

Geoghegan, Charles, 53

Geoghegan, Edward, 80–1

Gernon, Bartholomew, 40

Gernon, Nicholas, 89

Ginkel; see Athlone, earl of

Glin, knight of; see Fitzgerald

Godolphin, Sidney, 1st Baron, 83

Gorges, Robert, 25

Gormanston, Anthony Preston, 9th Viscount, 137–8

Gormanston, Anthony Preston, 11th Viscount, 161

Gormanston, Jenico Preston, 7th Viscount, 33, 34, 35, 137

Gormanston, Jenico Preston, 8th Viscount, 46, 137–8

Gormanston, Nicholas Preston, 6th Viscount, 14, 16

Gort (Galway), 91

Gort, John Prendergast-Smyth, 1st Viscount, 91

Grace, John, 108, 115, 136–7

Grace, Oliver (Courtstown), 115

Grace, Oliver (Shanganagh), 74

Grants of land, made by William, 82–95; objected to by English commons, 96–8; inquiry commissioners' estimate of, 107–9; resumption of, 111–14; excepted from resumption, 115

Grants, Book of (1699), 86–7, 91

Guy, Henry, 86, 93

Halifax, Charles Montague, 1st Baron, 97

Hamilton, George; see Orkney, earl of

Hamilton, Gustavus, 90

Hamilton, James (Tullymore): appointed to inquiry commission (1699), 98, 99 n.; and controversy over commission's report, 103; dies soon after appointment as forfeiture trustee, 118 n.

Hamilton, Richard, 32

Hardinge, W. H., 137 n., 163–4

Harley, Robert, 51, 110

Harrison, Thomas, forfeiture trustee, 118 n.

Higgons, Bevil, 74

Hollow sword-blade company, 151–4

Hooper, James, secretary inquiry commission (1699) and forfeiture trustee (1700), 118 and n.

Hore, Matthew, 74

Hospital (Limerick), 155

Howe, John, 96

Huguenots, 88–9

Hurley, Patrick, 123–4

Iar Connacht (Galway), 69

Inchiquin, William O'Brien, 3rd earl of, 125

Inniskilling; see Enniskillen

Portmarnock (Dublin), 130

Power, John, 76; *see also* Tyrone, earl of

Powys, William Herbert, 1st duke of (Jacobite title), 31

Poynings' law, 60

Poyntz, Charles, 80

Pratt, Benjamin, 154

Prendergast, Thomas, 1st bt, 90–1, 115

Preston; *see* Gormanston

Prittie family, 16

Private acts (Eng.), 41, 71 and *n*., 80, 89, 128–33, 140

Private estate; *see* James II, private estate of

Privy council (England), 32, 59, 60, 61, 63, 68

Privy council (Ireland), 27, 29 *n*., 46, 49, 51, 61, 63, 67, 75, 123

Proclamation of 7 July 1691, 27, 76, 77, 81, 130

Profitable land, 14, 16, 17, 133–4, 174, 193, 195

'Protestant purchasers', 101–2, 124–5, 139–41; act for relief of (Eng., 1702), 127, 148–9

Public accounts commissioners (England), 156

Puissar, Louis, Marquess, 88, 97

Purcell, John, 48

Purcell family, 16

Purefoy family, 16

Pyne, Sir Richard, 125

Queen's County (Leix), 34, 37

Quin, Thady, 40, 52–3

Quit-rent, 74, 122, 149

Ralph, James, 99

Rapparees, 53, 80, 123

Rathmore (Kildare), 48

Rathorpe (Galway) 81

Rawlinson, Thomas, forfeiture trustee, 118 *n*.

Reddy, Richard, 48

Reeks, McGillicuddy's, 46

Reilly family, 46

Repeal (of restoration settlement), act of (Jacobite, 1689), 21–5, 66, 74

Restoration settlement, statistics of, 14–17, 133–5, 193, 195; threat to maintenance of, 18–19; repeal of, 21–5

Resumption (of William's grants), act of (Eng., 1700): provisions, 89–90, 113–20, 148; controversies during passage

of, 110–12; hearing of claims under 136–47; attitude of Irish Protestants to, 44, 107–8, 124–8; conflict of, with Irish act, 89

Reynell, Sir Richard, 34, 36

Rice, Sir Stephen, 33, 58

Riverstown (Meath), 48

Roche, James, 89–90, 115

Rochestown (Dublin), 130

Rochford, William Henry van Zuylestein 1st earl of, 88

Rochfort, Robert, 99, 132

Rogers, George, 92

Romney, Henry Sydney, Viscount Sydney, later 1st earl of, lord lieutenant (1692–3), 43, 47, 78, 117; grant of estates to, 76, 84–5; sells estates to 'Protestant purchasers', 101, 125

Roscommon, county, 16 and *n*.

Ross Island (Kerry), 91

Russell, Bartholomew, 154–5

Sarsfield, Charles, 144

Sarsfield, Charlotte, 80, 144

Sarsfield, Mary, 80 and *n*., 144

Sarsfield, Patrick; *see* Lucan

Sarsfield, Patrick (father of Lord Lucan), 80

Sarsfield, William, 80 *n*., 144–5

Scawen, Sir William, 155

Schomberg, Frederick Herman, 1st duke of, 25, 32, 66

Seatown (Dublin), 154–5

Settlement, act of (Ire., 1662), 19 *n*., 21, 22, 66, 92, 107; *see also* Repeal, act of

Shaftesbury, Anthony Ashley Cooper, 3rd earl of, 112

Shanballyduff (Cork), 46

Shandon (Waterford), 74

Shannon river, 14, 19, 28, 34, 40, 90

Shaw, Robert, 69

Sheres, Sir Henry, forfeiture trustee, 118–19, 146, 151; in charge of survey, 122, 134; relations with Bishop King, 142–3

Sheridan, Thomas, 19

Sherigley, Folliott, 35

Sherlock, Balthazar, 41

Sherlock, Christopher, 145

Sherlock, Hester, 145–6

Sherlock, Mary, 145

Sherlock family, 16

Shower, Sir Bartholomew, 43

INDEX

INDEX

Waterford city, 33, 75–6, 102
Waterford, county, 41, 89–90
Wauchope, John, 28
Wesley family, 17
Westenra, Henry, 140
Westmeath, county, 34, 42, 99
Westmeath, Thomas Nugent, 4th earl of, 46
Westport (Mayo), 58, 160
Wexford, county, 13
White, Charles, 75
White, Mary, 75
William III: his negotiations with Irish Catholics (1689–91), 23–9, 32, 35–6, 48, 74–7, 116–17; attitude to outlawry proceedings, 38, 42, 43; and articles of Limerick, 46, 49, 51, 53, 55, 60–2; and articles of Galway, 68–72; his dispute with English commons on disposal of forfeited lands, 30, 82–8, 96–8; his land grants, 39, 82–95; and Elizabeth Villiers, 92–5; resumption of his

grants, 110–14; and Protestant remonstrance against resumption, 127
Winchester, marquess of; see Bolton
Wine, imported from France, 28
Wolsely, Richard, 142–4
Wolsely, William, 80, 142
Woods, destruction of, 158
Woodstock, William Henry Bentinck, Viscount, 87, 107
Wool trade, 107, 150, 159
Wyche, Sir Cyril, lord justice (1694), 93–4; forfeiture trustee, 118 and *n.*, 122, 151; *see also* Lords justices
Wyndham act; *see* Land act (1903)
Wyse, Thomas, 117–18
Wyse, Sir Thomas, 118

Yeomanstown (Kildare), 129
Youghal (Cork), 78
Young, Arthur, 160

Zuylestein; *see* Rochford

207